AMANI HAKI YETU

Thanks for the support!

Adam

AMANI HAKI YETU

PEACE IS OUR RIGHT

Adam Hummel

iUniverse, Inc.
Bloomington

Amani Haki Yetu
Peace Is Our Right

iUniverse books may be ordered through booksellers or by contacting:

iUniverse
1663 Liberty Drive
Bloomington, IN 47403
www.iuniverse.com
1-800-Authors (1-800-288-4677)

ISBN: 978-1-4759-0165-8 (sc)
ISBN: 978-1-4759-0166-5 (ebk)

Printed in the United States of America

iUniverse rev. date: 04/19/2012

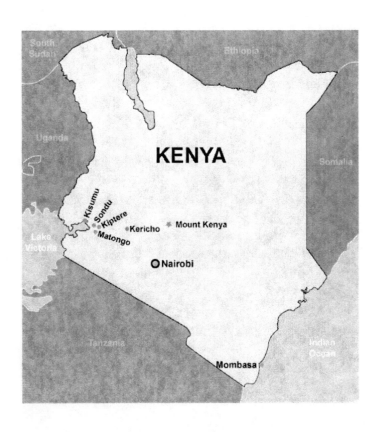

AUTHOR'S NOTE

As a consequence of the currency of this book, some of the events unfolding on the ground in Kenya may not match up with what I have written. In particular, the date of the next general election is in dispute. Throughout this book I have referred to elections that will be held in March 2013. Though this is the date that has been selected at the time of writing this book, it is very possible that as a result of numerous challenges to this date, the election may perhaps be moved to December 2012. In any case, I believe it is important to note that things are always changing on the ground in Kenya, and what may seem definite one day, can become very different the next.

Contents

Prologue

Peace is a concept that is both elusive and deceptive in today's world. It is a notion that far too many people have difficulty comprehending, and it is a concept taken for granted.

Peace is deceptive because it has no single definition. What may be perceived as peace may be either the absence of war, or simply a lull in times of tension. Only those who live in conflict zones however contemplate this difference, as those who occupy generally peaceful regions need not ponder such a technical, and yet practically important, difference. People who do not make these contemplations do not necessarily know whether they live in a time and place of peace, and the deceptive nature of peace leaves open the question of whether it must be achieved. This notion is difficult not only for impoverished villagers to grasp, but also governmental theorists and politicians whose role it is to shape policy and world peace.

Peace is a concept that is subjective, relative, and takes on different meanings depending on where you are, and throughout the project that I will detail in the pages that follow, it became abundantly clear that how people perceived peace in Kenya, in rural Africa, was entirely different to how people in western societies and developed nations view it. The reason for this distorted view is not only the fact that peace lacks consistent definition, but because the impact of peace, or the lack of peace, changes depending on your geographic, political, or social position. As our work in Kenya, developing a grassroots peacebuilding initiative, progressed, the relative nature of peace became clearer both to me and to others involved.

This book is about a project that has as its ultimate goal a practical peace, and it is designed to impact the lives of many who are overlooked by politicians, popular media, governmental reports, or popular causes. A quick Google search for "peace efforts" will yield results ranging from the Arab-Israel conflict, to the genocide in Darfur, to relations between India and Pakistan, to Afghanistan, and Iraq. When students on campuses wear t-shirts or buttons in support of peace, they dream of world peace and they preach brotherhood and togetherness, but they do not always consider the root causes of the lack of peace and are therefore unaware of how to achieve it. Now, this book will not purport to say that I *do* know what goes into making peace, nor will it claim that peace has been definitively achieved. This book will however detail efforts that have been made to make peace in a tiny part of Africa that is not given enough well deserved attention.

African tribal relations are sometimes considered a relic of the past, and many would be surprised to realize how strong a role these dynamics play today. Only by understanding the issue of tribal relations however can we understand the best approaches to its resolution. When the post-election violence in Kenya was reported on by the world media at the start of 2008, they did so until the cease-fire was signed at the end of February. Even that coverage was not necessarily done with the interests of the Kenyan people in mind, but some argued more so for the interests of western tourists who were on safari in Kenya at the time. When the cease-fire was signed, all news of Kenya's tensions stopped, attention on Kenya ceased, and it was assumed that because there was no more violence, there was no more conflict. What was not covered publicly was that with the cease-fire, bullets and arrows were no longer being fired, but tensions were still at a boiling point; little was being done to keep violent influences and radical elements at bay.

This book will look at the lives of people affected by the civil unrest that tore Kenya apart during the post-election violence in 2008 and how Kenya's numerous ethnic communities reacted to this conflict. It will consider factors and perspectives that should be understood and taken into consideration when bringing people together. I have tried to create a joint narrative that people from various backgrounds and heritages can contribute to, and the book will consider the power that both one person and a small group of individuals can have to influence change. That one person can be a poor villager from a rural region in Kenya who dreams of becoming a leader in their community, or a football player who wants to make an impact in his tribe, or a student from abroad who wishes to shed some sort of light on a part of Africa that has not received the attention it deserves. It is imperative that we consistently hold in our minds the power that one person has to affect change as we progress forward into a time where politicians, orators, focus groups and boardrooms increasingly make critical decisions alone. We must not forget the power of the individual, and the ability that each person has to shape the lives of others. This project demonstrated the drive that so many have to change their own lives as well as the lives of others.

This book is about one month I spent in Kenya, and the giant steps taken in a short period of time. As there continues to be, and will always be, work to be done, this book will detail the starting point of a movement that was inspired entirely by people on the ground, those directly impacted by the words of politicians, and by the violence committed by their fellow tribesmen. The point of this book is to serve as a launching point to understand what has happened in part of Kenya following its civil strife, how an amateur peace movement can be created and can succeed, and to inspire others to help ensure that these efforts continue to flourish.

Great men and women, who have shaped our modern understanding of the world, have provided numerous ways to understand peace. These definitions speak of heroic efforts, of mass movements, of world attention, and of influencing generations. Yehudi Menuhin, a renowned violinist and conductor, once said that, "Peace may sound simple—one beautiful word—but it requires everything we have, every quality, every strength, every dream, every high ideal." This idea that peace requires and deserves every effort served as the basis for my project. Yet it is through these efforts that I have realized that there is no real recipe for peace. In my experience, what peace needs is hope, the possibility of permanence, and the belief that your life and the lives of others will truly be affected by your efforts. These factors helped launched this project and where it will lead I am not quite sure. In the meantime, there has been progress, there has been change, and what is required is a continuation of these efforts so that the next general election is not plagued with the same violence, and that the people in even the remotest of regions feel comfortable moving forward together with other citizens of their country. It is because of these people, together, who inspire future generations both within and outside of Africa, that there is the possibility of peace. This project shows that all peace requires is one first step.

Introduction:
Welcome to Africa

Open your eyes and look up into the white cone that surrounds you. It takes a moment at first to remember where you are, and why you are waking up inside a mosquito net, but then you realize. You slowly adjust to waking up inside this shield that was supposed to prevent that mosquito from biting you four times last night. You scratch your forehead, neck, elbow, and big toe, and hope the mosquito's last victim was not some animal running around while the village slept. After all, you came to Africa for an adventure, not malaria.

You fumble to get out from under the net, get out of bed, and look around the room you are now standing in. You can feel dirt on the floor underneath your bare feet which will remain there despite how many times you sweep with a broom made from reeds of hay tied together. The brick walls are bare with dry cement seeping out from in between them. Look up at the white ceiling and find the crack that was fortunately big enough to shove a twister hanger into. This hanger will be used as a hook from which to hang your mosquito net-that-clearly-doesn't-work from. Look back to your bed, and see a mattress too wide for the wooden frame, so that it is sagging in the middle. This, you realize, is why you just literally had to fight an uphill battle getting out of bed, and also why you faintly recall dreaming about being a hot dog.

Before doing anything else, you bend over to roll up your sleeping bag. You were warned to take precautions from letting things crawl into your sleeping bag during the day, and shudder at the thought of what may potentially join you in bed that night. You hear some noise outside and look towards the window, its frame slightly ajar because it too is being held closed with a twisted former hanger. Sunlight has begun to infiltrate the darkness of the room, and you don't want to waste another moment inside. Put on some pants, put on your flip-flops, and open to the door to a beautiful morning in Africa.

As your eyes adjust to the light outside, you see orange and you see green, and you realize that at home in Canada you never really think about colours. The orange is the colour of the sky, but it is more like the colour of peaches and cantaloupes combined. It is shaded by the early morning almost-pink sun, and the light grey clouds that are rolling out from a rainy night. The trees, the tea plants, and the grass are green. It is a deep green, the green you would expect in an area where it pours with rain for an hour every afternoon, but not to be expected in Africa. It's the sort of green you have in your mind when you are imagining the perfect tuft of grass to put your head on, and it is the sort of green that makes you forget your initial hesitation that you'd be spending a month on a brown African savannah. You see Acacias, some donkeys, wild dogs, a barb wire fence, and school children in their royal blue and yellow uniforms heading off to school.

You remember that there was a noise that woke you. As this is your first morning waking up in Africa you expected to be woken perhaps by the roar of a lion, the crow of a rooster, or maybe, stretching your imagination for a moment, a giraffe sticking its head in through your window.

Turn your head left and your ignorance and idealism are instantly dissolved because the noise that woke you was nothing other than a group of men leading a cow to its imminent death. Before you have the chance to consider whether this is really the first image you want in your mind this morning, one foul tug of a rope gets the cow down to the ground. Without hesitation, its neck is cut, its lifeless body is hoisted up and is hanging on a shaky wooden frame which, as you find out later, is the village butchery, and three people are coming at it with machetes. They are preparing meat for the entire village and it's amazing to see (despite all the blood). Your first morning in Africa, and the lessons of the *Lion King* are already coming to mind: the circle of life being played out right here in your own backyard! You can't wait to tell your mom.

Your curiosity overpowers your natural inclination to turn green, and you slowly, extremely slowly, move closer. Excited by the presence of a *mzungu* (Swahili for 'white man') a man calls you over. You assume that he must be the butcher, because he's the one wearing a blood stained white coat. He holds out his machete to you, offering you to take the blade from his hand. Today, he wants you to help chop up a still-warm cow. As the option flashes through your mind for just an instant, you make the ultimately smart decision that your eyes are more curious than your hands. You politely decline, and prefer to stand aside and watch as the village's meat for the day is divided up between men who show up with all forms of containers and sticks on which to carry their meat. After a few moments, you walk back to your room and pass on the way the wild dogs that have run out of the forest to come and lap up the cow's blood which stains the muddy ground of this makeshift butchery.

Feeling groggy and dirty, its time for a shower, but in a village with no running water and no electricity you wonder how on earth you are going to get clean today. With further ignorance you wonder if someone is going to walk you down to the river to bathe yourself, or whether people do actually wash themselves at all here. Thankfully, one of your local hosts, Jessica, has gotten up early to help you out and make you feel at home. To do this, she starts by making a little fire from charcoal in a tiny cooking oven outside. She has gone to get water from a giant black-plastic water tank filled with rain water outside, poured that water into a cooking pot and boiled the water. Then, she poured half that boiling water into a big Tupperware bowl, the kind of bowl that you would use at home to serve a nice big Caesar salad in. To this, she adds some fresh rain water so that the water is warm, but not too hot, and voila: your shower is ready.

While you go and grab your towel and soap from your bag, Jessica goes and puts your "shower" down in a little concrete hut. You walk in, close the door and look around at this room that is about six-by-four feet in area, with a tin roof on top. There are spider webs and mosquitoes stuck to the walls, there is a crooked nail that you rotate to keep the door shut, and there is a rock covering a hole in the middle of the floor. Through this hole is a ten-foot pit that is your toilet for the next four weeks. You undress carefully, trying not to touch anything, keep your flip flops on, and squat next to the bowl to take the most unsatisfying shower of your life.

Put both your hands in the warm water. The warmth of it instantly makes you feel a little cleaner, but then you realize that you have to use this water to actually bathe yourself. Its easy to take for granted a shower at home, because the water is plentiful, and you can choose whatever body part you want to wash first. For this shower however you have to be strategic, and put plainly the strategy is: do I start from my head? Or from my feet? After thinking about it longer than you probably should have, you rationalize that if you wash your hair first, there will be soap in the bowl, and then you can wash the rest of your body with this soapy water and maybe that will get you clean. So, your process is wet hair, shampoo hair, rinse hair, use water to scrub the rest of your body. When you are almost done, take off one flip-flop, put your foot in the bowl, and scrub it clean. Then, take your foot out, put it back into your flip flop, and repeat with your other foot. Remember the most important thing: do not let your flesh touch the walls, the floor or the rock covering the pit latrine.

Your shower is done, and you are extremely thankful for the barber who cut your hair shorter than you wanted it to be before you left. Crouching down also hurts your back. And your knees. And your neck. You also know that you are likely going to be back later to move the rock off that hole leading down to the pit, so you pour the rest of the water out over the floor to give it a nice rinse because let's face it, it needs one.

You put a shirt on, put some shorts on, fling the now-wet towel over your shoulder, and turn the nail on the door to leave. You have mastered the African shower, and your new found confidence makes you stand up a little higher and makes you feel like you can now conquer anything. This triumphant feeling makes you shove open the rickety door to the new day. As you do however, you suddenly hear a squawking noise that scares the hell out of you! You have just opened the door onto a passing chicken that has become extremely protective over the five chicks walking behind her. It squawks, you scream, you slam the door shut, and you are now hiding inside a concrete hut that contains a pit latrine scared of a chicken. Good-bye confidence.

For these few seconds, shaking in the mud-shower-hut, you realize that your last encounter with a chicken were those nuggets you ate from McDonalds at Heathrow Airport. In a way you suddenly wish it had been this chicken you'd been dipping in barbeque sauce. After a few moments though, you compose yourself, creak the door slowly open, and look both ways. You think about that feeling you get when you trip in public, and then look around to see that no one saw you. Same feeling now, you're hoping that no one saw your chicken-freak-out, and realize that the coast is clear. You dart back to your room to get dressed. Once dressed, you head downstairs as thoughts of McDonalds, fresh beef and chicken have left you rather hungry.

It does not take long to find out that the pace of life in Kenya is slow. At home with your family you always joke about Jewish Standard Time, which is approximately 15 minutes behind actual time. In Kenya however, they talk of Kenyan Time, which is based on actual time but altered by any variety of factors. These include things like donkeys blocking the way, the desire to sit and drink another cup of tea, bumping into a neighbour you have not seen since the night before, stopping to talk about government corruption, or being slowed down by the mud created by last night's rainfall. As a result of these factors, Kenyan Time is extremely difficult to define, but for the sake of simplicity, I would say it is on average an hour or two behind regular time. This means that if you tell someone you will be seeing them at noon, they will not be too offended if you show up closer to 2pm. This will eventually take some getting used to, especially when you are on the receiving end of people showing up late, but in the meantime, you want breakfast as scheduled, at 8:30am.

Jessica comes to keep you company at breakfast, but the real reason for her coming is to order for you. As someone who does not usually eat breakfast, all you really feel like is a cup of tea. You soon learn however that as you are a foreigner eating at their establishment, the owners have found some eggs and tomatoes for you, and are insisting on making you a crude-looking version of an omelet, something the other customers will not receive. On your special request as well, this omelet will be served on a *chapati*, which is now one of your favourite African foods. It is essentially a pancake, made from a ball of maize flour and water, cooked with oil on a thick black dish over a fire. This *chapati*, with your egg-and-tomato omelet, rolled up into a sort of African breakfast-burrito, will be your breakfast for the next month and the only food that you will actually enjoy in the village. This suddenly transforms you into a morning person.

The place you are eating breakfast is a building that makes your room with the wobbly bed and mosquito net look pretty luxurious. It is a single storey building made from wood, with about eight tables and two benches to each table, and has the 'menu' written with a black sharpie on the wall. Before you enter there is a tub of rainwater that you use to wash your hands in, and the doorframe is used to wipe the mud and dirt from your shoes. It is dark inside, with only natural light trying to get in through the door, and you are instantly hit with a musty smell of smoke and cooking oil. On the walls are mosquitoes and spiders, and in the back of the restaurant there is one man doing all the cooking over a charcoal stove. The cash register is literally a drawer filled with bills and coins, and it sits above a glass box which contains *chapatis* and *mandazis*, a snack which is a ball of flour cooked in oil. The counter where Pastor David, the owner of the restaurant, stands is also used as the to-go counter, where people get their orders wrapped in yesterday's newspaper. When not used as wrapping, it is used as reading material for those dining alone. On the wall next to the menu are pictures of President Mwai Kibaki, Prime Minister Raila Odinga, and a calendar featuring the many poses of now-President Barack Obama (of Kenyan origin, as I will explain later).

Your food comes served on a tin plate, and is accompanied with a glass into which is poured tea from a giant tin pot. Unsure exactly of what you are drinking, you ask as to what is in the tea, and you are told that it is fresh cow's milk with ground tea leaves and some sugar. You take a sip, and refresh the description in your head: it is all sugar, with fresh cow's milk and some tea leaves. Nevertheless, it is delicious, and accompanies your meal perfectly. Little do you know this cup of tea is the first of approximately ten that you will have throughout the day. As you swat away the flies that have swarmed your meal, and pretend to take no notice of the other patrons of the restaurant staring at the only white man that has eaten in their presence in a long time, you finish your meal, ask for another cup of piping hot tea, and are ready to begin the day.

As you step out of the dark restaurant, it takes your eyes a moment to adjust to the sunlight. Though your sunglasses are on your head, you hesitate before putting them on. You are extremely conscious of people looking at you, and you do not feel like creating another barrier between yourself and the people in the village. You are already the only white person in the village and you do not feel like instantly confirming the widely held assumption that because you are white, you have more money than them. You naturally then do not want to be the only person wearing Ray-Bans in the middle of this small farming village. You feel like this minor act of putting on your glasses, something that you have never ever thought about before, will create a sort of division between you and the people of the village which is not something you want when on your first day in this village, all alone, you crave acceptance.

Squinting in the sunlight, you take a few steps and find yourself in the center of the village. You stand on a road made solely of mud and manure, lined with little wooden huts which serve as shops, restaurants like the one you just ate in, and tin-roofed houses on either side. You see people still walking off with pieces of meat from the cows that are being slaughtered, mothers walking with babies strapped to their backs with scarves, and children in their uniforms on their way to school. You see men in suits and ties talking about the day to come, and women and men walking with donkeys in tow behind them, donkeys with giant yellow water bottles strapped to their backs. With your basic needs of cleanliness, hunger and sleep satisfied, you have a chance to stand, look around, and absorb your surroundings. This foreign village, Kiptere, is where you have come to help build peace.

IT IS THEIR RIGHT, IT IS THEIR DUTY

Idealism and naïveté are two concepts that are often confused. Informed global citizens read the news and see only bloodshed and warfare, and then look to those people who dream of peace and believe in human goodness and consider them naïve. This perception is, some may argue, natural when one considers the state of global affairs today. But good news does not always fit into the parameters of what is considered popular news. Good news, which consists of progress, hope and often leaps of faith, does not find its place on front pages of newspapers or even the news ticker on the bottom of a CNN broadcast. Good news is often news witnessed by people who are so elated with what they have witnessed, that they are content sharing it with only those with whom they have experienced it. Good news is not reported on to the same extent as bad news, and it is for this reason that cynics may believe that peace-hoping individuals are naïve, as cynics do not see the good that these idealists have taken the effort to find.

Today the good news that I am referring to is the effort that is being made to build peace. Throughout history people have attempted to define peace in a variety of ways. Peace has been called the absence of war, the time when everyone stands around reloading, and the ability to cope with trying times. Peace is justice lived (Mahatma Gandhi), the way we arrive at goals (Martin Luther King Jr.), and a process of changing opinions (John F. Kennedy). Peace does not however only require definition—it requires proliferation.

An idealist is an idealist because they have seen potential. They have seen potential in an idea and they believe that this idea can take hold. Like me, those who are idealistic about peace have seen peace movements, despite how small some may be, and see them as the good that serves to balance out some of the bad.

The place where I have personally witnessed such a peacebuilding endeavour is in Kenya, by conducting a project that seeks to ease tribal tensions and ensure that youths will play a leading role in the political future of Kenya. This project envisions tribal communities coming together and celebrating their differences, not warring along archaic stereotypes propagated by their grandparents. Other likeminded individuals have seen African peace projects succeed in places like Ghana or Tanzania, or have seen success on other continents. A documentary recently made showing the process involved in creating the United Nations International Day of Peace, called *Peace One Day*, shows hundreds of peace movements celebrating on September 21 all over the world. When you see people, specifically youths, celebrating in regions once plagued by warfare and strife, one should, one must, be idealistic about the notion of peace; one should hope that the same trends make their way to those most reported-on war zones like Syria, Iraq, Libya, Afghanistan, and the Democratic Republic of the Congo that make people cynical about the prospects of any sort of progress.

As an individual involved in the creation of a peace movement, I think about the notion of peace every day. My mind changes daily and my attempts to understand how to make peace change with global events and new ideas and concepts I learn about. The one idea that remains consistently true to me however is the fact that peace is most easily understood either as a state-of-mind or a state-of-heart. Despite how cliché it sounds to ask people to look deep down inside before they begin to work on a peace project, this initial step is monumental because it will determine whether a lasting peace is realistically attainable. Unfortunately one's state of mind or heart is not clear cut and cannot be put down on paper, but a good initial understanding of one's thoughts or feelings at the outset of an attempt to forge a lasting peace will determine whether such a peace can and will last. As one of the youths I worked with told me, "Peace is possible when there is peace in each of us."

While the yearning for peace is a prerequisite, it must be followed with action. Many countries and international organizations have created days that urge people to take action. July 18 is Nelson Mandela Day in South Africa in which citizens are urged to spend time doing something good for someone else; December 10 is International Human Rights Day when people are urged to speak to their political representatives to ensure that human rights are observed in every corner of the world; January 27 is International Holocaust Remembrance Day in which people are implored to remember the lessons of "Never Again"; there are days devoted to fighting cancer or HIV/AIDS and days when people are urged to do any other number of positive acts. September 21 is the International Day of Peace, and it does not have to be a day when you have to go out and DO anything. All a peace day requires is that some form of peace is found within your own heart and mind. This is all that is needed by ordinary individuals: think about peace, think about how you can personally affect peace, and think about how peace can be spread.

To be an idealist means to believe in an idea. For the purposes of this book and our project, the idea is peace: peace within our hearts and minds, and peace in our time. Peace is always possible, and we idealists hope that though we may not be celebrating an actual international peace on every September 21, there is peace today in areas that did not see peace last year, and this is an accomplishment we can be proud of. Peace is possible. What it takes is will, self-reflection, and the acknowledgements of all the good that occurs daily in this tumultuous and hectic world.

As a self-professed book addict, the first step that I take whenever I begin something new is head to the bookstore. I rationalize this visit as a reason for going to find information about the field that I am trying to delve into, but in all honesty I think I just have a book-buying problem. Despite the stack of books that sit perpetually on my bedside table, I just want to buy more. Regardless of this addiction however, when I look through the shelves on world history and African affairs in big bookstores in Canada, I am unable to find many about Kenya. As I will attempt to demonstrate later, Kenya has a vibrant history and a troubled past, and though there are of course plenty of books written on every subject, I always had trouble finding books about what life is like in the villages in Kenya, or finding information about the people of the country. There are plenty of safari books, but not enough about life in Kenya. This is a little of what I will try to provide here.

At the time of writing, I have been to Kenya twice. The first time was on an organized trip with an organization that will remain unnamed. The reason for this anonymity is because I felt the trip was not what it could have been. To begin with, they misled me, in a ridiculous way. Before I get to that however, perhaps I should start with why I wanted to go to Africa in the first place.

Upbringing

I was born in South Africa but moved to Canada at a very young age. My parents, aware of the fact that there were soon going to be changes in the Apartheid regime of South Africa, wanted to leave for fear that crime in the country was about to spike. Another reason perhaps in the back of their minds was that there would be a full-scale revolution in South Africa when Nelson Mandela was eventually released from prison and power changed hands, but thankfully that did not happen, and it was not the reason for our swift departure. Despite the fact that I grew up in Toronto and could not have had a more opposite youth than I would have had we stayed in Johannesburg, I have always had a particularly strong South African identity (and when I was a kid it was always fun to tell friends that I was born in Africa and see their reactions. It's actually still fun).

The value of my African identity stayed with me throughout my adolescence and while an undergraduate student at York University in Toronto, I was also fortunate to get involved in a number of ways on campus. I was studying political science and history, but my primary extra-curricular involvement was with Hillel of Greater Toronto, the Center for Jewish Campus Life. Hillel is an organization that is present on most North American university campuses, and I can say honestly that Hillel changed my life. It has the unique ability to conform to the needs of the students. When you go to a Hillel office with an idea, displaying an eagerness and passion to get involved, campaign, and help, you can be truly surprised by how many doors are suddenly open for you. For this reason I have always had a special place in my heart for Hillel and they have done things for me that I will never forget. Having made my way through the ranks of Hillel to become the campus President in my third year, I had found that I was able to easily immerse myself in other forms of activism on campus. Unfortunately however, as a result of campus politics, I found myself primarily fighting on the front lines of the Arab-Israel conflict as it unfolded on my particular university campus. The Arab-Israel conflict is so overwhelming and all-encompassing at York that it distracts from so many other forms of activism that provide positive and productive outlets for students.

York University

Henry Kissinger once quipped, "University politics are vicious precisely because the stakes are so small." If there was any campus that could best exemplify this statement, it was York University. The campus is bogged down with the Arab-Israel conflict and though I was more than happy to take a central role in this dispute, and I grew greatly as an individual thanks to the experience, the negativity and the fight inevitably got to me. I have always been a pretty positive person, and within that positivity I have always sought to ensure that when there is a problem, a solution is found. I am a confrontational person, in both personal and professional aspects of my life. This is because I believe confronting a problem is the best way to move forward. If I do not see movement on an issue for a while, I get frustrated and tend to turn my attention elsewhere. I therefore became extremely frustrated on campus as I witnessed the daily protests in which anti-Israel and pro-Israel activists would square off and shout their views at each other. I began to espouse my belief not in the freedom of speech, which was quite clearly being exercised in the hallways of York, but rather the freedom to listen, which students rarely utilized. Caught up in their own views, they did not care to hear what the other side had to say. If you are not listening then there is no moving forward, as a one-way conversation leads nowhere. This is when I would swoop in to an argument. I would tell people that if they weren't listening to each other they should just back off and stop skipping class. They should only engage each other when there is the potential to learn from it. I tried this technique, met many interesting people, and came to be known as the often-heard-of-but-rarely-seen reasonable activist, but my efforts remained

7

futile. So it became that in this context, and amidst the utter failure of my conflict-resolution techniques and endless frustration, that I tried to get involved in another issue that had recently made a strong appearance on campus, which was the genocide in Darfur.

Darfur and Introduction to Africa

Along with some friends I got involved with an organization called Students Taking Action Now: Darfur (STAND), a group dedicated to bringing awareness to the atrocities unfolding in Darfur. Though, admittedly, we were unable to accomplish as much as we had hoped to at York, being involved in this form of activism got me thinking about what could be done to affect change in Africa from abroad. In fact, it made me realize that people abroad *could* actually affect change in a place like Africa. Coupled with my studies in political science and history, I became more passionate about African affairs and the idea was now planted in my head that I would love to spend some actual time in Africa trying to see what the situation was like on the ground there.

Jewish and South African Identity

It was not an accident either that my involvement in Jewish campus life coincided with my activism on African or human rights issues. My passion for these issues and my belief that we should all have a hand in helping the people of Africa most definitely stems from my Jewish identity. In fact I do not think that I can overstate the way that my Jewish identity and involvement pushed me to at least try to make some efforts to help others.

I have been fortunate to be brought up in a family that places much value on our Jewish heritage, with parents who have helped bring me up in a uniquely Jewish way. My formal education, having attended both Associated Hebrew Day School and the Community Hebrew Academy of Toronto for my respective elementary and high school education, has embedded in my consciousness ideas about Judaism that have helped shape and define me as a young adult. In these most formative years of my life, it has provided guidance for what sort of life to live. As I have grown up and realized how much of a product I am of this Jewish upbringing, I have come to appreciate how lucky I am to be brought up Jewish, a member of a religion, history, community, heritage and belief system that places the utmost value on human life and the ability of one person to improve the life of another. From Judaism I learned the universal principle that "he who saves one life has saved the universe entire", and the essential duty that we each have of *tikkun olam.*

Another one of the most widely known Jewish concepts is that of *tikkun olam*, fixing the world. It is a duty that is deeply set in Jewish values and it is found as the rationale for a wide variety of Jewish causes. It follows a belief that all men are created *b'tselem Elokim*, in God's image, which creates an innate responsibility that we all have for each other. These values ensure that members of the Jewish faith do not only care for the needs of their own communities, but that they reach out to those to whom they are not connected, in order to better the world. Jewish teachings state that it is important for people to contribute to the task of making the world a better place, and many Jewish folk tales end with the moral that you should leave the world a better place than you found it. This concept comes from many different sources, but with regard to helping lead the fight in preventing additional genocides, its modern form is undoubtedly shaped from the Jewish experience of the Holocaust. As second and third generation survivors of the Holocaust, those leading today's Jewish communities are all too cognizant of the responsibility we have to prevent genocide and the hatred that precedes it.

The idea of "Never Again" is one that I will attempt to tackle at another point in this book. With regard to Darfur however, it can clearly be seen that Jewish organizations worldwide have undertaken to advocate for the cause of the Darfuri people under the mantra of Never Again. The world permitted the Holocaust to happen to us, but we survived, and so now we will learn from this experience to ensure that similar atrocities do not happen to another group. I saw these movements taking place, and I saw people like Elie Wiesel, a renowned Holocaust survivor and human rights activist, standing in front of rallies calling on international support for the people of Darfur. This made me proud of my heritage. My South African heritage and upbringing in Canada as well as my Jewish ideals and perceptions all contributed to my desire to get involved with African affairs.

While adapting to my newly formed social-conscience, I also developed an idea that South Africans living in the Diaspora, those who had fled South Africa when things started to get bad, had a responsibility to assist those remaining in Africa. I noticed how ex-South Africans had this deep affinity and identity with Africa, and how it shaped their outlooks and perceptions of the world. I also noticed the lack of attention that ex-South Africans were giving to issues such as Darfur. Looking at just the South African community in Toronto I saw how proud people were of their African heritage and how they decorated their houses and talked about their pasts in Africa, yet they were disconnected with what was currently unfolding on the continent. It began to dawn on me that as the lucky group that was able to escape Africa when conditions began to decline, we must feel at least partially responsible for helping those in Africa who are significantly less fortunate than we are, and I tried to write about this issue and bring it up with like-minded individuals. Unfortunately I was unable to prompt people to act, and many did not want to hear the idea that we, as Jews who were also South Africans, had an even stronger moral imperative to reach out to Africa. Maybe this was another factor that spurred on my passion and activism toward Africa and its people.

Post-Undergrad and Life in London

After I graduated from York University, I moved to London, England for a year to do some soul-searching and dream-living. Ever since my first visit to London I'd fallen in love, and somewhere along the way I had decided that my dream job would be a tour guide in London. Shortly after moving to London I was fortunate to get a job as a tour guide for the Big Bus Company, and after spending the best summer of my life seeing London and teaching others about it, I had to find some other employment. I started working for the Union of Jewish Students in London as their Education Officer, and got involved in some of their campaigns, one of which involved bringing additional awareness to the genocide in the Sudan.

At this time in London, now early-2008, the atrocities in Darfur had been going on for approximately five years. While in Europe, I had the privilege of meeting with a number of refugees who had fled Darfur. I joined those helping them organize marches through the streets of London to bring awareness about their plight, and at a particularly moving conference in Amsterdam on the topic of genocide, I was fortunate enough to meet survivors from the Holocaust, the genocide in Rwanda, as well as Darfur. These experiences introduced me to the people most affected by these historical tragedies and failures of mankind, and it was then that I decided that I would actively try to spend some time in Africa in the near future. I started looking online for different projects and the one that I found was a peacebuilding project in Kenya, and more importantly at the time, seemed to fit my schedule the best. I called the organization to confirm all the details, registered, booked my flights, and was ready to go.

First Visit to Kenya

This first visit to Kenya, in the summer of 2008, turned out to be quite a different experience than I had expected. Firstly, I had a terrible experience with the organization that "organized" the trip. Though I had confirmed with them before booking that I would be participating in a work-camp for three weeks in Kenya with 14 other North American youths, when I arrived in Kenya I was . . . . startled, to say the least. I landed at Jomo Kenyatta International Airport in Nairobi, got picked up by one of the organizers of the trip, and as we got into the car, the conversation went something like this:

"Welcome to Kenya!"

"Thanks! When are we going to be heading to the village?"

"Oh, well the village is a six hour bus drive, so we're going to spend the night in Nairobi and head to the village first thing tomorrow morning. You are going to be staying at a host family tonight."

"Umm . . . ok, great! Where are all the other volunteers staying?"

"What other volunteers?"

"The other 14 that have signed up for this project . . ."

"Oh, nope, it's just you."

That's right. I now found myself alone in Nairobi, about to spend a night at a host family, and the organization had blatantly lied to me about the other participants. Thankfully however, I'm an easy going guy and came prepared for an adventure. Also, not knowing what to expect from a host family in Nairobi, I was pleasantly surprised to find that the first thing I saw in the house as I entered that evening was a big screen TV: thumbs up to globalization. Also actually, what was showing as I walked in was the movie *The Sentinel*, one of the only movies filmed in Toronto that shows actual Toronto landmarks, which I found to be the fates teasing me a little bit ("You miss home, don't you? Don't you???"). The rest of the night I sat nervously contemplating whether or not I should actually stay in Kenya or just back out while I had the chance, all the while watching whatever was being broadcast on Kenyan TV. That night I watched the finals of East African Idol, where a young Zimbabwean man took home the final prize, as well as a soap opera from Ethiopia. You think soaps in North America are overly dramatic? Wait until you see an African one where the husband is trying to avoid a confrontation with his three *legal* wives. No further explanation needed. I was intrigued with this place, and the next day I took the bumpiest bus ride of my life (I took off my seatbelt to see how far off the seat I'd go, and my head actually hit the roof of the bus at one point) west to the Rift Valley Province where I met a number of Kenyan youths who were warm, hospitable, friendly, and eager to make me comfortable.

I spent three weeks in the village getting to know the others and learning about Kenya. This did not involve a lesson about the history or politics of Kenya, things which I would later learn on my own, but rather learning about the people and how they had experienced the post-election violence which had torn the country apart only five-months prior to my visit. I spoke to school groups about Canada and got to ask the students about their own lives, and I was able to do some community service, helping clean up health facilities, marketplaces, and community centers.

The Beginnings of the Project

Without this initial experience in Kenya I would not have felt confident or comfortable coming back for a second time to try and start my own project. I suppose I was lucky in the end to be the only participant since I got all the attention and was able to get to know such a large number of individuals on a much more personal level. If I was not able to make these contacts and network with all those who actually lived and worked in these small villages, then much of what I set out to do during my second visit would not have been fulfilled, so I am thankful that the organization-that-shall-not-be-named misled me in such a way.

My decision to return to Kenya came about after having both formed close connections with people there, and having learned about all those issues that were dividing Kenyan society. Though I had lost faith in the organization that initially brought me to Africa, I left with an intense desire to return, and so decided that I could do it alone. I spent the next several months (also coinciding with my first year of law school at the University of Windsor) finding support for my idea to return to Kenya and help kick-start a grassroots peacebuilding initiative. I needed both financial and moral support for this one. Soon however, after having found the requisite minimal amount of funds needed to run an effective program, I was able to return and in the process, have a life-altering experience. This book is an account of my experience and is my attempt to illuminate what life is like on the most basic levels in rural Africa.

I wanted to run a project because I wanted to make a difference. I had met those recovering from the end of a horrible civil conflict, and had created intense and lasting connections with so many of them. Being pulled away from the country however, in the midst of my hands-on learning experience and simply as a result of scheduling, felt like a tease, and I believed that I had been given an opportunity, however small, to make a difference in the lives of others. If I could find the support, and the motivation, and the encouragement that I needed to pursue this objective, then I could not simply walk away from my three-week sneak-peek at Kenya with only my photos and souvenir Maasai blanket.

For a while I toyed with the idea of whether I should include this personal story into this account, and I had originally decided against it. I realized however that this project in Kenya is deeply personal and therefore a result of my particular experiences. I have also provided much commentary on the way that I saw things in Kenya and it is only responsible therefore to provide a context for my perspective on these issues. I want this book to be about the people of Kenya and about how they view the future of their country. In my time there however they made me feel as though I was one of them, and so perhaps it is fitting that I include a little about the way that I got to where I am today. My goal is also to encourage others to take the plunge and go and see Africa. I want others to know that the way that I got to doing this project was by no means through extraordinary circumstances or events, but that I was simply a curious young-adult who wanted to see a bit more of the world. George Kimble once wrote that, "The darkest thing about Africa has always been our ignorance of it." Seeing it once shatters all that ignorance and gets people to realize that there is a depth to the continent that is evident only through your own eyes.

The project I helped facilitate in Kenya is entirely grassroots and is all about the people of Kenya. The direction that it took, the way that it manifested itself, and the people it was able to touch was all a result of those youths steering it on the ground. I can comfortably say that I went to Kenya only wanting to facilitate some kind of a project based on my first visit to the country, but what kind of project would be created was entirely up to those who would be most influenced by it. I have been more than blessed by the results of what we started in Kenya but however much my life has been influenced by the progress we have made pales in comparison to the impact it has had on the lives of those in charge of it in Kenya. They have seen for themselves that they do not require the help of Westerners to improve their own lives, and that they are entirely capable of doing it on their own. They have been able to experiment and grow as a group, and the different ideas they consistently propose when I ask them "What's next?" are evidence of this. This is grassroots activism at its finest and my goal is to share with you these successes to demonstrate that there is hope for peace in an area of the world that has largely been overlooked by outsiders. What we accomplished also gives me the conviction to proudly call myself an idealistic-realist.

Goals of the Project and Book

This book will detail the project as it stands at the time of writing. Currently, there is a group called the Youth Ambassadors for Peace whom I had the privilege of training over the span of a one-week workshop. These youths then went on to form a number of peace clubs in local high schools to try to inspire students and instill in them the values of peace from a younger age. A few members of the group then formed a drama club that has been successful in terms of activism, and they in turn created a chicken farm, designed to help people in a few communities who are suffering from HIV/AIDS. This project also includes a soccer tournament that has seen great successes and has spread the word about the overall project to those who would otherwise not have heard about it. Our strides have therefore been great, and the projects themselves shed much light on village life in Kenya.

In the American Declaration of Independence, there is a line that I love. It says,

> But when a long train of abuses and usurpations, pursuing invariably the same object evinces a design to reduce them under absolute despotism, it is their right, it is their duty, to throw off such government, and to provide new guards for their future security.

I am not attempting to imply here, as others do, that absolute despots necessarily rule Kenya. This affirmation however means that governments should listen to their people. To use a line from the movie *National Treasure,* if a country's people do not feel that their government is acting in their best interest, then those who have the *ability* to take action have the *responsibility* to take action.

The challenge is determining that one has that ability to take action. Once that ability is recognized, by performing any number of self-actualizing activities or exercises, it is then realizing one's responsibility to take action that becomes important, and this is what the project aspires to do. This project has served as an indication to Kenyan youths involved in it that they have the ability to affect change, and that this ability is limitless. Once they stopped telling me that they thought they needed the help of Americans, Canadians, Europeans and, well, white people in general, then they realized that they as youths, as the majority of Kenya's population, had the responsibility to help shape their country's future. This is what we are trying to do in Kenya, and this is what I have tried to highlight in the account that follows. I also feel that others should take responsibility for what happens in the world, and the more we know, the harder it should be to close our eyes to it.

Idealism is important because it provides hope as well as a goal. The goal that was set for this project was to ensure that there would be a peaceful general elections process in Kenya in March 2013. There are however many ways to achieve a goal. A famous adage says that "A goal is a dream that is simply written down," and when I was younger my dad always bugged me that the most important way to ensure that you reach a goal was to write it down. So Dad, here it goes.

Peace is Precious — If you don't trust me, taste war

There are around fifty different tribal communities in Kenya. They are spread around the country, the larger ones recognized for land that is historically theirs, and the smaller ones interspersed between the larger ones. Despite Kenya's history and the age of these communities, some have managed to stay distinct without being absorbed into the other, larger communities and have maintained clear cultural differences. Tribal communities are differentiated most distinctly by language, as each different community speaks a different tribal language. This means that every person in Kenya speaks at least three languages: English and Swahili (the two official languages of Kenya), and their own tribal tongue. There are at least 52 different languages spoken in Kenya, a country with a population of roughly 30 million people.

As much as I would love to include some information about all the tribal communities mentioned in this book, and as much as I'm sure you'd love to read a survey of the ins and outs of every tribe (obviously), I am going to stick to the three communities I know best: Luo, Kisii, and Kalenjin. Before I get into the details of these specific communities, I would like to offer a few words on the issue of tribal communities in Kenya. This is relevant and important to my peacebuilding project and it may also be useful at this point to include a survey of the events that led to the post-election violence in Kenya, which is the ultimate reason for our work in the region in the first place.

For those of you interested in all the tribal communities in Kenya however, aside from a brief historical overview of the development of these communities and their impact on modern Kenyan society, I will give you a list of the approximately fifty different tribal groups currently in existence in Kenya. They are the: Ameru, Bajuni, Bakusu, Embu, Isukha, Kalenjin, Elgeyo, Kipsigis, Marakwet, Nandi, Pokot, Sabaot, Terik, Tugen, Kamba, Kikuyu, Kisii, Kore, Kuria, Luhya, Luo, Maragoli, Marama, Maasai, Sengwer, Mijikenda, Kenda, Chonyi, Digo, Duruma, Giryama, Jibana, Kambe, Kauma, Rabai, Ribe, Ogiek, Orma, Oromo, Pokomo, Rendille, Samburu, Somali, Suba, Swahili, Tachoni, Taita, Taveta, Turkana, Yaaku.

Say that three times fast.

When people ask me about the goals of my project the first reason I give is the eradication of tribalism. By this I am not calling for the eradication of tribes or identity along tribal lines. I believe tribalism is like racism. Racism is roughly defined as an irrational hatred or prejudice of people based on their race. In this same way, tribalism is an irrational hatred based on membership in a particular tribe.

Tribalism exists in many forms across both Kenya and Africa, and a clear example of tribalism and its potential to do harm is the Rwandan genocide. At the start of April 1994, the Hutu tribe in Rwanda began a campaign to cleanse Rwanda of its native Tutsi population. This hatred was based solely on tribal tensions, the differences between the two tribes perpetuated greatly by the Belgian colonizers of Rwanda. This instance of tribalism led to the murder of approximately 800,000 Tutsis and also moderate Hutus in only 100 days. This provides clarity with regard to the potential devastation that this social trend may inflict on a certain population. As you will see later, some of the trends from Rwanda were similar to those in Kenya; thankfully, however, not nearly to the same extent.

On my first visit to Kenya I discovered tribalism. I went to Kenya not knowing much of anything about the country, and throughout my time there, I was introduced to the notion that the country was divided into many different tribes. To me this seemed a relic of the past, and as one gets to know the system, one learns that it essentially is. However, tribes were historically formed; the model dominated at a time when people were able to remain separate, only married within the tribe, and essentially considered the other members of the tribe to be an extended family. Many of these preferences still exist today, but in modern Kenya where 30 million people are spread out all over a small piece of territory, it is difficult to remain separate. People can get along, and there are plenty of examples throughout Kenya of tribes coming together without giving a thought to the fact that they come from a different collective history.

The problem in Kenya however was the way that tribes were treated when Kenya was still a British colony. It is an understanding of this issue that contributes to the modern understanding of tribalism, as well as the reason for the outbreak of the post-election violence at the start of 2008. Much of what follows is taken from an article called "Who are the Kikuyu?" by Michela Wrong, who is a brilliant commentator on many issues and events taking place in Kenya.

Prior to Kenyan independence in 1963, British colonialists ruled East Africa in much the same way as they controlled the majority of their other colonies: the rights of the British came first, and the native Africans were treated for the most part as second-class citizens. In the tribal context, the Kikuyu tribe, the largest single tribe in Kenya at the time, turned to face-off with the British when they felt that they had gathered enough strength. The Kikuyu desired more land for their tribe to expand and so in the 1950s, the Mau Mau Uprising against the British commenced, with Jomo Kenyatta leading the charge.

When the Mau Mau Uprising ended and the British eventually left Kenya, independence was declared in 1963.

The Kikuyus were not only the most numerous tribe in Kenya (and still are), they were also the most educated and privileged. This affluence and education came as a result of Kikuyu physical proximity to the British colonial administration as well as the influence of British missionary schools in largely Kikuyu areas. This ensured that the Kikuyus in central Kenya were best suited to benefit from British rule, and they did benefit when independence was declared.

Today the majority of Kikuyus live in and around Nairobi and the Mount Kenya region, and remain the dominant tribe in Kenya in terms of both political influence and population. There are approximately 5.3 million Kikuyus in Kenya, making them 23% of Kenya's overall population. There have been three presidents in Kenya since independence and two of them have been Kikuyu, Jomo Kenyatta and currently Mwai Kibaki.

This survey on the Kikuyus is relevant for having made the assertion that the British placed serious emphasis on the notion of tribes, which has survived to this day. The tribal divide impacting political influence as a partial relic of British colonialism has contributed heavily to the current realities on the ground and has resulted in the Kikuyus being the dominant tribe in Kenya. In the literature on this subject, it becomes clear that Kikuyus also see themselves as the dominant tribe in Kenya, and as a result they tend to look down on the other communities, which understandably creates resentment. Tribal dominance and favouritism have been particularly accentuated during the Presidency of Mwai Kibaki, in power since 2002, and are considered direct reasons for the outbreak of the post-election violence at the end of 2007. This is evidenced in the common nickname for Kibaki's inner circle as the "Mount Kenya Mafia", alluding to the fact that the most powerful men in his government are all of Kikuyu descent. The reference to Mount Kenya is an interesting quick history lesson as well.

Mount Kenya, located geographically in the centre of Kenya, was historically the birthplace of the Kikuyu tribe and is also the location where the Kikuyus believe mankind was created. In fact they believe that Mount Kenya was where God, Ngai, resided. On the outskirts of Mount Kenya there is the *Mukurwe Wa Nyagathanga* or "Tree of Gathanga", which could most easily be equated with the Biblical Tree of Knowledge. The Kikuyus believe that Ngai created the first man, Gikuyu, in the shadow of Mount Kenya, and then later sent the female Mumbi to be his partner. Sound familiar? Together Gikuyu and Mumbi created a homestead, and today, right near *Mukurwe Wa Nyagathanga,* there are still two small mud huts, one for Gikuyu and the other for Mumbi. From this region, the Kikuyu tribe spread throughout Kenya and members of the tribe became farmers, developing a special affinity for the land.

As I will demonstrate later, some of the tribes in Kenya believe they have special connections with various natural elements. The Kalenjins, for example, believe that all the cows in the world belong to them. The Kikuyus believe in a special connection with the land and soil. They not only believe that they must own land, but all Kikuyus believe that they must build a home on that land, to which they can invite visitors to eat and drink. Borrowing a quote from

Wrong who quoted Jomo Kenyatta, "A man or woman who cannot say to his friends, come eat, drink and enjoy the fruit of my labour, is not considered a worthy member of the tribe." In this sense one can appreciate the deep-seated belief that Kikuyus possess with regard to owning land and building a home. It is as a result of this desire that they felt the need to expand and drive the British off the land, in particular from the arable and fertile land that they had taken as colonialists.

Now, back to politics: When Mwai Kibaki was elected President in the 2002 general election, he made no secret of his ethnic favouritism and promptly embarked on a policy of nepotism. This ethnic favouritism, avoided somewhat by his Kalenjin predecessor Daniel Toroitich arap Moi, naturally bothered the population of Kenya immensely. Now, the old elements of traditional Kikuyu snobbery combined with the institutional dominance of the Kikuyus secured by Kibaki, put into place a shaky system that most analysts believe led directly to the post-election violence in 2008.

In the December 2007 elections, Mwai Kibaki, seeking reelection on behalf of the Party of National Unity (PNU), squared off against Raila Odinga for the position of President. Odinga represented the Orange Democratic Movement (ODM). He is a member of the Luo community, and the son of Kenya's first Vice President, Jaramogi Oginga Odinga. Leading up to that election, and in the five years of Kibaki's first term, many rumours circulated from Kikuyu leaders, in the form of fear mongering. While Odinga preached a proposed policy of federalism, many Kikuyus took this policy to mean that Kikuyus would be kicked off the land that they owned in largely non-Kikuyu areas. An even larger rumour then circulated about a proposed culling of the Kikuyu population because of their size and influence. With sabre-rattling occurring on all sides of the political and tribal spectrum, violence seemed inevitable at some point. All that was required was a single shot to ignite the situation.

This was not the first time that violence would erupt between tribes in Kenya. What made this most recent post-election violence unique however, was its scope and the fact that it reached across the country from Kisumu in the West to Mombasa in the East. In conversations I had with locals about the situation, they all referred to prior violence that had erupted in towns where members of different villages resided, and said that election years have always been tense for tribal relations.

In one particular situation in 1992, major clashes erupted in Sondu, a village on the border of Kalenjin and Luo territory. The violence was initiated by a group of Kalenjin individuals who attacked a Luo man for wearing a political t-shirt that advocated for a Luo party called Forum for the Restoration of Democracy (FORD). Despite the claimed spontaneity of the violence, those who witnessed it said that the Kalenjins were well equipped with their bows and arrows, meaning that they had come prepared for a confrontation. A Luo villager told me, "a community with warriors will always go to war; otherwise there is no point in having them in society." Despite this apparent provocation however, it was only one event in a long line of cold relations between the Kalenjin and Luo tribes.

In September 2007, a few months before the last elections occurred, violence again broke out in Sondu between the Kalenjin, Luo and Kisii communities. During the campaigning period before the election, houses were burned down, families were uprooted then forced to leave, and some political leaders were banned from certain tribal regions leading up to Election Day. The youths with whom I worked lived in and around Sondu, and described to me the fear they felt around election time.

They feared attacks spurred on by revenge from members of other tribes, and they described how even the local police took different sides in the conflict, sometimes only helping people from their own communities. The youths described how gangs of youths would attack others at night under the cover of darkness, and how one never knew who would be targeted next. One of the girls who participated in the workshop told me that her own cousins had set fire to her home with the family still inside because her parents were in a mixed-marriage. The family escaped but the house and all their belongings were entirely destroyed. Again, this was even before the election took place and accounts for the vast number of Internally Displaced Persons (IDPs) whose tents dot the countryside as one drives west through Kenya.

The election was held on December 27, 2007. On December 30, Kenya's Electoral Commission declared Mwai Kibaki the winner, despite the overwhelming belief that Odinga had won the popular vote. Allegations of fraud arose on both sides amidst claims that the members of the Electoral Commission were simply loyal to Kibaki himself. This declaration of Kibaki's victory provided the spark required to ignite the fire. Soon, ethnic violence erupted throughout the country as a result of Kibaki's perceived corruption and the wider underlying societal resentment of the Kikuyu people.

Many Kikuyus were targeted during the post-election violence, and members of Kenya's other communities were determined to ensure that the Kikuyus would not spend another undeserved term in power. In Kisumu, on the coast of Lake Victoria, members of the Luo community began to loot Kikuyu owned shops, while Kalenjin militias in the Rift Valley Province drove the Kikuyu owners from their farms. As the country rapidly descended into chaos, the tribal tension that had always been simmering just below the surface of Kenyan society suddenly reared its ugly head.

This post-election violence continued for just over two months, leading Kenya to resemble a number of its African neighbours. Almost 1500 died and upwards of half a million were displaced internally, with thousands more severely injured. Former UN Secretary-General Kofi Annan persuaded Odinga and Kibaki to agree on a power-sharing deal, and this agreement formed a new Unity Government with Kibaki as President, Odinga as Prime Minister, and an approximately equal number of ministers from the two opposing parties. This power sharing deal has been held in place from the time of the ceasefire, yet most maintain that this imposed ceasefire was very much a band-aid solution to the larger problem of tribalism.

The emphasis that the British placed on differentiation based on tribal adherence, translated into very real results with the advent of Kenyan independence, and this relic of the past is still clearly seen in modern day Kenya. The

2008 post-election violence occurred directly along tribal lines, and it is from this context that I came to understand the idea of tribalism and many of the other problems that plague Kenya.

In the same way that racism is defined as an irrational hatred of a person or group of people based on their race, I have found that tribalism is an irrational hatred of persons based on their tribe. It's a simple definition, and within only a short time in Kenya I personally witnessed plenty of examples of tribalism throughout the country. A number of experiences really stuck with me, but none as clearly as the day we were visiting an elementary school, during which time an eight-year old student stood up and told me that all Kikuyus deserved to be killed. Common sense dictates that an eight-year old likely did not come up with this bold assertion on his own, so one inevitably would point to his parents as the source of such hatred. In any case, tribalism exists and bares its teeth in even the most remote areas throughout the country.

In another instance, one of the participants in our project named Gordon told me about his upbringing. Growing up with his grandmother, Gordon had always been taught that the only enemy in the world was the Kikuyu. As a Luo living in the Sondu area, Gordon grew up witnessing tribal animosity and violence. He described the comments that his grandmother made to him throughout his youth. She told him that members of the Kisii tribe were witches who practiced black magic, and she suggested that he marry a Kalenjin girl because they were the most passive. She told him that he could beat a Kalenjin girl as much as he wanted and that she would never leave him because of her submissive nature. Though he asked questions and resented his grandmother's hatred of the other communities in Kenya, he saw this as the attitude of the elders in the village and came to realize that if there is to be peace, these stereotypes and generalizations had to be overcome. His grandmother dismissed his objections as him "talking too much" and not realizing who his neighbours really were. Gordon turned out to be one of the most energetic and passionate participants of the program, regularly running seminars and singing songs that stemmed from his deeply tolerant and religious beliefs.

Our peace project's message is clear: tribalism is irrational, is rooted in archaic and colonial notions of tribal supremacy, and has no positive impact on the Kenyan way of life. To borrow a line from one of the participants, "We are all Kenyan, the rest is just bad history." Eradicating tribalism is a practical change only in the sense that it would eliminate both the negative element of hatred from society and the potential for Kenyans to harm each other simply as a result of an unexplained animosity. Nothing positive is lost in the eradication of tribalism, as this eradication does not, by any means, imply the eradication of tribes. The purpose of this endeavour would be to change the thinking of the youths in society in order to realize that tribal difference should not be a divisive trend, but rather a beautiful concept that should be embraced and fostered throughout the country at all possible opportunities.

After my first visit to Kenya, prior to the initiation of this peace project, I remember learning about the concept of tribal communities and then experiencing this feeling of extreme helplessness. I came to learn about a history of divisiveness that led, more often than not, to violence and hatred. I heard negative comments from eight year-olds, from grandparents, and even from some youths, and realized that Kenya was just like any other place in the world. Irrational hatred exists everywhere and to anyone who pays attention, this fact should be extremely saddening. My feeling of helplessness, however, was overcome by the dedication and compassion that I encountered in a group of youths who I came to learn much about during my second visit to Kenya. In deciding to initiate a peacebuilding process, we tried to attack this hatred from a grassroots level and tried to chip away at the helplessness that I, along with some others, felt. Through the initiation of this project, we were able to help found a peacebuilding project that these youths wanted in order to better their own inter-tribal relationships. They were able to help me realize that irrational hatred can become the exception, not the rule.

When we began to speak about tribalism in the workshop setting with the youth, one of the youths stood up, looked around at the others and asked, "Did you apply to God to be born into your tribe? Did you? Please, show me your application form if you did!" He told me afterwards that in asking this question he was trying to demonstrate that we should not simply resign ourselves to feeling helpless just because of the circumstances that we were born into. It is only by chance that each of these youths belongs to a specific tribe, but it is by choice that they found themselves in a peacebuilding workshop, attempting to shape their own futures. These youths therefore accepted the situation that they were born into, but promised that they would not let the future resemble the past.

THE OPPOSITE OF LIFE IS NOT DEATH, ITS INDIFFERENCE

For many months at the Nairobi Gallery, the former headquarters of Nairobi Province, there was a photo exhibit displaying photography of Kenya's 2008 post-election violence.

Set amongst the downtown core of Nairobi, the gallery is next to a government building where people line up all day to receive visas to travel abroad. A fence surrounds the gallery and as you walk into this large property, you notice that the Nairobi Gallery is actually quite small.

The sign that greets you when you enter the building is a poster for the exhibit that says, "Never Forget, Never Again: Kenya Burning" above an image of a camera on fire. Next to the poster is a simple sign hastily printed off a computer, which says, "SOME OF THE IMAGES YOU ARE ABOUT TO SEE ARE DISTURBING."

I entered the exhibit feeling as though I had been tripped, suddenly feeling caught off guard. I was not surprised necessarily by the content of the photos, but by the context in which they were being shown, here, in a brightly lit building in the middle of Nairobi in the heart of beautiful Africa. As someone removed from the conflict and its beginnings, I felt like it was a photo exhibit like any other. But it wasn't.

Here I found some of the most explicit photographs I had ever seen of people brutally killing each other. The kinds of images there made me gasp audibly and cover my mouth. On display in the nation's capital, the purpose of this exhibit was to show the people of Kenya what they resorted to and what they became in a time of desperation and to remind them that it could never happen again. Another thought was that this exhibit likely incriminated many Kenyans involved in the violence and slaughter that took place. Many of those who took part in the violence had now likely faded into the background and were again living life as if the violence had not occurred, and they were lucky to not to be held accountable for their actions. Those perpetrators would probably not pay a visit to the Nairobi Gallery to see this exhibit that portrayed their heinous behavior, but for those who did perhaps wander in, this gallery served as a stark reminder and condemnation of what they had become in a time of utter lawlessness.

Then I thought that this was perhaps the exact point of this exhibit: incriminate everyone. If not the whole country, then it at least incriminated the leaders, the new President and Prime Minister, shown in one of the last images of the exhibit smiling, shaking hands, and drinking tea after signing the cease fire and unity government agreement.

The photos that stand out in my mind from that visit are of a field littered with people standing with bows and arrows ready to fight. Another was a picture of a dead man with an arrow in his face, with a photo of an x-ray next to it showing how deep into his head the arrow penetrated. Another picture showed an angry mob pulling people out of a *matatu* (a Kenyan taxi that seats 15) and beating them on the ground with sticks and machetes, while another picture showed a funeral service. The coffins used in the funeral were too small for the people they contained, and so the ends of the coffin were cut off so that the feet could stick through the bottom. The pictures varied from the bright, hope-filled photographs of politicians at election rallies amid throngs of their supporters, to the darkest potential of human activity, one person smashing the head of another with a boulder as he lay bleeding on the grass.

The images evoked in me not only a sense of desperation that something like an election could lead to such human disaster, but also that this violence follows a similar pattern of human history. The images on the walls of the post office were not new. Images with the exact same content are found from conflicts all over the world: from the fight to topple Apartheid in South Africa, to the Arab-Israel conflict, to the standoff in Tiananmen Square, to the civil rights riots in the US, and the newest images that have emerged from the recent Arab Spring. All over the world and throughout history violence has been demonstrated in photographs like these. All over the world this violence occurs out of a sense of desperation and a sense of last-resort, yet people are always quick to pick up a gun or machete and risk their lives for some greater struggle. My comparison here does not mean to equate all these conflicts to each other, and it is not my purpose to pronounce on what was or is a "just" struggle or not. My point is that time and time again people manage to get to the point where picking up arms and fighting becomes an option. The goal, from the beginning, should always be the prevention of such violence.

This display was intended to teach a lesson, and though such exhibits are rarely created so soon after the time of hostilities, the timing here worked well. It was at a time when the memory was still fresh enough in people's minds but removed enough so that they could learn something from why an exhibit like this was being shown in the middle of Nairobi. I purchased the official book of the exhibit that contained all of the photographs and my experiences simply carrying this book around demonstrated that people in Kenya were ready to learn about what they had done and confront the past by talking about it. I used the book to talk about the conflict during my workshop with the youths from the Kisii, Luo and Kalenjin communities. I brought it with me sometimes to school visits that I would later hold to talk to the older students about what they remember as having happened, and it often became a topic of conversation when I least expected it to.

When I was at Jomo Kenyatta International Airport leaving Kenya at the end of my month there, my suitcase was a little overweight. As such, I was told to open it up and shuffle things around and put some items in my overnight bag. I opened up my suitcase on the floor of the airport in front of a line of others waiting to check in, and on the top of my suitcase I had placed this book. One of the security guards, who had just been standing joking around with a friend of his, picked it up out of my suitcase to look through while I was hastily reorganizing my things so that I could make it to my plane on time (overweight bags and running late . . . the story of every one of my airport visits).

As soon as he and two others opened the book, well, their faces changed. I could tell by their reactions and by their sudden intense interest in the photos that they had personally experienced something, and I asked them about it. They told me that members of their families had been injured during the conflict, followed with the common expression of disbelief about how this could possibly happen in a country as peaceful as Kenya. Almost making me late for my flight, they continued to leaf through the book speaking to each other about the pictures and lamenting the fact that their country had taken such a turn for the worse. They asked why I had the book and what I had been doing in Kenya, and each one of them shook my hand after I had explained the essence of the peace project. This seemed to be the reaction of everyday Kenyans to the violence that tore apart their country.

In a room at the back of the photo exhibit at the Nairobi Gallery there was a film being screened about the conflict. A young Kenyan man sat at the back of the room, with his cell phone in his lap and white headphones running into his ears. His job was to make sure the film kept running. The film was to be playing on repeat without any breaks in between, and this man got up each time the movie ended, walked over to the DVD player connected to the 20 inch TV and hit STOP and then PLAY. Once the movie started afresh, he would go and sit back down, take out his phone, and continue to listen to his music.

I sat and watched the movie with two women from a volunteer organization in Nairobi who were helping me get my logistics organized on the ground in Kenya. As we watched, my eyes widened as scenes of violence flashed by in front of me. It was done as a documentary, interviewing people involved in the violence, Kenyans who had relatives murdered in the villages, people in Nairobi stranded in their apartments for fear of wandering into the streets, and journalists assigned to cover the violence. The video was done well and incorporated scenes that I had just seen illuminating the walls of the gallery. As startling as the photographs were, the shock only really registered by seeing the raw video footage and the people in action.

A Kenyan reporter who worked for the Al-Jazeera news agency made one comment that struck me and has remained in my mind. While being interviewed he said, "I always have covered conflicts around Africa, like in Rwanda, Darfur, Zimbabwe, and have always felt lucky and comforted in being able to go back to peaceful Kenya. Now, here I was watching my country experience the same thing." Here was a reporter lamenting that his country had become like the rest of Africa, and it saddened him and others. The corruption and other negative societal elements were things that can be understood and lived with in Kenya, but people were really disturbed by the fact that the people of their own country would resort to such primitive violence. I spoke about this idea at length with the participants of the workshop, and I found widespread consensus on this issue among Kenyans with whom I spoke.

One of the women with whom I was watching the video experienced the post-election violence from her apartment in Nairobi. The neighbourhood she lived in was close to Kibera, one of Africa's largest slums, and so the riots were visible from her windows. She was fearful because she could see the city burning, whether the slums of Kibera were on fire, or *matatus* were torched, or roadblocks were made of burning tires. Aside from the visual experience, she could also hear the screams of women and children and smell the wood and rubber burning. These were the screams of vulnerability, of people both being attacked and of those mourning the loss of a loved one. Afraid for the lives of those living near her, she also did not want to leave her apartment fearing risks to her own life. Despite her reluctance to leave, even if she had wanted to go there would have been no way to get there, as taxi services had ground to a halt and most stores and businesses were shut down. She had limited food in her apartment and had to be careful with her rationing, as she was unsure how long she would be trapped for. Adding to the physical destruction she was witnessing, emotionally she was terrified as she was unable to contact her husband and six-year old son who were stuck in the village of Taita, near Kenya's east coast.

Her husband had been away in his home village with their son when the violence erupted. Far from Nairobi, they were unable to make their way back as transportation around the country was sparse, and the phone services around Kenya, most people using pay-as-you-go cell phones, were limited. You simply could not buy more airtime for your phone. People did not have enough minutes to stay in touch with their loved ones, and so her family was separated by the inaccessibility to communications, divided by a burning country. In comparison to the story of other families, this experience of just one family is rather mild. They were apart and emotionally distraught, but no one was killed or injured, and they were ultimately reunited. This was not so for many others. Again, 1500 were killed at that time, and more than half a million were left internally displaced. The diversity of the stories that you can hear from Kenyans living through the conflict demonstrates that the elements fueling the conflict came together to encourage a bitter crisis that raged for over two months. The experience of those outside of Kenya however, is all quite similar.

When the violence broke out in Kenya at the start of 2008 I was living in London, England. I had heard that ethnic tensions had broken out in Kenya but did not hear much else. To me and those in my immediate circle, violence in Africa was all the same. For the last few years I had been intensely interested and involved in advocating about the genocide in Darfur, and was aware of similar trends in the Congo. I knew about politics and considered myself quite well informed, but 53 countries in Africa is a lot of information. When you hear about civil infighting in Kenya most people tend not to give it too much thought, and I did the same. And why not? Violence seems almost typical and expected in a continent that sees so much strife with the added touch of some extremely ineffective and usually corrupt leadership.

To be honest, the only real reason I was aware of what was occurring at all, besides my addiction to cnn.com, was because my English friend's parents had booked a 10-day safari holiday in Kenya and were about to leave when the post-election violence broke out. He expressed to me his parents' dismay at having to postpone their vacation, and told me that although some British tourists were still going and just staying away from the hot spots, his parents had decided to cancel as the news showed the violence intensifying. After that I didn't pay much attention to the crisis, and suddenly there were no more 10-second news clips about hostilities gripping East Africa. I also imagined that it couldn't be *that* bad if people were still vacationing there.

Knowing what I know today and seeing what I've seen, it surprises me when I think back to what I knew or did not know at the time this all started. Then again, maybe I shouldn't be too surprised. News has always been a product of who is covering it and the people who are covering it, frankly, rarely spend that much time on Africa.

To generalize that the world doesn't care about Africa is not fair. There have been admirable commitments to Africa made by world leaders, the United Nations and their millennium goals, the G8 and G20 nations, massive pharmaceutical companies, and individuals who have traveled to the continent to do their part to help. A search on the Internet for volunteer opportunities in Africa yields a massive number of results and this is the way that I myself got involved in Kenya. I would therefore say that people do care, maybe just not enough.

My opinion about Africa is not that people don't care, but it is that today people are more willing to act to fix something if it affects them directly. They care about what will have a negative impact on them, what will do them harm, and what those doing the judging in the future will say about them if they stood idly by. Unfortunately, Africa does not always fit into the above categories and so the tragedies that continue to affect Africa occur daily, without so much as a word of condemnation or a lone voice of opposition from the world as to what has happened. As I wrote earlier, it is important to stop this violence before it becomes violence, and this prevention requires care, thought and action. Though this may upset people and is just my personal opinion, I believe that Africa has been left behind because of factors like disaster-fatigue and the fact that in terms of perceived real and immediate threats, what happens in Africa does nothing to influence our lives elsewhere.

Disaster-fatigue is easy to understand, and actually makes sense. Bluntly, the world today sucks. A great indicator of what has happened in the past year on an international level are the video montages that the people at CNN and Google put together every year that is showed on New Year's Eve. They show video footage and photographs of the year in review that hopefully make you sit, watch and reflect. Increasingly over the years you realize that there are fewer and fewer good things happening, and more and more terrible things happening. Of course bad news always gets more coverage than good news, but the fact that there are so many terrible things happening in the world means that people at some point, to maintain their sanity or whatever positive outlook they may have, feel like it is best to shut themselves off from certain things. If they turn off the TV or radio and are unaware of the bad things that are happening, they remain unaffected and can go about their lives focusing only on the good things that happen, things that occur on a more human and private level. By this I mean good things that happen on a daily basis that do not require news coverage. Disaster-fatigue is obvious when considering such tragedies as the 2010 Haiti Earthquake, in which people opened up their hearts and wallets to the people of Haiti. When however another earthquake hit Pakistan later in the year, as well as Chile, people for whatever reason did not place as much emphasis on those events and may have potentially rationalized not helping because it was just too much. Disaster-fatigue is something that many people likely frequently feel, but deciding what you can and will shut yourself off from is a matter of priority. The most obvious things to close your eyes to are those events that you do not perceive to affect you in any way. I would argue that this thing, to many people, is Africa.

Fine, what happens in Africa does not necessarily have an immediate impact on too many people. There is certainly an argument to be made about the long term global effects of matters like the HIV/AIDS crisis, Sudanese oil, Somali pirates, mining for coltan, and blood diamonds from Western Africa, but these are not considerations that people make right away. In some way or another when shutting yourself off as a result of disaster fatigue you go through a list of what has a stronger impact on you personally. You prioritize among local issues, national concerns, conflicts in countries you're connected with or have visited, and then issues in places that you can't point out on a map. The fact that Africa falls into the last category for so many people in one form or another is a reason why when something terrible happens in Africa, people turn a blind eye.

For anyone who has ever been involved in programs that have to do with the Holocaust or really any genocide, the phrase "Never Again" is commonplace. The phrase evokes a sort of guilt in the world that "this is what you once allowed to happen, so let's try make sure it does not happen again." By acknowledging and remembering that prior atrocity we vow never to let such things happen again. You'll have to excuse my upcoming cynicism about the phrase "Never Again" though because when reflecting on the history of the phrase, it seems more theoretical than practical in its usage. After the Holocaust people vowed never again; after the genocide in Cambodia people vowed never again; after the genocide in Rwanda people vowed never again; and people talk about never again today while there is an ongoing genocide in Sudan and arguably also the Democratic Republic of the Congo, a place today referred to as the "Rape Capital of the World." Though it is difficult to take this phrase seriously with the history of inaction that it evokes, it is a nice idea that people grasp onto when they have not yet heard it.

For example, at the end of my first visit to Kenya one of the members of the community put together a list of all the funny comments that people had made during my trip. At the very end of this list, he acknowledged that I had used the phrase "Never Again" in reference to the post-election violence. This was of course not a funny saying nor was he saying that it was, but he included it on the list because he wanted the locals involved to think about this message and internalize it. Their cynicism has not yet sunk in.

What happens in Africa on a daily basis is not really reported on or covered by the mainstream media. I think people in a way expect such terrible things to be happening in Africa so it tends to become more important to inform them about other wars that are ongoing. It may also detract from the world's obsession with the conflict in the Middle East. Aside from an obvious critique about the news that it rarely reports good things because 'bad = sexy', the media does not always act in a manner befitting a group of people who have the ability to change the world, or at least our perception of it.

With modern technology we have all become obsessed with having things done instantly. When we send an email we expect an urgent response, and when we hear about something that has just happened we expect an article or news story printed immediately. There is Facebook, there is Twitter and these outlets are used constantly and with a tremendous result. This is what these 24-hour news stations now do best, and it is precisely because of the fact that new news is the best news, that old news becomes irrelevant news. This is why crises like the genocide in Darfur are no longer reported on, and it is why you rarely hear about the struggles of the people in Africa. Only when there is widespread violence that suddenly breaks out will it occupy the headlines for a day or two until the news gets back to pushing Israel around or questioning whether Obama should have worn that awful red tie today. People know that there is a problem with Africa, and perhaps in a sense they don't always want to be reminded of their failure to help in a certain part of the world, so they resort to willful blindness, and it receives no attention.

This unwillingness to face Africa is a problem not only because people there often turn to violence as a means of solving problems, but also because the problems in Africa are exactly so significant. Though people are seemingly content on leaving the people of Africa alone to sort out their own fates when it comes to violence, there is one problem that the African continent faces that absolutely requires the assistance of the outside world, and that is AIDS.

Aside from the physical bloodshed that occurs (overlooked) on a daily basis throughout Africa, the biggest threat to the African population is the scourge of HIV and AIDS. Firstly, not enough people know what these acronyms actually stand for: HIV = Human Immunodeficiency Virus; AIDS = Acquired Immunodeficiency Syndrome. I am not going to attempt to delve into this issue at length since I am not nearly qualified enough to do so, nor is that the purpose of this book. I must however mention it because a discussion about apathy with regard to African affairs is incomplete without some kind of an illustration of the way that HIV and AIDS are also destroying Africa.

On one of my first evenings in Kenya I was sitting with a group of youths after dinner in a room lit dimly with a kerosene lamp. I had just arrived and I told them that I wanted to get to know them, and they responded that they in turn were interested in learning about me. One of the youths proposed we go around the circle and everyone can talk for a few moments about themselves like a typical icebreaker we would play at home in North America. As the visitor (and resident *mzungu*) I obviously had to go first. I told them my name, where I was born, what I studied, what I thought I wanted to do with my life, a bit about why I was interested in Kenya, and then wrapped it up. As I finished, someone asked me: "what is the main crop you grow in Toronto?" Hardly a surprise coming from a small agricultural community, I laughed nonetheless and said that Toronto wasn't exactly what you would call an agricultural centre, which they eventually accepted. Then someone asked if I could ride a bike. Thankfully the answer to this was yes. Then a third hand went up.

"What is your status?"
"I'm single."
"No, I mean your HIV status."

Boom. I was hit by what felt like a ton of bricks. Think to yourself when you have EVER considered this question or ever even thought about the possibility of HIV/AIDS as being a factor in any thought process you have ever had. Why would we ever think about a question like that? Even if we had thought about it, there would be a very good reason with extenuating, possibly devastating, circumstances. Either way, here I was sitting with a group of people my own age and one of the first questions I casually get asked is whether or not I am HIV positive.

Not knowing what the look on my face was, I know that my reaction was to not speak. The question had caught me totally off guard and when I eventually did come back to my senses I felt almost bad brushing off the question, as if it's something that I've never thought of (because in truth it is something that I have never thought of). I felt bad because I felt bad! I knew that there was an HIV and AIDS crisis in Africa, however I could not comprehend that this is the way it was spoken about (though in truth not all Africans speak about it so openly and candidly) and here I was getting asked one of the most intense questions of my life.

This really opened my eyes to a lot of the issues faced in Kenya, but I suppose one of the positive aspects—as I believe one should try to find the positive in even the worst of situations—is that people are talking about it. Though there are of course many who would prefer to keep their status to themselves or not even find out their status at all, there are groups of people who understand that this is a problem in Africa and that AIDS, like most problems, needs exposure if it is to be tackled. It is because of people like this who understand that the first step to overcoming a problem is saying that there is a problem, that there is room for positive thinking in this sense. It must also be mentioned that this is set in the Kenyan narrative, and the story in other African countries is indeed much more devastating.

Throughout the countryside when you come across a market day or events being held in village centres, you will often find VCT tents. VCT stands for "Voluntary Counseling and Testing." The tents are equipped with testing kits to take a blood sample to determine your status, and information about HIV/AIDS to provide whoever is seeking support with someone to whom they can speak privately. The tents are used for mobile services, whereas there are numerous permanent clinics set up across the countryside as well that perform the same functions. I assume that since it is a tent it is supposed to be confidential, but people encourage others to go and seek the assistance of the counselor inside the tent.

People who want to be tested or get further information go to the tent. There, they are asked why they have decided to take this initial step. This pre-testing counseling conversation includes questions about the reason for why they are getting tested, what the tests actually look for, how to read the results, and what to do once you are given the results. If you are found to be HIV negative, then you are taught what precautions you should always be taking to prevent infection. If you are determined to be HIV positive, then these counselors will help link you to a hospital or clinic, which can provide you with antiretroviral therapy and drugs (ART/ARVs). In hindsight I do wish I had gone inside one of those tents to speak to the people who have volunteered their time to help, but I couldn't really bring myself to do it.

One night in our village we held an event for some local youths to come and hang out. We found someone to be a DJ for the night, rented a generator, got the word out, and people came to dance. It was a nice break from the usual 9 o'clock bedtime (since there's not much to do when the sun goes down) and it gave me a chance to meet those not participating in our peacebuilding program.

While planning the event someone mentioned that we had to set up VCT tents outside the building where we were hosting this party, and so it was arranged. When these are set up at night it is apparently called "Moonlight VCT". I need not stress how insane this must be to North Americans to hear, but imagine going to a party where you can take a break for just a few moments to step into a private tent and quickly check to see whether or not you are HIV-positive. While I was speaking to a group of people someone had noticed that I had not actually gone to get tested yet, and implored me to go since, "It is important that we all confront this important issue face-to-face."

I thought about going, I really did. And at the risk of suddenly sounding hypocritical and super-Western-oriented, I had two initial thoughts. Firstly, I know I'm not HIV-positive. I just do. Secondly, and I don't love admitting that this is my thought but its true I suppose, I didn't really want to go near any needles in Africa. There, I said it. Here I am in the middle of a chapter about ignorance about Africa, praising the amazing work of the VCT workers, and I didn't want to go near one of their needles. I don't know how to reconcile this thought with what I really believe, and I guess it was in a sense a selfish act by someone not really sure of how to proceed. I think this thought also put a wall between me and those who I really wanted to create some sort of a bond with, and I don't really have any excuses. The only thing I will offer however is that perhaps my thoughts and my hesitations to get near anything like that is pretty indicative of our ignorance on the issue of African AIDS in the West, and our ability to build a barrier between us. This is just not something we consider a threat in our part of the world and so I had difficulty coming to grips with it, especially in the time-span of one evening.

After that moment and for the rest of my visit, despite the fact that my trip was focused on peacebuilding, I always had this HIV and AIDS issue in the back of my mind. It is one thing to read a book about the crisis and be passionate about it, but my interaction with these youths really put the issue front and centre in my mind.

The other *mzungu* in Kiptere, where I was staying, was an elderly Irish nun named Sister Lucy. Having met her when I was first in Kenya I was impressed when I returned that she was still there. We were able to finally bond as a result of my prolonged stay in Kiptere and as a result of her finally getting a car to get around a bit more easily.

Sister Lucy always told me that the work she did in Kenya was behaviour change. This useful little euphemism essentially means sex-education in Kenyan classrooms with a religious Catholic twist. Not entirely sure how to broach this subject with her, for a number of weeks I toyed in my head about the conversation that I had to have with Sister Lucy about how she confronted this issue with these youths, and how she was able to handle so much of it at once.

On one of the last days of my trip I was invited to see the Catholic compound just outside Kiptere where Sister Lucy and another nun lived. I brought my friend Marion, one of the local Kenyan youths, to come visit with me as she was actually quite close with Sister Lucy herself and wanted to visit too.

The grounds of the compound were beautiful. There was a church, a school, and even a few small houses used by a number of Kenyan families who live on the grounds of the compound. There was an orchard and flowers everywhere, red and orange, and it seemed like I had just stepped out of muddy Kiptere and into a secret garden. Everything was immaculate, the church itself was actually a spectacular sight, and I was most relieved to arrive at Sister Lucy's door to have her offer me a slice of toast with butter, and a cup of tea. I sat speaking with her for a while on all sorts of topics, using this chance to improve my knowledge of the Catholic faith, and we slowly approached the topic of the AIDS epidemic in Africa. This was my chance to find out a few things.

I asked her rather bluntly what exactly she did in the classrooms she visited. She told me that her role was to go in and talk to the students about life decisions like having sex, and to coach them to make the right decision when it comes to that. Not having to prompt her further on this point, she told me that she of course advised abstinence until marriage. Unable to hold back a whole swath of things I had in my head, I told her that a week before our conversation, Pope Benedict XVI was in Cameroon speaking to an assembly of nearly a million people. Here, in front of a crowd of faithful, in a country heavily affected by the AIDS crisis, the Supreme Pontiff of the Catholic Church told his followers that the usage of condoms makes the AIDS situation worse. That's right: the Pope told a million people in Africa that condoms exacerbate the AIDS crisis.

Ya.

I was angry. I was disappointed. I was stunned. I was overcome with this sense of confusion that no part of me could possibly make sense of. Understanding religious dogma is one thing, but, and excuse me if you feel like I am blowing this out of proportion, AIDS is essentially a death sentence in Africa. I do not need to cite the number of studies to tell you that condoms are used to prevent the spread of sexually transmitted infections, and do not make the situation worse. The Catholic Church's stance on birth control aside: this is just wrong. Religion and belief are important, but what the Pope did was make a million people question whether they should use condoms in the future. He is making them choose between a possible fatal disease, and listening to the Holy Father. In Africa, a religious continent where you do what the Pope says, THIS is what is bound to exacerbate the AIDS crisis.

Ok, so I didn't say all of this to Sister Lucy. One, a nice Jewish boy doesn't have to sit and lecture a nun about what he thinks the Pope did wrong, and two, she reacted instantly. She too was not pleased by what the Pope had said. Here was a religious person who can see for herself what the situation on the ground is like, and I am happy to say that she was not blinded by faith but rather acknowledged that the preservation of life is the ultimate goal. She told me that she does not echo the sentiments of the Pope, but rather tells the students she speaks to that abstinence is best, but if they feel like they absolutely must engage in sexual activity before marriage, then use a condom. Bravo.

With this out of the way I wanted to speak to her more about the AIDS issue. I wanted to explain to her that I had read a few books about the crisis before coming to Africa and that it was an issue that I really wanted to learn more about so that I could perhaps incorporate something about it into our wider peace project. This is how the conversation went:

Adam: It's really interesting speaking to you about this and I'm so glad you're on the ground in Kiptere working to educate about this issue. I'm actually really . . . . (I paused to think about what word to use next)

Lucy: Promiscuous?

Adam: . . .

Lucy: (turns red)

Marion: (bursts out laughing)

Adam: . . . interested in learning more about the impact that AIDS has had in Kenya.

Ok, so a bit about what Sister Lucy had in her head about me instantly became clear.

I want to highlight the fact that Sister Lucy is in Kiptere because it is important to know that there are people working on the ground to make sure that this issue is confronted. Whether the mechanism of confrontation is religion, health awareness, or just plain common sense (or a combination of all three), it is imperative that this movement to confront the HIV/AIDS crisis head on continues. Kenya is a somewhat positive story with regard to this African crisis but there are many countries that suffer endlessly. The reason for this suffering is that confronting the situation is something, but it is only a start. Confrontation of HIV/AIDS requires government support and intervention, the availability of antiretroviral drugs in order to counteract the negative effects of HIV and to minimize the transmission rate to offspring, and the help of outsiders. There is a dire need for volunteers in AIDS clinics across the African continent and they need people, even those without medical backgrounds, to go and help distribute drugs that are made available and to teach about how and when to take these drugs. Organizations like the *Clinton Foundation* and the *Bill and Melinda Gates Foundation* have taken great strides in helping to provide these essential services to the people of Africa and Bill Clinton's efforts specifically in this respect are incredible, but there remains much to be done.

The point: Never again is a vague term. It is left open-ended so that it can be applied to any variety of situations, and those situations are not limited to man-made genocide. The Armenian Genocide, the Holocaust, Cambodia, Rwanda, and Darfur: these are events that must be seared into our collective memory and prompt us to act. I believe that these global experiences should leave us with a sense of embarrassment, a sense of embarrassment that we allowed something like this to happen to others. Stand by while atrocities are happening, and you should be considered a perpetrator. "Never Again" is brief because the message is simple, so it necessarily confounds idealists who believe that people are rational, sympathetic and peace-loving. This is with regard to genocide.

In Africa however we cannot be allowed to forget the way that AIDS is ravaging a beautiful continent. There are many factors working against those who want to work to end the AIDS crisis such as the sheer magnitude of those infected, the amount of medication that is required to combat AIDS, and the ability to control or at least limit the detrimental behavior of those infected. People on the outside do not necessarily understand how those infected live, or how they make their decisions, and I of course do not purport to know myself. There is however a need for some basic generosity and understanding to ensure that we do not condemn the people of Africa to the future that is so clearly almost in sight.

Across Africa there are funeral ceremonies held every week for the approximately 1000 people who have died as a result of AIDS. Every week: 1000 people. In an aptly named book *No Place Left to Bury the Dead*, Nicole Itano details the lives of AIDS-infected people in South Africa, and neighbouring Lesotho and Swaziland, and encourages education on the issue. It is a phenomenal read, as is Stephanie Nolen's *28: Stories of AIDS in Africa*. There are so many ways to help and one need only look at countries like Uganda who have identified the problem and vowed to fight it, as success stories. The AIDS crisis in Africa affects everyone and only by understanding the scope of the problem can we begin to counteract its effects. In terms of AIDS, the issue may not necessarily be "Never Again" but rather "Enough" and in this way people can and should be called on to act.

Yitzchak Rabin, the former Prime Minister of Israel, once said the following:

> Just as no two fingerprints are identical, so no two people are alike, and every country has its own laws and culture, traditions and leaders. But there is one universal message which can embrace the entire world, one precept which can be common to different regimes, to races which bear no resemblance, to cultures that are alien to each other. It is a message which the Jewish people has carried for thousands of years, the message found in the Book of Books: *'Ve'nishmartem me'od l'nafshoteichem'*—'Therefore take good heed of yourselves'—or, in contemporary terms, the message of the sanctity of life. The leaders of nations must provide their peoples with the conditions—the infrastructure, if you will—which enables them to enjoy life: freedom of speech and movement; food and shelter; and most important of all: life itself. A man cannot enjoy his rights if he is not alive.

Looking at photographs, like I did in the gallery in Nairobi, you are often able to see a glimpse of our fragile humanity in a snapshot. Mothers crying over their lost children, husbands preparing to fight and perhaps die for their community, and children encouraged to take up arms because they have nothing better to do. This is not the life that these people desire nor should they be condemned if they are born to a mother who is HIV-positive. Humans are products of their environment and because of this simple fact, some people are better equipped to help others. So, help others. It often takes a little bit of effort, but imagine taking that lesson of "Never Again" and making it last. Edmund Burke said that evil triumphs when good men do nothing, and Elie Wiesel said that "The opposite of love is not hate, its indifference; the opposite of faith is not heresy, its indifference; the opposite of life is not death, its indifference."

Education, understanding, empathy and action: these four factors will ensure that the people of Africa are not left to simply fend for themselves.

WHEN FORMER ENEMIES APPEAR TOGETHER, THE WORLD TAKES NOTE

A study habit that I've picked up over the years is to underline and write comments in margins of books instead of highlighting. This is not only with textbooks for school, but also in books that I read just for fun. My habit of writing in books is also my own rationalization for buying books, not taking them out of the library because I'll likely vandalize them, and so I stick with purchasing. I also tend to write in books because for me, like many others, the best way to retain information is to actually write it down. Whether these comments make sense to anyone else is irrelevant, and I've noticed that what I frequently do is write single words in the margins. The recent books that I've read have margins filled with comments like "good!", "yes!", "use this!", and "amazing!" These words are often accompanied by various symbols like stars, arrows, square and round brackets, and a slew of random lines pointing in every which direction.

The book I used as the ideological foundation for my project was the book *Peace First*, by one of Israel's lead peace negotiators, Uri Savir. Needless to say, this text is covered with my own blue ink.

I used *Peace First* throughout my project for guidance and clarity into issues regarding a peace initiative. It is a brilliant piece that outlines the concepts behind creating a modern day peace, and provides both functional and theoretical ideas of how to go about creating such a peace. I have written all over this book, and in one particular margin I combined all my symbols and words, writing, "YES! USE THIS! GREAT IDEA!" in a sort of over-enthusiastic and ridiculous tone combined. Savir postulated that if he had his choice he would bring peace to the Middle East by carpeting the region with green turf so that there could be thousands of soccer fields. He notes how people tend to come together when they are playing sports, and soccer is of course the most popular game in the world. He writes that if he were able to unite the people in the Middle East by playing games of soccer, he would get it done and instantly see results. I was thrilled to see this written because it confirmed what many of others have already said and done, and it gave weight to my own idea to help initiate a soccer tournament in Kenya.

On my first visit to Kenya it was actually the idea of one of the locals with whom I was working to have a one-day soccer tournament. Though my local hosts and I were only working with youths from one community, the Kalenjins, we thought it would be a great way to bring people together for a day and also enable me to meet and interact with a variety of youths all at the same time. We put out the word a few days before to a few different leaders who would spread the news among their peers, and we told the teams to prepare themselves for a daylong tournament that would take place on the grounds of a nearby elementary school. The day of the tournament the youths showed up, in taxis and on the backs of pickup trucks, all very excited to play. Some of them came all wearing the same colour, some actually had old uniforms, but they all had the same drive and excitement and had come ready to compete. As they arrived on the field I saw members of all the different teams greeting each other, and was told that many of the youths had gone to school together and had not seen each other for a while prior to this meeting on the field. This initial moment was the first time that it had occurred to me that soccer could be used to bring people together.

We began the tournament by speaking to the youths who had arrived, six teams in total, and telling them why they were here and who I was. As the token white boy in the crowd, they were all of course curious as to who I was and after my brief introduction they got over the fact that there was a stranger in their midst in order to get on with the game. Though not much of a soccer player, I was personally invited to join each team, and told them that I'd let them play a little first before I joined in with one of them. It did not really matter in the end which team I would join because as a result of my skills I was likely to be more of a liability than an asset to whatever team was unlucky to receive me.

I was astounded by the skill of these players, all of them, and the way that they interacted with each other during the games. They were friendly and smiling the entire time, as expected, and their skills were really remarkable. Despite the fact that I was one of the only players on the pitch actually wearing shoes, they were destroying whatever ego I may have had and were playing phenomenally well. One of the older youths was the self-appointed referee who enforced all the rules in a balanced way, and spent half of his time laughing at me and shouting "Adam! RUN! Why have you stopped running?? Jump! Get to the ball! Kick it! Why are you so slow?!?!" and other morale defeating comments. In any way, I probably lasted about ten minutes before I decided to make the shift from out-of-breath player to overly fatigued spectator.

From this one-day experience I recognized the popularity of soccer in a rural African setting and hoped to be able to expand on this idea, ensuring that there would be additional tournaments in which more youths from more tribes would be able to compete with each other. This was my idea, and this was going to be the only thing I would try leave behind my first time leaving Kenya.

On my last night in Kiptere at the end of my first visit I was debriefing with one of the local community leaders in a dimly lit room in the village's community centre (also doubling as my room for the duration of the stay). He asked me how my experience had been, what I had learned, and then asked what, if anything, I would like to leave behind. Based on my experience with some of the villagers, I had the feeling that this request to leave something was really asking for me to leave a wad of cash behind for them, which was something that I neither had nor was willing to do. I told him how impressed I had been by the success of the one day soccer tournament that we had quickly put together and told him that I'd like to try establish a soccer tournament to be played on an annual or bi-annual basis. We brainstormed some of the details and roughly concluded that the next tournament, for which I would send funds, would see the participation of a number of communities. I told him that I would go back to Canada, find some funds, and send it to them to hold the tournament.

A few weeks after my return to Toronto, I visited Western Union and sent about $300 to Kenya for our first attempt at an inter-tribal soccer tournament. I learned that youths in Kiptere had been planning it for weeks after my departure and was told that it would be held in two months' time, in November 2008. The money I sent would cover the purchase of a trophy, some banners and advertisements, payment for the referees, and refreshments for the players. I asked them to please keep me updated on the progress of the tournament and let me know if there was anything else that they required. A few days before the tournament began one of the youths involved in the organization process sent me an email asking me to please send a speech to be read at the opening of the tournament. The village elders and a number of local politicians would be present for the opening introduction, and another international volunteer from the United States was there and she had volunteered to read whatever speech I sent to be read. What I wrote, and what she read, was as follows:

Habari yenu! (Hello everyone!),

Before the tournament begins, I wanted to take this opportunity to speak to you from overseas and tell you how thankful I am that you have come to participate today.

Today, you are making history in Kenya. Today, you are uniting because you are tired of fighting and conflicts, and you are tired of violence that can tear your beautiful country apart. You are making history, and I want you to remember this starting today.

Sport, specifically football, has always been able to unite people and bring people together. The Olympics, held every four years, does just that, as does the Soccer World Cup, or Rugby World Cup, or any other international sporting event. For as long as those events take place, the participants put aside their political opinions, and they come together for the love of the game. They compete against each other as fellow human beings, and do not consider skin colour, race, religion, or gender as issues that divide them.

There is a big difference though between the athletes at the Olympics and World Cup, and everyone gathered here today. In general, athletes who compete at the Olympics just spend their time training in sports. They don't get involved in their country's affairs and most likely do not fight in their country's conflicts. The difference is that you, every one of you, have the unfortunate chance of being involved in a conflict in Kenya. If a conflict starts, you may decide to pick up a spear, or a bow and arrow, or a gun, and you can go into a conflict and fight. In doing so, you would be making sure that the conflict continues, and that peace fails. Today, hopefully, you will understand that you have the ability, each and every one of you, to stop a conflict. You can look at someone handing you a weapon and refuse, say no, and state that you believe in peace and dialogue. Do not for a minute think that this makes you weak. It makes you stronger than any soldier or politician in your country or continent, and it gives you the chance to change the world. Always remember that.

I came to Kenya with an open mind and not knowing what to expect. I knew that there was post-election violence, but I did not know the scope of the violence, and I did not know how many normal, everyday citizens, were involved. I thought it was just the army or the police fighting with small gangs of violent people. I did not realize that violence reached throughout the whole country, and I did not know coming to Kiptere that there were people here who were actually fighting in this conflict. As I left Kenya, I still could not believe, after meeting so many of you, that you were involved in the fighting and that you were pulled into the unnecessary violence. I came to Kenya to try and assist with peacebuilding and was lucky, because I did not realize how much everyone here already wanted peace.

I come from Canada where we do not fight over election results. In fact we do not fight about anything, which we are very lucky about. There is peace in Canada, and Canada tries to help in different countries around the world to maintain peace. In university, I studied politics, and specifically studied the conflict in the Middle East, the conflict between the different groups of Arabs, the conflict between the Jews in Israel and the Arabs in the rest of the Middle East, and the conflict with other countries in that region as well. In studying these subjects, I decided that I want to help create a lasting peace in the world. I would love to say that I have made peace in the Middle East, but for now, my efforts are focused on Kenya where I believe peace is possible, as it is already present in the hearts and minds of all of you.

I also come from South Africa, and so I am African myself. I know that there have been many problems in South Africa, but thanks to the efforts of Nelson Mandela, my hero, when the terrible racist and Apartheid system crumbled in 1994 and freedom was felt by all the people of South Africa, both black and white, no violence erupted, and many white people there were saved from the violence of revenge. In this way, we can all see how peace can be achieved easily. Believe in the goodness of everyone, and find similarities with others, even if they are in a different tribe or live in another area of the country.

My experience in Kenya taught me many things and I must thank each of you for this education, which I could only find in Kenya and never in a classroom. Tribalism must be defeated in this country. Defining people by tribe should only be used by people in Kenya to pride yourselves of your rich tradition and heritage. It should not be used to justify why someone is better than or worse than someone else. It is a form of hatred that can easily be resolved as soon as you all see each other as equals. This is not only possible, but it is simple. Each of you can look around today, and play football against each other, and make sure that when the game is over, you shake hands with each other and look each other in the eye when you do so. You will see in that other person the same values that you believe in, and the yearning to live in a peaceful and calm Kenya. It is just that easy.

Nelson Mandela once said "I dream of an Africa that is at peace with itself." Well Adam Kipkoech (me) says "I dream of a Kenya that is at peace with itself." I know it can happen, and my vision is that this tournament will extend to the borders of Kenya, and bring people together. My dream continues that when this tournament reaches the border, it will show the people in Uganda, in Sudan, in Tanzania, in Ethiopia, and Somalia that the people of Kenya can come together. Maybe this will inspire them to try come together themselves. The idea of this tournament should spread throughout the country and continent in order for Nelson Mandela's dream to come true. We dream of a united continent and a united Africa. Unity brings understanding, education and can help problems that afflict this continent such as violence, poverty, and HIV/AIDS. This dream may seem too big, but you would be surprised how much of a difference a little understanding can make. After visiting you in Kenya, I know that this is possible, and I dream of the success of this tournament.

I am sorry for this being so long, but I miss you all and have lots to say as always. Please do not think that I am just a *mzungu mjinga* (crazy white man), but I want you all to experience peace for yourselves, and I want you to help me achieve this goal. Hopefully one day you can visit me in Canada and I can show you my country and how different things are here. But for now, enjoy the tournament, learn from each other, and spread the message of peace around the country. If you do this, you will make history and impact the future generations of Kenya and Africa for many years to come.

In hindsight, this speech included aspects of the project that I would run a mere six months later. In this short address (which was simultaneously being translated into Swahili as it was being read) I tried to suggest to the youths involved that a soccer tournament is much more than just a sports game. It is the act of bringing people together, bringing them to ground onto which they would not have otherwise stepped, and making them look at each other face to face, eye to eye. In playing a game of soccer they were judging each other based solely on their athletic abilities, which do not take into account tribal history or irrational stereotypes. Athletic ability is clear and evident, and so in this sense a game of soccer is the chance to demonstrate who they are on the most basic level. It shows a side of people that is hidden when they speak or participate in other activities, and people are generally amicable and fun when it comes to a game of soccer or any other sport.

The tournament turned out to be a huge success, and I was fortunate to receive by email a number of photographs taken as the tournament began. To my surprise, delight and embarrassment, the first picture I received was one of all the elders and politicians present holding up the trophy and a giant banner that read, "Adam Hummel Coexistence Football Tournament. Theme: *Vijana Tujipange*." The Swahili at the end means "Youths preparing themselves." As honoured as I was that they had chosen to name the tournament after me, it was a bit surreal seeing my name written in big like that, and I had argued with them afterwards, saying that they should have named it something else.

"Why did you put my name on it?"

"Because you sponsored it Mr. Adam!"

"But usually you name these sorts of things after people who have died, or after the President or something, please change the name."

"Mr. Adam, we do not like the President, but we like you, so this is the name we chose."

Not realizing that this was an argument I'd be having a few more times in the future, and touched and flattered at the same time, I realized there was no winning and slowly adjusted to the fact that my name was now posted in a number of small villages in rural Kenya. More importantly however, I realized how successful this soccer tournament was. In the next few months as I expanded my ideas for a peacebuilding project, the soccer tournament became the core component of the project which would launch the initiative and be played over the span of two weekends, sandwiching the peace workshop that I would be hosting with some other youths.

To return to the idea of soccer as a peacebuilding tool, it cannot be understated how widely believed this view is, and my ideas are anything but new. Soccer, and sports in general, have always been used as tools that cross political boundaries and enables all sides to put aside their issues for a short time while competition plays out. As far back as Ancient Greece when the first Olympic Games were held, athletes from a grouping of nation-states would assemble to compete despite political alliances or long standing military conflicts. The modern Olympic Games were modeled on the same ideas of people being able to put their differences aside for a short time to ensure that the spirit of competitiveness reigned supreme for the duration of the games. There has also been much emphasis in international organizations, such as the United Nations, on using sports to foster peace and understanding between nations and peoples who would not otherwise be inclined to join together.

In 1993, a United Nations General Assembly resolution recognized the powerful role of sports as well. Through its ability to educate and empower youths the United Nations recognized the role that the Olympic Movement had in building a peaceful and better world. The following year was then proclaimed the *International Year of Sport and the Olympic Ideal*, and another tradition was initiated which is a powerful example of the power of sports in the international realm. Since 1993, before each Olympic Games, the *Olympic Truce Resolution* is adopted by the General Assembly, usually initiated by that year's Olympic host country. This resolution is titled "Building a peaceful and better world through sport and the Olympic ideal." The truce, echoing similar motives intended by the ancient Greeks in the 8th century BCE, asks nations to observe a truce from seven days preceding the opening of the games, until seven days following the closing ceremonies. This resolution epitomizes the true value of the Olympic Games and the value placed on sports.

In the UN Millennium Declaration, adopted in 2000, Member States of the UN were also urged "to observe the Olympic Truce, individually and collectively, now and in the future, and to support the International Olympic Committee in its efforts to promote peace and human understanding through sport and the Olympic Ideal". Furthermore in the 2005 *World Summit Outcome Document* it is stated on behalf of Member States, "We underline that sports can foster peace and development and can contribute to an atmosphere of tolerance and understanding." Like I said, the idea of using sports to bring people together is hardly a new idea, reaching as far back as Ancient Greece. The very fact that this idea is so well rooted in the modern psyche however further proves why these sporting events are required in conflict zones.

With regard specifically to soccer, the World Cup is a good example of politics being marginalized for the good of the game, and the recent games in South Africa epitomized the world coming together to compete. Even though the next tournament that would be held in Kenya at the time of deciding to hold this tournament was still two years before the World Cup would be held in South Africa, it still managed to give momentum to the project from the fact that this was the first time the World Cup was to be held on the African continent. This fact alone encouraged the Kenyan teams and demonstrated to them that in some respects the world was about to turn their eyes to Africa.

A book (and subsequent film) entitled *More than Just a Game* demonstrates the power that soccer can play in enabling its participants to overcome obstacles. In Apartheid South Africa, Robben Island was the personification of the police state that taunted and punished the black population. Located only a few miles off the coast of Cape Town, Robben Island was South Africa's Alcatraz, a place where the most notorious political prisoners were sent after they were arrested and sentenced to prison by the white government. Robben Island is where Nelson Mandela spent 18 of his 27 years in prison and was also home to a plethora of other political prisoners from the rise of Apartheid to its demise in 1994. While imprisoned on Robben Island these prisoners were deprived of basic elements of humanity. They were treated with disdain by the guards, fed poorly, and were given little time outside during the days. The prisoners however noted that one of the only perks was that for the most part they were held together in large cells, unless they were particularly important and therefore 'dangerous' individuals, like Mandela. The prisoners who were held in

71

these large cells said later that the biggest mistake that the warders had made was putting them together because as a group they became hardened in their convictions. The prisoners referred to this collusion as "cross pollination", whereby the more senior prisoners could pass on their ideas to their juniors. This system of "cross pollination" strengthened the resolve of the prisoners in a few ways.

When they were not held indoors, their time outside was spent in the quarry, digging up and smashing pieces of slate. Though one can hardly imagine the suffering imposed on these men in such conditions, looking back the prisoners note that the quarry actually unified them and they came to refer to Robben Island as 'The University'. The prison was labeled thus because of the weight placed on education by the prisoners and the belief that they must be prepared for their ultimate freedom. The more educated prisoners would teach the others, and they would confer on each other bachelors and masters degrees, and prepare themselves for life after Apartheid. They said that if the prison in its entirety was a university, then the slate quarry received the designation of 'Main Auditorium'. In conceiving of their surroundings as a place of higher learning, the prisoners fought back by ensuring that they would not allow the way they viewed themselves to be shaped by the way they were viewed by white South Africans. It was this defiance in the face of segregation and suffering throughout South Africa that led Steve Biko, the renowned anti-Apartheid activist, to develop his Black Consciousness movement, which ensured that black South Africans saw themselves as equals to South Africa's white population. He believed that overcoming prejudice required not just an alteration to a specific way of living, but also changing the black population's state of mind. While the prisoners developed this sense of togetherness on Robben Island, and out of a desire to make sense out of life in prison, they realized that they needed a way to actually congregate in a social way with each other, and their solution to this problem was to play soccer.

After persisting for years with the warders of the prison, the prisoners were eventually given the right to play soccer together once a week. What was originally understood to be down time and the chance to stretch their legs by doing something recreational for a few hours each week quickly became an organized activity and later blueprints for life after their release from prison. The prisoners promptly created a soccer league called the Makana Football Association (MFA) named after a Xhosa warrior held by the British on Robben Island, who died while trying to escape in 1819. Through this organization they not only were able to interact with each other on a more personal and basic level, but they were able to share with each other something other than their education. They trained those players who were weaker than others, and for those who were older and could not play, they made them referees and the administrators of the league. Jacob Zuma, the current President of South Africa, was a referee of the MFA, and the current Deputy Chief Justice of South Africa's Constitutional Court, Dikgang Moseneke, was at one time the chairman of the MFA. These administrators and players came together to draft a constitution for the MFA, made posters for the games, and even had three leagues, each consisting of a number of teams. This capacity to organize even in prison ensured that these men did not lose their drive and motivation to help organize a new South Africa after their release from prison.

The various accounts of this football association detail how the players got involved to help shape their own destinies. This soccer association was not just a social or recreational club. It became a way of life on Robben Island, and as a result, "Soccer saved many of us on the island," said Anthony Suze, one of the prisoners. The guards were sent to purchase colourful uniforms from mainland South Africa which introduced colour into the primarily grey and brown life in the prison, and though many of the teams were originally divided along the lines of political allegiances, primarily between the African National Congress (ANC) and the Pan African Congress (PAC), the teams were soon integrated and mixed so that people could learn from each other while they played and organized the future of the association. As the MFA progressed in its development, so did its bureaucracy and membership, and the club soon became a way of life on the island.

In a particularly poignant part of the club's history, there was a game played between two teams, the Blue Rocks and the Atlantic Raiders. As a result of what some players deemed to be unfair play by the other team, there was a six-month spat between the teams that saw the involvement by the MFA's disciplinary committee and management. At one of these disciplinary hearings one of the prisoners stood up and asked the others why they play soccer on Robben Island. He asked whether the point is to win games, score points, or be awarded trophies. He remarked that aside from all else, the ultimate goal of this endeavour was to make their stay on Robben Island less unbearable and less intolerable. He stated that though the disciplinary committee met in order to ensure the fair play of the game, whatever conflicts occurred on the field should stay there, and not affect their lives in any negative way while in prison, as their living conditions were bad enough. The purpose of the game was to improve their lives, and it is this 'noble ideal', of making the most of their lives even in the harshest of circumstances, that mattered the most. "If we had no noble ideals," he stated, "would we have been here on Robben Island today?" By affirming their common convictions, he ensured that his fellow prisoners realized that they were prisoners of conscience and in prison simply because they stood for something greater than themselves, for these noble ideals. As a result, they could not let their attempts at making their own living conditions better do what the prison itself intended to do to them, which was to crush their spirits and aspirations.

This survey of what happened on Robben Island is relevant to show how soccer can play a role in changing people's lives. Although the situation of the prisoners in South Africa was starkly different to the situation of the youths we intended to work with in modern Kenya, their aspirations were the same: improve their own lives by taking control of their own destinies. Sports have a unique way of enabling people to put aside their differences and see each other as equals. It pushes people to compete as a result of their drive, competitiveness, adrenaline, and physical abilities. It makes people equal, so that people from perhaps a higher socioeconomic background can play against wealthier or affluent people, and therefore breaks down social barriers. It has also shown that it is able to break down racial barriers, and has brought together people from all different kinds of backgrounds. It further enables those who have the least to be able to contribute in a meaningful way because all you need in order to play soccer (and sports in general) is yourself and a ball.

Uri Savir describes a particular game of soccer that was played in Rome's Olympic stadium initiated by the Vatican as well as Palestinian and Italian NGOs. This 1999 game saw a group of Italian soccer stars and pop singers playing against a team made up of both Israeli and Palestinian players, together on the same team. On the day of the game, sixty thousand people watched as the match was played and transmitted live to both Israel and the Palestinian Territories to ensure that the people were watching. Savir writes that this transmission of the game illustrates, "that when former enemies appear together, the world takes note." Savir details further that the money raised from this game was used to build a soccer infrastructure in schools on both sides of the Arab-Israel conflict. As a result of this game and the attention of the international community there are twenty-four twin schools that participate in playing soccer, and a joint indoor soccer team made up of both Israelis and Palestinians. Savir also notes that aside from their matches in Israel and the Palestinian Territories, in 2002 this joint Israeli-Palestinian team played a match against a Rwandan team that included players from both the Hutu and Tutsi tribes. As Savir continues with the description of this incredible initiative, he states that, "For the youth who participated in this project, soccer changes their attitude toward the Other more than any governmental policy initiative could." I was overjoyed to read of this connection between the conflict in the Middle

East and an African conflict, and appreciated the succinct way in which the impact made by a simple game of soccer was described.

In a further account from the book *Small Acts of Resistance,* the authors detail how soccer came to affect the war torn Ivory Coast. In 2002 Ivory Coast was divided between North and South as a result of political and ethnic tensions, leading also to a civil war. This division mirrors many African conflicts that end up dividing countries such as Sierra Leone and Sudan, leading citizens to stay away from the parts of the country that they do not belong to. In many of these countries it is also impossible to cross from one side to the other, as an unofficial border takes shape and keeps both sides separate. Although the political landscape seemed hopeless as the conflict dug in its heels, it soon became apparent that soccer could play a role in changing the bleak status quo in the Ivory Coast.

Didier Drogba is from the Ivory Coast and is a well-known soccer player for London's Chelsea team. Aside from playing in England, he was also the captain of the Ivory Coast team, the Elephants. As well as insisting that this team itself be ethnically mixed, which was achieved, he wanted to unite the country in a way through sports that would bring together both the North and South. After seeing how the entire country came together to support their nation's team when they qualified for the 2006 World Cup, Drogba had another idea of how to use soccer to unite the country. For the 2007 qualifying game for the African Nations Cup, Drogba declared that the game would be played in Bouake, the rebel capital of the North of the country. This region had been off limits to government forces as well as people from the South in general, and by encouraging the playing of a soccer game there he hoped to bring the country together to ensure that people would be encouraged to cross this physical, political and ideological threshold. On the day of the game, 25,000 spectators were present and the Ivorian team beat Madagascar 5-0. The authors of this story provide numerous accounts of the joy that people experienced at the time, and also share a headline from a prominent Ivory Coast newspaper from the day after match, which read "*Five goals to erase five years of war.*"

Steve Crawshaw and John Jackson, the authors of *Small Acts of Resistance*, have put together a wonderful account that details how small acts can lead to massive results. Their section on sports captures perfectly the way that soccer can play a guiding role in changing the world and shaping peoples' perceptions of each other and their surroundings. At the start of their section on sports they quote the manager of the Liverpool soccer team, Bill Shankly, who once said, "Some people believe football is a matter of life and death. I can assure you it is much more important than that." Soccer is important both for what it is able to accomplish, in terms of what unfolded in the Ivory Coast, as well as what it stands for, in the example from Robben Island, and it is this dual role which encouraged me that as the centerpiece of our project in Kenya, soccer would make a huge impact.

After the first game was played in Kenya in November 2008, the next tournament was to be held on my second visit to Kenya six months later. When I arrived, nervous and excited to put into motion the project that I had spent much time preparing and planning for, the first task that I had to do was kick off the Second Annual Adam Hummel Coexistence Football Tournament, literally.

The day after I arrived back at Kiptere, I was woken early, enjoyed my African breakfast burrito (omelet and *chapati*) and jumped in a *matatu* to go to Matongo, deep in the heart of Kisii land, to kick off the first tournament. This particular tournament would involve the Luo, Kisii and Kalenjin communities, and I would be kicking off the tournament in each community this weekend. There were five teams playing on the first weekend in each community, and then the winning teams from each would come together in Sondu the following weekend to play a day of games to determine the ultimate winner. The first tournament held was only within the Kalenjin community so this was the first time that it would be expanded to include the participation of others. The objective was that as the tournament proceeded each year more communities would be able to compete.

Arriving in Matongo I was greeted by Geoffrey, an older youth who would also be a participant of our workshop the following week. As we got out of the *matatu* and started walking through the village I was informed-slash-blatantly-lied-to by Geoffrey that the school where today's games were being held was only a five-minute walk away. It being a scorching day and me stupidly deciding to wear jeans, we started walking . . . and walking . . . and walking . . . for an hour, along a mud path. Thoroughly unimpressed with Geoffrey and just about ready to boycott my own tournament, my foul mood instantly evaporated when we arrived on the grounds of the school. I found waiting for me a group of probably 150 people, consisting of participants, their parents, their young siblings, and an assortment of other spectators, waiting for the games to begin. Hanging in the trees over the field was a sign with the name of the tournament designating the division that they were playing in, and in the shade lounged the players, getting antsy and frustrated that I had taken so long. When I arrived, I was introduced to the players, and shook hands with almost everyone there, while the younger children who had come with their parents just stared at the *mzungu* in their midst. Some of them ran over just to touch my skin and touch the hair on my legs, something lacking from the legs of everyone else present.

Once everyone had gathered around, I stood on the field, apologized for my tardiness (while giving Geoffrey the death-stare) and introduced both myself and the purpose of the tournament. I told the players that they were about to get involved in their own mini-peace movement and echoed many of the same ideas that I had written in the speech given in my absence only months before. In hindsight, speaking to this first group of players in Matongo, initiating this next tournament, I had no idea what we were starting. I did not realize that what was simply supposed to be a sports game designed to bring people together would actually become the foundation of a peace project that would see the involvement and dedication of so many. When I think back to that moment, I could not be happier that the soccer tournament was the centerpiece of this project because all the other projects require people who want to stand out and be leaders in various ways in their own communities. These soccer players however are not loud and outspoken and do not dream of being leaders in their communities: they just want to play sports. Despite the fact that they were content with being one of a group of many athletes, I wanted to make sure that they realized the role that they would be having and the importance that has been placed on football so many times throughout history in so many places in the world. These are all things that are difficult to impart to a group of athletes who you have delayed from playing a game, and also when you have to speak particularly slowly because they do not all understand English as well as others do there. I tried my best, but the purpose of my speech and my actual presence at the start of the tournament in Matongo was to try conveying to them the fact that they were now easing the cornerstone of this peacebuilding project into place.

After watching the first game I had to make my way to Sondu to kick off the Luo tournament. To get there my local hosts called people on dirt bikes to come and pick me up, resulting in my first dirt-bike/motorcycle ride ever, taking me to the nearest *matatu* stand. I jumped in the next *matatu* and headed to Sondu, where I found a familiar scene: a sign hanging in the trees, soccer players lounging under the tree, and a restless coach pacing up and down the field waiting for me. After being lectured for a few minutes about the importance of punctuality (this was rare because as I described earlier Kenyans are typically running two hours late, however this coach also happened to be a high school teacher) the coach decided that the games would begin. I gave my speech, shook some hands, and was given the game ball to kick as far into the field as I possibly could. Making sure that I was ready to make the kick, I adjusted the straps on my crocs so that they did not fly off, and did my best, launching the ball farther into the field than I had expected. Being in Sondu and not having any other engagements for the day, I was able to stay and watch the games, have lunch with some of the players, and meet some of the local community.

While in Sondu participating in this tournament I came to meet a group of people who were living a short distance away from the soccer field on which we were playing. While standing watching the game, I was approached by an elderly man named Peter. He was wearing a yellow and brown button-down shirt tucked into a pair of dirty blue dress pants with a belt that was far too big for his narrow waist. He had a pair of sandals on his feet, grey hair, and lines on his face showing his age. He greeted me with a hand that was big, strong and calloused, which told me that he had lived his life doing some kind of labour, likely agricultural, considering the surroundings. He had seen the commotion created by the soccer game, asked someone what was happening, and had been directed to me. A short, fat little woman who also wanted to meet me accompanied him. It was the warmth of both of their smiles and the goodness in their eyes that attracted me to them immediately.

They came over to see what had been going on with the football tournament, but they also wanted to tell me about their own situation. They were Internally Displaced Persons (IDPs) who literally lived in a field around the corner, and they had been displaced as a result of the post-election violence. They wanted me to hear their stories, what their living conditions were like, and see it for myself. After ensuring that this was safe and that they were genuine, I grabbed my friend Jescah to come with me to see the refugee camp that had been set up, and act as my translator if need be.

I was led behind some small buildings, through a field, past a church, and into a clearing. In front of me were ten tents. Each was probably around five-feet high and ten-feet long, with a curved roof, each looking like a mini-airplane hangar. Emblazoned on the side of the white fabric were the giant pale-blue letters UNHCR, standing for *United Nations High Commission for Refugees*, the agency that had supplied these tents and those mandated with assisting refugees in need anywhere in the world. After taking a look inside the tents, my skepticism about this UN agency was confirmed, and I was informed that the last time an agent from the UNHCR or the Red Cross had visited was eight months prior. Inside the tents were ripped and broken mosquito nets hanging from the top which could hardly be called effective, and some thin sheets on which the IDPs slept. They slept on no other padding between them and the ground, and the only other things inside the tent were some various pots, bowls and cutlery. Unable to imagine living in such conditions, I was told that not only had no other agencies visited these refugees in months, but that they had been living in these tents for the last 14 months, since the time of the post-election violence.

I met the other refugees, none of whom were too far away when I showed up to visit. There were approximately 20 of them and I would say that Peter, who I had met, was one of the youngest, probably in his late-60s. These refugees were elderly, and the last remaining refugees from this particular tent-village, out of a population of what were once around one hundred. Remember that I had said ten tents: that means that when this was set up there were ten people per tent, and they were by no means just one family per tent. These refugees lived in these tents with their neighbours and total strangers, many of whom were eventually given the chance to relocate, find jobs and find other housing. These twenty elderly Kenyans were those left in these tents, and they were stuck there because they were not employable or able to be the first in line when a new shipment of food showed up from some international agency in the village or when people showed up looking for workers for a particular project. They were hungry, they were idle, and they were living in broken tents in a field.

After being given the privilege of meeting each one of these individuals, I was given a tour around their living area. Ok, so the tour only took about five-minutes because aside from the tents the only thing that they had to show me were the latrines, a hole dug into the ground around which was built a very crude wooden wall without a door. There was also a clearing with a small tarpaulin over it, where they dried out the millet and maize that they received as a donation from surrounding farmers. Millet and maize are common crops in this region and are used to make basic food so that they had something to eat aside from assorted scarce donations from other people in Sondu.

Meeting this group made me realize that their situation was a product of their circumstances. They told me that the people in Sondu helped them out when they could so that they were not starving, but that many of their families had fled the area and so were unable to visit or offer much in terms of assistance. They were refugees because they were targeted by the post-election violence and their houses and belongings had also been burned down. They had been left with nothing, as was evidenced by the emptiness of the tents, and had now been abandoned by an international agency that had only paid them attention at the outset of their new living conditions. This was the band-aid solution that I continued to see that was a result of the post-election violence. The government, as well as the UN, saw the fighting after the elections happen for a while, but as soon as the fighting ended, they assumed that the conflict was over. They gave tents to the refugees, they stopped people from killing each other, but these were all only temporary solutions as the real issues that led to the post-election violence were still lurking below the surface. It broke my heart to see the living conditions of this group of Kenyans and the way they had been largely ignored by their government and international agencies. It did however confirm my suspicions that more was required on the most basic of levels for people to begin taking control of their own lives again.

This was an experience that I was not anticipating. I knew that such IDPs still existed and had personally seen the fields and fields of UNHCR tents dotting the countryside as I sat on the bumpy bus ride between Nairobi and the Rift Valley Province. I knew the issue existed but I had not thought about what the conditions in camps like these looked like, nor had I thought about the kinds of Kenyans who made up the camp populations. This particular one was made up of the elderly, but in the other camps throughout the country there were populations that largely resembled those refugee camps that you see in movies like *Blood Diamond* or any documentary about Darfur. These camps house children, adults, the sick and elderly, and a wide spectrum of individuals who need assistance but are just not getting it. It was unfortunate that I was not anticipating this experience because I wished that I had come prepared with something to give them. When I met Peter I was in the middle of a day just kicking off these football tournaments and therefore had not come prepared with much cash on me, but I really wanted to help them when they asked me for something. I gave them whatever money I had in my pockets which probably only added up to around $2, and then I told them what I was doing in Kenya and told them I'd look at my budget and see what I could give to them. I asked them if they just wanted money, or if they wanted something specific.

Sugar. They told me that whether I was going to give them cash or buy them something particular, they wanted sugar. They wanted sugar so that they could make tea, as milk was easy to come by as were tea leaves, but sugar was the one expensive commodity that they needed. This was probably the last thing that I had imagined they would have asked for as to me, sugar seemed like more of a luxury, but they wanted it to make their tasteless maize and millet meals taste a little better, and wanted it for their tea. I made a little reminder for myself in my notebook so that I got back to them at some point before I left, and asked them how much money they needed to buy the sugar.

"Well, we would like one kilo of sugar for one person," Peter said, "and there are 20 people, so that would be 20 kilos of sugar please Mr. Adam." I quickly thought about how much or little 20 kilos of sugar was, and then asked, "So how much does a kilo of sugar cost?" to which they responded, "50 shillings." Now a pro at converting Kenyan Shillings to dollars in my head (1 Dollar = around 80 Shillings at the time) I suddenly realized how little they were asking for! Well, maybe not to them, but to me, they were telling me that the only donation they wanted for a group of 20 refugees was a contribution of $15.

This was strange, and I think I quickly told them they would get double that, because well, it was worth the donation and was by no means a significant dent in my finances. I was not being scammed because they had not anticipated my visit, I saw their living conditions, and I heard their stories long before they themselves told them to me, but this was all they were asking for. True, after doing the conversion the amount does not seem like much since the dollar is obviously much stronger than the shilling, but I was still stunned by both requests: they only wanted $15, and they wanted it for sugar. More than happy to oblige I told them that I would give them the money next time I was in Sondu, which would be the following weekend for the final game of the soccer tournament, and that one of them should come and find me.

On the day of the tournament, Peter showed up by my side wearing the same yellow shirt and dirty dress pants, smiled at me with his crooked teeth, reached out his rough and calloused hand, and said *jambo*. We spoke for a while, I gave him the money, and he hugged me, invited me to his tent to have a glass of tea with him, and thanked me on behalf of his fellow IDPs. I was happy because I had been given this personal opportunity to learn about the situation of people affected in different ways by Kenya's post-election violence, in small places that have been overlooked or forgotten. I do not include this story for the purpose of highlighting my donation, but rather to demonstrate how easy it is to assist people in the direst of needs, and how a small contribution can go such a long way. If there is anything that you are going to take away from this story, please let it be that and the knowledge that this is how many refugees continue to live even as the next general elections in Kenya approach.

Though this issue of IDPs is not directly related to the issue of soccer, it was the facilitation of the soccer tournament that brought me to Peter and the others. They lived literally a stone's throw away from the soccer field but had they not approached me I would not have known who they were, what they were doing there, and how they got there. They were also a group who were not only directly affected by the post-election violence but most directly affected by the poor attempts of their government and international organizations to provide only minimal assistance to their plight. Seeing the conditions in which the IDPs lived, and seeing the ages of the inhabitants of those tents made me realize how much more needed to be done for our peacebuilding project to be truly effective, and affirmed to me that whatever I was able to accomplish, that at least it was something. Something is sometimes all that is required, and the rest can easily fall into place. What is required is for someone in need to make 'the ask'. Once this first step is taken, there are enough people in the world who are able to help, they just need to be shown how they can assist, how little is actually needed in order to make a difference, and how they can change lives even as far away as East Africa. People are not always hard wired to offer their services, but when confronted with a request, whether it is guilt kicking in or the mere realization that they are in a position to help, often that initial push is all it takes to get help for those who need it most. After that, we hope for the best.

Leaving the IDP camp I returned to watch the last soccer game on the field in Sondu. Afterwards we had an early dinner in town consisting of tilapia, and headed back to Kiptere as my friend Courtney would be arriving from overseas to help conduct our peacebuilding workshop that would be starting in two days. I wanted to meet her when she arrived and she would be accompanying me the next day to kick off the third part of the tournament with the Kalenjin teams.

The next day we stood on the now Kalenjin field, with the sign in the trees and the players lying in the shade, and I told them about what they were doing to help change Kenya. This time I incorporated part of what I had learned from the IDPs, and I was able to say with conviction that this soccer tournament was bringing people together in a fragmented region of Kenya. I told them that soccer not only brings players together, but that Courtney and I were able to meet them as a result of the game, that the spectators supporting the various teams could interact with each other on equal footing, and how soccer would be the first step in the creation of a movement that would one day sweep across the eight provinces of Kenya.

I was given the game ball that I walked with to the middle of the field. I dropped and kicked it as hard as I could, as this kick now essentially locked in the participation of three communities who had last been brought together with bows, arrows, and machetes. Today, they committed (excuse me for borrowing the phrase) to more than just a game.

A week later we woke up early to make our way back to Sondu. On the soccer field behind the police station we would be holding the final day of games of the tournament, and the best teams from the Luo, Kisii and Kalenjin communities would be joining us to compete for the trophy. We arrived to find the three signs from the three villages tied to the trees each side by side, the three referees making their way to the field and greeting each other at the start of a busy day, and some of the youths walking around the field with paint cans, painting lines onto the grass. Others were pushing the cows off of what was quickly being transformed into our soccer field, while *matatus* began to show up next to the field, out of which jumped entire soccer teams wearing their colourful uniforms. I went for a walk around Sondu trying to collect my thoughts and think about what I would say when called on to speak to all the participants and the spectators.

On my walk through the paths that made up the town of Sondu, lined with garbage, old women selling goods and dried foods, and wooden stores and restaurants painted in bright colours, individuals came up to me asking if I was Mr. Adam. Unsure how they knew my name, I responded in the affirmative, and the majority of them welcomed me to Sondu or to Kenya ("*Karibu Kenya!*"), thanked me for coming, or made various requests for me, asking if they could have my hat, sunglasses, shorts or running shoes. As I continued to walk I realized that signs had been plastered all over Sondu telling people to come out to the tournament that was being held today, and that since they had of course named the tournament after me, those who had seen the signs knew the name of the *mzungu* in their midst.

I returned to the field and found that the teams had all now arrived, loudspeakers had been set up, lines were painted on the field, the referees were in uniform ready for play, and swarms of children were standing on one corner of the field eager to cheer on their favourite team. Sondu was chosen as the location because it was a village where members of all three communities lived and we wanted to ensure that all teams were evenly represented from the sidelines. I arrived, was called up to the middle of the field, and suddenly found myself surrounded by a huge group of players, children and adults standing ready to hear me speak:

> I'm so happy to be here today and so happy that there are so many of you here today as well. Today you are all here to play football and because you are not happy with the way things are in Kenya now, right? You are here because you want to make change, right? You are no longer going to rely on

other people, not going to rely on your community leaders, you are going to rely only on yourselves to make changes to your lives. In order to show you how you can do that, I want to tell you a little bit about what I have been doing in the last week leading up to this tournament.

This last week a group of 25 youths from Kiptere, Sondu and Matongo came together and worked to put aside their differences and make sure that everyone knows that they are Kenyan. You are Kenyan, and will not be divided by tribes or communities, and you are here together because you want to make the country a better place. Together, with these 25 youths, we created the Youth Ambassadors for Peace, and we drafted a peace treaty yesterday, copies of which I now hold in my hand to distribute to those of you who want to know how to move forward. We drafted this treaty to show what is needed for there to be peace, and we discussed how to tackle issues like corruption, poverty, and idleness, and what everyone here can do to change their own futures.

You all know President Barack Obama. Obama says that people have to change their own lives, and that they cannot just expect change to come from somewhere or someone else. All of you are here today because you are going to follow what Obama always talks about, and you are going to shape your own lives. You are going to make change on your own, and not rely on people from outside to come and make that change happen. This is something you have to do yourselves.

The most important thing that is required for peace is that you have to find that peace within yourself first before you can go and find it with someone else. You can think long and hard about what you think peace is and how you can find peace within yourself. Once you have found peace within yourself, you go to your friend, and you tell them that you want to talk about peace, and you find others, and go to the community, politicians, and make this dialogue spread around the country to ensure that the violence that happened last year does not happen again.

Ok, I am here to watch a football game, and that is what we all came here for. I hope everyone is excited, and thank you for making this possible. Next year and in the future we will make sure there are many more tribes playing and we will make it spread across Kenya to ensure that everyone is coming together to play and to make peace. That is the goal, and that is what you are here for.

Ok so I did my best, and you can see my written speeches are a bit better than my actual speeches. I also may have spoken a little fast because I was nervous, and noticed that people weren't really responding to anything that I said, never a good sign. Nevertheless, what I said was a combination of ideas I had discussed during the workshop that we had held the week in between the two weekends the tournament was held. Today however I was not speaking directly to the teams, as I had already spoken to them the week before when I launched the tournament. Today I was trying to reach out to the spectators and demonstrate to them that their presence at the game directly contributed to peace. The players would interact with each other on the field and would see each other as equals beginning today and proceeding into the future. I wanted the spectators present to realize however that they were also contributing by supporting the tournament and by engaging and interacting with everyone present. Soccer today would embody an attempt to bring together people from a variety of backgrounds and histories, whether they were the aggressors or victims during the post-election violence or those who simply dreamed of a Kenya at peace with itself.

Despite a massive thunderstorm in the middle of the day, cows constantly wandering onto the field, puddles, and plenty of mud, the day was a success. The Luo team won the tournament, and tears poured down my face when I witnessed the captain of the Luo team run toward the trophy, grab it, and run through Sondu carrying it high for everyone to see. Behind him followed his entire team and probably 200 other people parading through the streets singing, dancing and shouting in joy that they had won. I could not believe this reaction and knew that such a positive display of joy, affection and sportsmanship in the middle of Sondu was a big change from the usually violent or hostile outbursts that had previously erupted on these streets. Once the parade had made its way around the town, everyone returned to the soccer field where the district officer was waiting to make the official trophy presentation to the winning team, and where I stood, teary eyed, unable to speak or address the group in any coherent way in either Swahili or English. I simply waited for the district officer to finish speaking, handed the trophy over to the captain once again, and watched as joy filled the air and the players filtered back onto the streets singing and dancing.

It had worked. Beyond my wildest dreams and pushing beyond the limits of my imagination, what unfolded on those two weekends had worked. We were not attempting to make peace right away, as that obviously does not happen in two weekends (but it would have been sweet if it did). The purpose was to create that spark, to act as a catalyst to bring people together. From the beginning of world history and in even the darkest days of human history, sports, and in particular soccer, have brought people together and made them forget about all that divides them. Here in Sondu, a place that has seen so much violence, these youths helped create the largest soccer tournament held in years, and was the first time that these communities had come together in any official program or capacity since the outbreak of the post-election violence. The players and those who came to watch and support them sent a clear message to all onlookers that they wanted to contribute to a peaceful future in Kenya, and committed themselves to the ideals of sportsmanship and competition.

Thrilled with the success of this part of the project, I thought that this could have been enough. Why attempt to put all these other projects into place now that one of them, which was somewhat easy to make happen, had found so much success? Why? It was because of those standing and cheering on the sidelines. Those spectators, and children, and the people in the village who came up to me to introduce themselves made sure that regardless of the fact that sports clearly played a positive role in the creation of a 'peace consciousness' in the village, that there was still much to be done: we needed to engage those who were not just athletes. I knew that there was much more to be accomplished, but for now we had a successful starting point.

A final story about how soccer can change the world and change individual lives comes from the town of Clarkston, Georgia. In this small town there is a team called the *Fugees*, made up of young refugees from all over the world including Afghanistan, Sierra Leone, the Congo, Sudan, Bosnia, Liberia and Iraq. These youths were previously child soldiers and others affected by the scourge of war in their respective countries, some of them forced to see their parents killed in front of their own eyes and many who are today orphans as a result. Though they have been brought to America by different humanitarian agencies, many are left to fend for themselves with limited resources and as a result of language and cultural barriers have a difficult time fitting into school and other social settings. Soccer is the one way that they are able to join together with other similarly affected youths and feel, in some way, like everyone else.

A resident of Clarkston, Luma Mufleh, is an immigrant from Jordan. Having lived an affluent life in Amman she was sent by her father to university in America, with the expectation that she would return to Jordan following her graduation. Upon completion of her studies she decided however that she wanted to remain in America, and upon learning of this decision, he cut off her financial support and limited contact with his daughter. Jumping from job to job, Luma later discovered a group of youths playing soccer which reminded her of life in Jordan, where every piece of grass would be used by youths to kick around a soccer ball. She thought that maybe she could try to work with these kids to bring them together as a team, try improving their soccer skills, and ensuring that they at least had the right clothes in which to play the game. During some of the first few games that she watched, she found kids playing in flip-flops, wearing only boxer shorts and flannel shirts, and very few of them had the right footwear. She saw an opportunity and though she felt in some way like a refugee herself, she was able to witness what life as a real refugee in America was like.

On one particular occasion, they were playing on Armistead Field, the usual location for their afternoon soccer games, when somewhere nearby someone started to shoot off fireworks. Innocent as this action was, most of the kids suddenly dropped onto the field, the noise of the fireworks evoking memories of bombardments and rebel attacks from their home villages. Luma then realized that the kids needed much more than just soccer; they needed help better integrating themselves into American life, needed help with their schoolwork, and needed assistance fitting into local social circles. To overcome their status as refugees they both needed and wanted to fit in, and this was exactly the task that Luma took upon herself. Over the last few years, she has been working hard to integrate these kids into society in Clarkston, Georgia, and she has seen overwhelming results. Some of the teenagers with whom she works have been granted scholarships to play soccer in universities and colleges around the country, and every youth's marks have improved. Together with other volunteers and forms of financial and moral support, they have created a diverse family, like the ones that so many of these youths had taken away from them early in their lives. To this effect, Luma is a hero and is indeed someone who selflessly works to change and improve the lives of others.

Soccer did this. Soccer brought these youths together not on a field in Africa but in the middle of Georgia, a place now far removed from ethnic conflict and civil war. Hearing of these stories and the way soccer continues to touch lives all over the world fuels the notion that sports should be used to help quell tensions and violence. Do a search online for "inspirational soccer stories" and what you will find is tremendous. Sports has always brought people together, and whether it is in America, Kenya, Afghanistan, Israel, Congo or Sierra Leone, soccer has the potential to defy all odds, bring together those who would not otherwise have looked at each other, and bring a smile to the faces of youths who have not smiled in a long time. We often underestimate how powerful a role sports plays, but you show up to a schoolyard and throw down a soccer ball, and you will hear laughter and see smiles within minutes. This, I can guarantee.

THERE IS A TIME TO BE FRIENDS, AND A TIME TO BE ENEMIES

The first time I stood speaking in a room on the third floor of the village's community centre was on my first visit to Kenya. On my first morning waking up in Kiptere, after experiencing my first cow execution, first shower out of a bucket, first chicken attack, and first *chapati*, I was told that I would be attending a meeting with the village elders. Still unsure of what I would be doing in Kenya, and not having met that many people in the village as I had just arrived the evening before, I was both nervous and uncertain what they were going to have to say to me. I thought it would be a standard meeting with the new volunteer, thinking that it was the sort of meeting that was not uncommon for someone in my position.

As I walked up the stairs and entered the room where the elders were sitting, I found about twenty men, wearing suits of different colours, a few with walking sticks, with shined black shoes, grey hair, and big smiles. I sat down at the side of the room, and after a brief introduction, each elder took a turn standing up and saying a few words to me. Most welcomed me to Kenya and to Kiptere and thanked me for traveling all the way to their village. One of the final men to stand up and speak was named Joseph, and he said to me, "Mr. Adam, *Karibu* (welcome to) Kenya, and we thank you for coming to our little village of Kiptere. We hope that with this experience you will learn much about our country, and be able to go back to your home to act as a goodwill ambassador for our village." Goodwill ambassador eh? Well, now that I was joining the likes of Angelina Jolie and Bono, I could really get used to this Africa thing! They asked me to stand up and speak, which I was NOT ready for, and I nervously stood up in front of this group of elderly men and said the first thing that came to my mind.

"Thank you for having me and for appointing me your goodwill ambassador before you have even heard me speak! We should make a deal first before I say anything else: If, after my time here is complete, you are happy with the work that I have done, then you can tell everyone your goodwill ambassador is from Canada; if you do not like the work that I have done . . . please tell them that I am American."

Getting a surprisingly excited laugh from the men present, I continued to tell them how excited I was to be there . . . and that was all. Not really having much else to say, I took a seat not knowing that the next time that I would be standing and speaking to a group of people in this exact same room, I would be helping to start my very own peacebuilding project and speaking to a group which was on average thirty years younger than the present audience.

The academic in me said that although an ideal, and potentially more fun, way to start a project of this sort was to just initiate a whole lot of projects that would bring people, specifically youths, together and get them excited about the prospect of a grassroots peace movement, that there would have to be a sit down, discussion and educational aspect to such a project first. Though projects like soccer tournaments and drama groups are able to get people moving, they do not provide much impetus for commitment and so I thought that maybe the best way to create a base for this project would be to find a group of dedicated youths from each tribe involved, and give them a bit of training to enable them to understand the concepts that other projects were designed to tackle. I had zero idea whether they had learned anything about civic education in school or in their own individual experiences, and was unsure how they would feel about taking some time out of their personal schedules to come learn about war and peace with me. Though unsure of many factors, and admittedly not having planned too much until I actually arrived on the ground in Kenya a week before the workshop began, I had a few things to do: find the participants, draft a sort of framework for our workshop, and figure out the actual logistics of the project.

In order to find the participants, I was lucky to have made connections in Kenya who could travel to a few villages and find ideal candidates for this project. Considering the notion of leadership, they asked me what kind of a person I was looking for, and I spouted the usual adjectives: outgoing, friendly, smart, active in their community, and the ability to take initiative. Though these are pretty standard descriptions of a leader, a week after we began the search for participants, I sent another email with one more adjective: passionate. After thinking for a while about the project, the situation in Kenya, and what we were trying to achieve, I realized that passion, and the ability to really internalize the situation, was the most important adjective. It was social empathy that I was looking for.

I have learned that being passionate and being able to care can be the most critical aspect of any involvement. A girl that I once met in Paris while I was traveling around Europe told me that she was in the process of writing a book dedicated entirely to the idea of passion, and after asking her how she chose this topic she told me that in her experiences in politics and humanitarian work, she believed it was passion that truly drives people forward. Passion can be the difference between getting work done and getting work done well. It gives one the ability to thrive and succeed, and if one is passionate about something then they will overcome any obstacle or challenge with ease. The German poet Christian Hebbel once said, "Nothing great in the world has ever been accomplished without passion," so how could I go wrong with asking that the people who participate in my project are passionate? I was not looking for a specific type of passion. On the contrary, I was looking for a group of youths who were dynamic and different, with different experiences and beliefs and backgrounds, all enabling them to add to the mosaic that would hopefully be the makeup of this newly formed peace movement.

Once the search was on for participants, I had to then plan the content of the actual workshop and decide how to best facilitate the event. The thought of running this workshop alone overwhelmed me, and I was extremely privileged that my friend Courtney, with whom I used to work in London, was able to travel to Kenya for a week to help me both run the workshop and provide support regarding the overall direction of the project. Having a second voice and a sounding board to help me develop some of my nascent ideas was invaluable, and what she brought to the project, including her insanely positive attitude, energy, excitement and charm, ensured that all the youths who attended quickly made a new friend. Aside from all the work that she did in helping me prepare, it was mostly gratifying to be able to share this experience with someone, and know that there was now someone else in my life who would both witness and develop, with her own experiences and training, the future of this program. This being Courtney's first visit to Kenya also gave a refreshing perspective on the whole experience, and sitting and speaking with her, explaining to her the tensions and the conflict in the country and what we would be able to accomplish together, set me at ease likely more than she realized.

As the date of the workshop drew nearer and the pieces gradually fell into place, we were slowly able to put together a framework for what would be one of the most interesting, meaningful and insightful weeks of my life. The plan was to have 24 youths, equally divided between the Kisii, Kalenjin and Luo communities, and having an equal number of boys and girls, come to Kiptere and spend the week with us. They would arrive on Monday evening when we would do some icebreakers and other opening activities, and we would then spend the rest of the week together probing what were the most critical issues and problems that they wanted to confront. We would find host families around Kiptere who would accommodate the visitors in their homes, and the financial donations that I came with from Canada would be used to cover all the food and requirements for that week.

In Nairobi I had also gone shopping for stationary and bought notebooks, pens, easel paper, markers, nametags, and a slew of other supplies for the use of the participants. Organizing food for 30 people for a week, we struck a deal with a local "restauranteur" who would be doing the cooking for us. Hitting up a few supermarkets and grocery stores, we bought bulk products like rice, beans and corn that he would prepare for us throughout the week when needed. Reviewing the records I kept for the amount of money spent during each phase of this project, I am still blown away by how little the food cost for thirty individuals, three meals a day, for a week: $130. Total. This incredible fact served only as a reminder that any little bit of money could go a long way out here.

Food, supplies and accommodation in place, we were set to begin.

On Monday night the selected youths made their way to Kiptere. They each brought with them a small bag with some clothes, and as they arrived we took them to meet the host families where they would be staying while in town. Their accommodation ranged from couches in some of the nicer homes, to the hard floors of others. Once they had all congregated in the village, we made our way to the room on the third floor of the community centre to do some icebreakers. They each got a chance to introduce themselves as both Courtney and I spoke to them about what we sought to accomplish during the week. We told them that the ultimate plan was to make them ambassadors to both their own and each other's villages, and provide them with the information and materials necessary to understand and appreciate some aspects of both war and peace. At this point we both decided that we wanted to make it very clear that we were not there to impose a project on them, and we were not by any means going to pursue a plan that we, Courtney and I, had concocted. We had come to Kiptere as facilitators, and it was their role to tell us what they wanted to do.

Volunteers are often criticized for their approach to these sorts of projects, specifically when it comes to white volunteers traveling to Africa. Before coming to Kenya I had heard countless stories of failed idealists who went to Africa with a plan to make peace. Often however, this plan failed simply as a result of insensitivity to the fact that our values and beliefs in the West do not always square up with those of the people in Africa. I knew as well how ridiculous it sounded when I expressed my desire, the exact same as many others, that I wanted to help start a peace movement in Kenya, but I knew that the key to its success would be its ability to be shaped, developed and executed by youths in and from Kenya. They know best what works and what is needed. I did not want people to misconstrue my motivations but knew that without understanding the details, it was pretty easy to perceive of this project as a foreign imposed solution. I wanted to make it clear to the participants from the beginning that the success of this project, and the ideas for this project would come entirely from them and that we were only there to push the process along. As a result, Courtney and I did not make a plan for the workshop, but only prepared a few things to do on the first morning that we were together. After that it would be entirely up to the participants to decide what would happen next and what we would do. Both Courtney and I would be there only to help keep the conversation on track and remain facilitator-observers, so that we could get as much done as possible in the four short days that we had with each other. Just to drive this point home, it was truly important to us that this project was not pre-planned or directed by

105

us. We wanted these young leaders to feel empowered from the start, and it quickly became clear that they were more than eager to take advantage of this situation. We all were.

As we wrapped up this first evening's events and were heading for dinner, one of the younger participants put his hand on my shoulder, looked me in the eye and said, "There is a time to be friends, and a time to be enemies: this is the time to be friends." He then shook my hand and we walked to dinner together.

It was important that the youths involved were at least able to feel a sense of belonging and brotherhood amongst each other, for if they were to create a coherent group then they could perhaps find the support from each other that they lacked from the outside world. Before they were able to overcome prior challenges however, it was important for them to know who they were working with, and our first educational exercise proved to be one of the most interesting parts of the entire project.

LET'S MAKE OUR OWN TRIBE CALLED THE YOUTHS

Though there are indeed a plethora of ethnic communities in Kenya, I was fortunate to get to know members of three of them intimately: the Kisii, Kalenjin, and Luo. These three communities, prominent in the Rift Valley Province, have a diversity that contributes to the strength and resilience of the Kenyan people.

Before getting into the meat of our workshop bringing together 25 youths from these three different communities, we only conducted one exercise in which the participants were asked to divide up along tribal lines. In every other exercise and activity they sat together, united. Though the workshop was designed to bring youths together and ensure that they do not make associations of each other based on tribal identity, the purpose of this exercise was to smash stereotypes and destabilize prejudices that were previously held. One of the youths actually compared the beginning of the workshop to group therapy, which I thought was a pretty funny analysis. The more I thought about it however, the more it did sort of feel like it and, in following with the therapy analogy, the first step of overcoming a problem is realizing that you have one. So, what better way to deal with this problem than to highlight differences, and alter this paradigm in which differences are seen to be negative? On this day in group therapy we changed the entire model of thinking to ensuring that the youths primarily know that differences mean diversity. This will hopefully also be the lesson that you as the reader take from this chapter as well. Today, the participants would stand up and teach about each others' communities.

I should also take this opportunity to comment about my usage of the word 'tribe'. The people of Kenya refer to their ethnic groupings as tribes, and though many both in the developed world and elsewhere outside of Africa put a negative connotation on the word and use others like 'group' or 'community', tribe is sometimes just an appropriate word to use. It is by no means intended to imply primitiveness, backwardness, or any lack of civilization. When I use 'tribe', though I often switch between the different synonyms noted above, it is a result of speaking to many Kenyans who refer to their communities as such, and I intend no ignorance, malice, stereotyping, or negativity.

As I have said before, tribalism is like racism, and so I felt that it was important for these tribes to be able to represent themselves fairly. By enabling youths to essentially present themselves to the others, we tried presenting them with the opportunity to speak proudly, openly and honestly about their traditions, history, culture and beliefs in a trusting environment. I would say that the purpose of this exercise and the workshop in general, was to demonstrate that differences make people unique. The fact that we are each unique means that we each have the ability to contribute to society and the world in our own specific ways, and these differences should be seen not as divisive factors in society.

These differences should simply be viewed as the results of a beautiful history.

This idea played an important role in a project designed to tackle the elements that contributed to the post-election violence, which was essentially a civil war. A civil war itself is characterized as people of a certain group fighting with each other, which is why I suppose the Hebrew term for civil war, translated, is a "war of brothers." Civil wars and the post-election violence that destabilized Kenya are a result of peoples' tolerance failing them for a moment. When this happens, people perceive each other as, well, "the other". It is this concept of "the other" that has plagued academics for ages and has contributed to much hatred and intolerance that has seen results as minor as petty racist slurs ranging to full blown genocides. When you consider this notion of "the other" I believe that the one idea to keep in mind is that you yourself are "the other" to someone else. It is for this reason that the Golden Rule, as has been enunciated throughout the ages, is "Love thy neighbour as you love yourself." If people did this, then all could potentially be a little better in the world. Fairly straightforward, no?

President Obama, having a certain way with words, wrote about this concept in his book *The Audacity of Hope*, when he wrote,

> The danger to our way of life is not that we will be overrun by those who do not look like us or do not speak our language. The danger will come if we fail to recognize the humanity [of everyone different]—if we withhold from them the rights

and opportunities that we take for granted, and tolerate the hypocrisy of a servant class in our midst.

Talking with reference to the Civil Rights movement in the United States, this statement itself is telling in terms of understanding the importance of tolerance and not "othering" people with whom we share a neighbourhood, country, continent, or planet. Making someone the 'other' contributes to an unnecessary amount of harm which is entirely avoidable by the simple idea that you should treat others the way you want to be treated. Simple tolerance has always bridged gaps and made even the most different of people stand together hand in hand.

Now, to actually tell you about the differences of these three tribes! Again, *differences highlight diversity*. Say this a few times over in your head before you read this section, or I can just provide this mantra for you: Differences highlight diversity, differences highlight diversity, differences highlight diversity, and differences highlight diversity. Don't forget it.

To conduct this exercise, I divided up the youths into their three different communities, and asked them to each prepare a presentation about the strengths, weaknesses, and some interesting aspects of their individual tribes. The results were brilliant and what follows is what they presented. There was no research done in presenting the following information, and I've tried to keep my own commentary and perceptions to a minimum. The information we heard was really eye opening and it was interesting to learn the intricacies of three of Africa's many tribal communities, and I hope that you enjoy the information in the same way.

Kisii (Gusii)

The Kisii youths broke down the section of strengths into a few different types of strengths, beginning with social strength. They told the others that the Kisii people were kind, generous and loving to all, and that when a visitor comes to their village they are extremely hospitable. I can personally attest to this as I had never had as much food forced on me as I had when I went to visit the Kisii village of Matongo (and I have a Jewish mother, so that's saying something). They stated that their tradition is welcoming guests in a special way, going over and above trying to make them feel welcomed, even giving the guest something to take with them when they leave. Me, I got a bunch of freshly picked bananas.

With regard to intermarriage, that is marriage between tribes, the Kisii youths said that they can marry from any tribe as long as there is attraction (always important) and they can live peacefully together (equally important I suppose). Intermarriage is one way to interact with other communities and tribes, and they said that they fear nothing as a result of their ability to interact well with everyone. This interaction is accentuated by their self-professed skill of forgiving-and-forgetting things of the past, and they said that they do not keep negative things in their heart for a long time. They are a community united in their social development, and they listed their schools as an example of such development.

Playing on the adage of "Good fences make good neighbours", the Kisiis said that they are keen on boundaries to avoid conflict. They actually listed as a weakness however their habit of erecting a fence as soon as land is bought, and said that they saw this physical barrier as an obstacle to better interaction with others. They quickly rationalized the fence not as a way to keep neighbours out, but as a way to keep their animals in, which, incidentally, makes a good marker for their boundaries.

With regard to their economic strength, the Kisiis said that they are hardworking individuals, and this is exemplified in many of their various occupations, such as beekeepers, agricultural farmers, and poultry farmers. They are able to excel in these areas and in their economic strength since they are creative and good planners, and they told me how they make carvings from soapstone to sell to tourists (Yes, I bought some).

Kisiis are anxious of development and competition. By competing, they say, you are simply trying to out-do the others, but they believe that competition breeds development which is ultimately a positive societal element. By fostering positive competition, community members encourage each other to get involved, push their limits, and test their ability to grow. They also said that as a result they have the best spirit of investment anywhere in the country, and that they start investments anywhere. This I presume means that when they see a project that has the ability to succeed or develop into something bigger, they help foster the growth of this project and invest any resources they have into it. They also keenly see economic strength as a way to promote peace and that when people are financially successful, they are less eager to wage war or pick fights. They strongly feel that conflict decreases investment, which is of course an acute observation, since at times of war priorities shift, and economic growth is marginalized for mere violence or survival.

In terms of their political strength, they proudly stated that they were democratic, and that anyone from any Kenyan political party can campaign on Kisii territory. One of the youths said "we have an ear for any person who comes to speak into it." Along this democratic line, the Kisiis said that they are not partisan and do not only vote for one party or group based on what the entire tribe is doing, and that they will support a wide variety of politicians, making the effort to not neglect even the lesser known politicians or public faces. In terms of their own tribal politics, they proudly stated that they have a hierarchy in leadership that involves elders at the top, and other followers going all the way down to the youths. They also expressed a desire that the youths would rise up through the hierarchy to ensure that their voices are heard.

The weaknesses that the Kisii listed were extremely interesting. The first one requires no paraphrasing and was listed as "an uncircumcised community cannot lead a circumcised community." They stated that they used to believe this maxim, which obviously means that you must be circumcised to be a fully participating member of the community. This tradition, shared amongst numerous communities and religious denominations worldwide, is important to the Kisiis, though they did profess that this is not necessarily a belief that they adhere to as strongly as they once used to. Another interesting tradition that they listed as a weakness was that an unmarried person could not speak before a married person, which, as youths, was concerning. Perhaps this practice insinuated that the unmarried voice is not worth hearing, and they described this practice as archaic and unreasonable at a time when the number of youths is overwhelming in proportion to the older generations. They told me that "Today, this tradition has changed slightly because the unmarried are sometimes wiser than the married." So true Kisiis, so true.

A final weakness that they suggested was that women were not allowed to attend meetings of males, and that the perception of women was that they were "to be seen, not heard." Acknowledging this and other traditions as a weakness was demonstrative of the Kisii youths' willingness to part with many elements of their heritage that they felt could not, and perhaps should not, be maintained in an increasingly modern and progressive world.

As if those tid-bits were not interesting enough, the Kisii then went on to describe a list of things that they believed were interesting about their community which I perceived to be a direct attempt at shattering those widely held stereotypical beliefs about their tribe. This is a tribe that is commonly believed to practice witchcraft and have a reputation as "Night Runners", meaning that they are believed to get naked at night and run on the roofs of houses while holding torches of fire. Get excited.

The Kisii have an innate fear of being bewitched. This fear means that they approach certain societal elements with caution, in particular the modernization that has come from the western world such as technology and other developments. They also detailed very specific rites that they have with regard to paying their last respects to someone who has died. One of these special rites is that the body is brought into the person's house for a certain period of time before they are buried, in a ceremony which seemed to me similar to the tradition of a wake. When they conduct this ritual, the body is brought into the house through one door, but it must be taken out of the house through another. This practice of using different doors of the house came up a few other times in various Kisii traditions.

Here are some other interesting facts: When Kisii boys are circumcised at the age of 18 (yes, 18) they reside in special huts for the duration of their recovery, and their parents are not allowed to see them for this period of time. Furthermore, circumcised boys are not allowed to enter their parents' bedroom, an action which was deemed "highly prohibited." If, however, a young man does transgress and enters the room, they must sacrifice a goat or a white chicken to apologize. The only time that this entry would be permitted would be in instances of an emergency or a particular concern.

Here is one that some may be jealous of: Parents-in-law are not allowed to enter their son-in-law's house. As well, a son-in-law that has not yet paid a dowry to his wife's parents is not allowed to enter his in-laws' house through the regular door—he must enter through the window.

Luo

The youths from the Luo community began with an interesting history of their tribe, which they felt was necessary since a way of understanding much of what they currently believe and do is a result of how they perceive the past.

The word *Luo* actually comes from the tribal word *lupo* that means "fishing". The Luo people originated from South Sudan, and gradually moved to settle in Uganda and other regions around Lake Victoria. This is where the fishing aspect of their history comes in, and they became a predominantly fishing and farming community that was persistently searching for water to fish and pasture for their animals to graze.

The beginning of their presentation focused on physical strength, an aspect that translated into very real terms within their tribe. A common tradition they have is the removal of a man's six lower teeth. This practice demonstrates a man's strength by proving his tolerance of pain, and makes my coming into manhood of simply reading out of the Torah on my Bar Mitzvah seem . . . well . . . wussy (I then told them, as a way of consolation, that the *bensching* at my bar mitzvah consisted of me single-handedly lifting a bench on which sat my entire immediate family, but they didn't buy it). This Luo emphasis on physical strength is a result of one of their historical narratives, which involved a strong individual named Luanda Magere.

Luanda Magere was an enormous individual with great strength derived from his shadow. This story is similar to the Biblical story of Samson, who similarly derived his sheer strength from his hair. Luanda Magere fought the Kalenjins, another tribe in Kenya who were considered the fiercest fighters of all. When the Kalenjins threw spears at Luanda Magere however, they could not kill him because of his near invincibility. As a trick, the Kalenjins gave Luanda Magere a woman, who he made his second wife (Luos are polygamous to this day). One day when

Luanda Magere fell ill, his first wife went to retrieve some medicine to help him recover, at which point his new second wife asked him how she could assist in his recovery. He asked her to treat him by making a small incision in his shadow, which he then revealed to her to be the source of all his strength. Once this was revealed to her, this 'Trojan Horse' wife went back to her native Kalenjin community and disclosed to them the secret to Luanda Magere's strength. The Kalenjins then attacked his shadow and killed him. This show of weakness is one of the reasons why the Luo place so much faith in the importance of physical strength.

The Luos spoke at length about their strong traditional values. They believe that "He who follows tradition has the strength of the community," which is quite a touching sentiment and a statement about tribes which is overlooked when focusing on the negativity of these societal divisions. Aside from sheer strength, the Luos emphasize education and told me, "We are the learned people. This is obvious since even Obama is a Luo," which is also true.

Their other strong characteristics are that they are loving, caring, and care deeply about helping each other. They themselves told me that there is no point in having a tribe if it is not treated as a support structure, and so it is critical that every member supports the others. They are hardworking, which leads to their success in their traditional role as fishermen and farmers, and they also insist on keeping to their boundaries. They believe that a polygamous man, someone with many wives, is strongest within a community, and they are firmly democratic and supportive of one another.

117

As a weakness, the Luos primarily confessed that their political leaders misuse their strength, perhaps alluding to the current Prime Minister of Kenya, Raila Odinga. They also lamented the fact that their community members are easily susceptible to political manipulation and that they are easily incited to violence and to act by their political leaders. This was brought into stark realization by the post-election violence. Unlike the Kisii who maintained a strong "forgive-and-forget" characteristic, the Luos told me and the other tribes that they kept hatred in their hearts, and that if they hated a particular community, they had a difficult time convincing themselves otherwise. A final weakness, which is certainly the black sheep in the list, is that they dislike funerals because there is lots of eating and food distributed at the ceremonies, and that many people from their tribe attend funerals simply to get free food. Maybe we Luos and Jews aren't that different after all . . .

With regard to the interesting aspects of their tribe, the Luos are proud of the fact that they are creative, and they believe that this creativity is espoused through, for example, the formation of parties in Kenya's political system. They also mentioned their in-laws but unlike the rules that the Kisiis noted, the Luos simply said that they highly value their in-laws, and told me that this natural extension of a family meant much to their tribal development.

Finally, and perhaps most interesting, in returning to the idea of hatred that they mentioned as a weakness, one of the youths stood in front of this group of youths from two other communities, in the midst of a peacebuilding workshop, and said plainly, "If you are making peace with other communities, you will find the Luos at the finishing line." As I wrote this line in my notebook tears formed in my eyes, which have returned even while writing this down here, because this is the essence of this entire exercise. Despite their own self-professed difficulty at overcoming historical hatred and the differences between tribes, these youths, sometimes the most judgmental of society's members, stood up to tell the others that despite their differences and their history, that they want to be a part of the healing process. Perhaps in this way the above statement was the incision in the shadow of the Luo representation, which maybe needed more than any other tribe to enunciate these truths out loud in order to make progress in this endeavour. This statement alone exemplified the personal impact that some of the youths were feeling in the context of this project, and it made me both emotional and proud.

Kalenjin

Finally the Kalenjin youths had a chance to address the group about their strengths and weaknesses. The Kalenjins, perhaps more than any other tribe in Kenya, are perceived by the others as the militant group that excels at physical warfare. With this in mind, as well as realizing that this entire workshop was taking place in Kiptere, a Kalenjin village, led me to contextualize the importance of what the Kalenjins were saying to the others in the room.

The Kalenjins began by telling the others that they were strong in sports, leadership, and hospitality. With regard to sports, they told us that their community is known to produce excellent marathon runners. With regard to leadership, they informed us that the longest serving Kenyan President, Daniel Arap Moi, was a Kalenjin, serving from 1978 to 2002 (succeeding Jomo Kenyatta, and preceding Mwai Kibaki). With regard to hospitality, the Kalenjins said that they were willing to live with anyone and everyone from every part of the world unless something bad or personally harming is done to them. As someone who was a guest in Kiptere on two separate occasions I cannot omit a comment here that I was the recipient of the most incredible hospitality from the Kalenjins, and that they were most definitely correct in this regard.

The Kalenjins also noted as a form of their strength their farming abilities, and said that they were adept at growing maize, a wide variety of vegetables, and that everything is green in Kalenjin land. Assisted by the heavy daily rainfall in Western Kenya, my plethora of pictures do not do justice to this description of everything being green, and it is abundantly clear how agriculturally motivated their community is.

The Kalenjins are most proud of their livestock rearing, and in this sense they are particularly obsessed with their cows. As I mentioned earlier, the Kalenjins have an old belief that God made the cows for them, and a common warning to other tribes goes, "You can take the milk, but leave the cow." As a result of this divinely-inspired receipt of the earth's bovines, the Kalenjin people regularly engage in "cattle rustling" or cattle raiding, which is stealing cows from neighbouring villages and communities. This leads to great tension among the communities, and in fact the day before the workshop began two young Kalenjin boys were killed while attempting to steal the cattle of their Luo neighbours. Though we feared this event would create some hesitation among the participants of the workshop, we were fortunate that no one was deterred from coming to participate in this event. Cattle raiding nevertheless continues to be a trend in the region that regularly contributes to minor tribal clashes, and is something that was recognized by these Kalenjin youths as a tribal weakness as it bred more conflict than anything else.

As the warrior group, the Kalenjins described as their strength their ability to wage war, noting in particular both their bravery and their techniques. They value the asset of being brave in the face of harm, and so they also practice the tradition of circumcision at the age of 18. Their weapon of choice is bow and arrows, and during the post-election violence these arrows were tipped with poison, forcing even the Kenyan military to back off when faced with row upon row of Kalenjin archers.

Aside from their physical strength, the Kalenjins place much emphasis on unity and tribal togetherness, stating that they always have one voice despite the fact that there are many sub-tribes in the Kalenjin tradition and that this is perhaps not the most democratic tribal makeup. Despite this unity however, they are not necessarily an insular tribe, and also value the possibility of intermarriage, particularly with the Kisii and Luo communities as a result simply of their regional proximity (there may also have been in this group of Kalenjins a young male who was interested in a particularly attractive Kisii female . . . so it is all relative). In addition to intermarriage, the Kalenjins are also polygamous, and believe that having numerous wives gives a man pride, leverage and security within his community. More wives also means more offspring, which means that the patriarch of the family will have a good labour force in the future.

Despite the perceived strength of polygamy and intermarriage that the Kalenjins detailed, the item that topped the list of Kalenjin weaknesses was "wife battering". They listed as a weakness the fact that women are regularly beaten in the Kalenjin community, and listed as a second weakness the fact that there is extreme gender inequality within their tribe. They said that their men in general do not value women enough and rarely help in the family setting. This negative trend is further accentuated by the fact that there is widespread alcoholism amongst males in Kalenjin society as a result of the popularity of local brewing. These youths acknowledged that local brewing contributes to a weaker community, irresponsibility on the part of men, and general alcoholism. I can also say personally that I tried this Kalenjin local brew (purely as a social experiment of course) and could not believe that this most disgusting liquid I have ever tasted contributed to so much addiction in Kalenjin communities.

Returning to gender inequality though, there may be many reasons for this extreme trend, but part of it stems from a variety of their other traditions, such as marrying off their daughters at young ages. They told the group that the reason parents send their daughters to get married at a young age was financially motivated, and that the parents just wanted the dowry offered for their daughter. This objectifies females, making them appear more as financial assets than as members of the tribe. The trend contributes to gender inequality, and as a result many females forgo the opportunity to receive an education. The Kalenjins said that their tribe does not always place a heavy emphasis on education, specifically for girls, and that many perceive a female's role as being primarily a mother, capable of being traded for a dowry. I must say that I befriended a number of young Kalenjin females throughout my time in Kenya, and I was particularly impressed by how acutely aware they were of this expectation of them, and how determined some of them were to break this mould. This determination sometimes resulted in them defying the will of their parents, but their moderation and deference to the will of their parents meant that they were able to find a balance between pursuing their own future, and fitting into the form of a traditional Kalenjin female.

Another weakness noted with regard to Kalenjin females is the practice of female initiation or circumcision. This activity, today considered to be one of the most barbaric of human practices, is still often practiced by Kalenjin families, though not to the same extent as it traditionally was. This practice involves the mutilation of the female genitalia to curb any sexual pleasure. In some Kalenjin families, if the daughter refuses to go through with this rite of passage, she may be rejected by her family and peers, and some males are instructed specifically to marry girls who have gone through this procedure. Traditionally, this initiation implied that the girl has demonstrated her own strength and was ready for marriage and the responsibility of a family, but today again, that tradition and perception has thankfully been marginalized in Kalenjin communities.

A final weakness that the Kalenjins noted was that they were a segregated community, in the sense that they isolated themselves from other tribes in Kenya. They told the group that they like to do things alone, like to speak to each other in Kale, their own tribal language that other communities do not understand, and do not always enjoy mingling with members of other tribes. They said that although they are hospitable to strangers and encourage intermarriage, it takes them a long time to grow to trust a stranger in the midst of their community, and noted this hesitation particularly with regard to someone who is running for government. They said that as a result of this political hesitation, they tend to trust only their own tribal members for government, so that they will be unlikely to support or vote for politicians from other backgrounds.

The Kalenjins went on to detail some other interesting tribal practices for the group. They spoke of how important circumcision was to members of their tribe, and that when these 18 year old boys were circumcised, they were made to wear a leather-beaded head set (one of which I later received as a gift—a headset . . . not circumcision). The Kalenjins also wear animal skins throughout the circumcision ritual, a tradition which they use for other rites as well such as weddings. They told us that during the circumcision, although boys are encouraged to demonstrate strength throughout this rite of passage by keeping their cool and not screaming, many faint—obviously. After the ceremony, bulls are slaughtered and eaten to celebrate. This tradition is one of many that come from a tribe that also has Medicine Men and Fortunetellers performing these ancient roles of prophecy and magic.

As a byproduct of their love of cows, one of their traditional drinks (which I also had the misfortune of trying) is called *mursik*, which is a Kale way of saying sour milk. Not letting any part of the cow go to waste, the Kalenjin people will make as much use of the cow's milk as possible which includes beverages such as tea (essentially milk and sugar), *mursik,* and also taking milk and mixing it with the cow's blood which is apparently a nourishing drink. This is the one thing that I did NOT try while there.

The Kalenjin value understanding their past and abiding by their traditions, and so every night while waiting for their wives to prepare dinner, they tell stories of their past, a tradition that has contributed to a rich oral history.

Like other communities, the Kalenjins place much emphasis on their tribal hierarchy, with elders sitting at the top. A short stick called a *rungu* identifies these elders. Any picture of former President Moi will show him holding a *rungu* in his hand, and this tradition essentially dictates that in order to speak in the community as an elder, you need a stick like this to hold. On my last day in Kiptere a group of Kenyan elders presented me with my own *rungu* which I was incredibly humbled and honoured to accept. The presentation of this gift led a number of the youths whom I was sitting with at the time to break down into tears as a result of how touched they personally were to see the elders praising me this way. Their reaction to this gesture demonstrated that this list of facts still plays an integral role in the life and values of the community, and shows that the tribe is a living, breathing entity that is very real in the lives of all its members.

Observations

After the presentations by each of the tribes the entire group had a chance to discuss what they had learned and reflect on anything they felt relevant. Their ideas afterwards were thoughtful and pronounced, and I was impressed that many of them had taken notes, promising me they were going to take much of this information back to their own villages. It was unbelievable to me to hear this as they had all grown up with each other, in a way, and yet there was so much that they had learned from this short and simple session on each other's tribes. Living without truly knowing your neighbour was a strange idea to me, but I was glad that at least some of the stereotypes and misconceptions had been shattered, and that some of these youths were able to at least thoughtfully reflect on what the rest of the workshop would be like.

One of the participants, Ibrahim, took detailed notes on all the presentations and made some pointed comments at the conclusion of the activity. He noted that all tribes are hardworking, as is evidenced by their tendency to be farmers and/or fishermen. He noted in particular the unity that each tribe demonstrated when faced with adversity, and talked about how in times of trouble, the tribes unite to protect each other. He commented that this is the sort of unity that needed to be both intra-tribal and inter-tribal, so that when there is danger in Kenya, this ability to come together unites everyone as Kenyans only. He said that each group had mentioned that the purpose of having a tribe was to create a common bond with others and to ensure that this connection is not easily severed. He said that tribes, being an archaic concept, are merely an older expression of modern states and countries, and that modern political entities are essentially new tribes. Therefore, as one of the participants named Jescah said, "I can now say you are my brother, not my Kisii brother, but my actual brother." This analysis, equating countries to tribes was a simple but profound way of saying that all Kenyans should come together, particularly those youths who see, feel and believe many of the same things. It is this feeling that prompted Ibrahim to proclaim that "we should make our own tribe called the Youths, and this would be a very positive achievement indeed."

Noting the emphasis that each group had placed on traditions, Ibrahim saw that the preservation of traditions is a good thing, and that it highlights the values of our beliefs and practices. Hospitality, a practice common to all the tribes, is a tradition that should be fostered to promote peace, and he said that peace was a concept that should always be spoken about in the context of welcoming people into your village and into your home. This leads to intermarriage, which should always been striven for, and Ibrahim said that if the tribes can successfully achieve chances of intermarriage, then it should not be that hard to get along as equals. There are common weaknesses that were noticed amongst the tribes too, but the fact that they were all so willing to admit to their weaknesses and discuss them in a room of their peers, including some who are not always friendly in the relations with each other, means that they are willing to overcome weaknesses and press forward in the spirit of forgiveness and change.

Ibrahim said there are always changes as time progresses, and noted as an example the change in religious beliefs of the tribes. He stated that many communities believe in their own primitive creation stories before basically becoming Christian in their beliefs and actions. This change is exemplified in the storytelling that all communities engage in, and by discussing the past and the advances that have led to the current situation, the tribes can learn from their histories and be sure that they do not repeat past mistakes. The aspects of bravery and strength that are central to each tribe should be used for good, evoking the lesson from Spiderman that says "with great power comes great responsibility" (my idea, not theirs). Ibrahim however concluded that it is crucial that everyone uses their bravery to be brave in terms of peace, and use their entire bodies to embrace their neighbours not violently but with a handshake. He said they must look each other in the eye and lend each other an ear to hear their ideas for what is best for Kenya. In that sense, they are taking their future into their own hands and demonstrating to the older generation that tribalism is a relic of the past that must be forgotten if there is to be a lasting peace in Kenya.

Before our seminar ended, one of the participants, also a local Pastor, stood with a bible to read a quote from the Book of Leviticus, chapter 19 verses 17-18, which reads,

> Do not hate your fellow kinsfolk in your heart, rebuke your neighbour frankly so you will not share in their guilt. Do not seek revenge or bear a grudge against anyone among your people, but love your neighbour as yourself.

Included in this verse is again the Golden Rule, and the warning against hatred and seeking revenge. As devoutly religious Christians the youths sat and nodded their heads as the pastor read these powerful lines of the Bible, a book intended to provide guidance for everyone, regardless of any perceived differences. I watched as these youths absorbed the words of the Bible and came together as members of the same faith, and noted that in the same way, they should unite as kinsfolk of the same country. A belief in shared identity, albeit with minor differences, brought them to this workshop. It is their unimaginable inner strength however which enabled them to stand and face those who are so often perceived to be the enemy and share with them their perceived strengths and weaknesses and admit that they are both different and the same as one another. It is for this reason that the experience of this session, a true form of group therapy, both simple and straightforward, stayed with these youths for the duration of the program and throughout their experiences in working as peace ambassadors to other communities in subsequent programs that they themselves initiated.

Three days after this eye-opening meeting, the District Officer of the region came to our closing ceremony to address the newly formed Youth Ambassadors for Peace. He said that, "If there was a way to take an eraser and erase tribes and just call ourselves Kenyans, we must do it." This session detailed above acted as that eraser, but the sort of crappy pink eraser that you find on the ends of those cheap pencils that does a decent job but still leaves a mark so that you know there used to be something there. The point is not to erase tribes entirely. Rather, we should ensure that the lines are blurred just enough to make certain that people are able to maintain their traditions and cultures, but also feel as though they are one people in a larger, united group of Kenyans. In this way, both youths and elders will find no distinct boundary when they leave their village, be able to wander onto each others' territory, and share a cup of disgusting sour *mursik* while toasting to the peaceful future of Kenya.

Day One — There is Nothing Hard in This World if You Have Motivation

The first day of the workshop started early and was the only day we had planned out in advance. As everyone was still strangers, we wanted to gauge the group's interests, expectations, purpose for attending, and their perceptions of each other. Drawing upon my prior experience as a day camp supervisor back home, I created a few icebreaker activities to help everyone get better acquainted.

After our group breakfast of *chapatis* and tea, everyone made their way upstairs to our conference room. Sitting on white-plastic garden chairs that made a creaking noise on the concrete floor every time they moved even the slightest bit, the youths settled in, taking a cursory look at each other as they sat in three distinct groups according to which community they belonged to. This was a trend that we hoped would take a day to get over, and by the end of the week we saw good quality intermingling, and even a few couples that had formed as a result. It also became clear why there was so much talk of encouraging intermarriage, but I will get to that later.

Before starting anything, we wanted to establish expectations and get the participants thinking about their reasons for being here. Writing things down creates a strong foundation for these thoughts, so we asked everyone to rip a piece of paper out of their notebooks and write down answers to the following four questions:

1. What are your expectations of this seminar?
2. Why did you decide to join us in Kiptere this week?
3. What do you hope to take back to your communities after this seminar?
4. What is peace?

They spent some time thinking about their answers and writing them down, and though I would love to include all of their reflective responses, I thought I would provide a few of the more poignant answers.

What are your expectations of the seminar?

"I am expecting a great deal of knowledge and empowerment that will help me facilitate peace preaching out there in the community. I also expect effective proclamation techniques that will help me give out effective information to the community."

"I expect to be able to be empowered so that I can change the Kenya we have today and be one Kenya. I expect to make friends from the other communities."

"The expectation from this seminar is that we go back to the communities we have to see that all young people are taught about good behavior and encourage them to be self-reliant."

"My expectation from this seminar is to acquire some knowledge of how we can relate well with each other despite the differences in background and views and at least be able to go out there and tell or rather spread the message that I will have acquired from this workshop to those who never had the opportunity to come and attend this workshop."

"We expect to find solutions to the problems that face our nation and gain leadership qualities that will enable us to eradicate the inter-tribal differences"

"I expect that every one of us will see the other as a brother or sister and children of God."

"I expect to learn more about each other and make peace within ourselves."

"To be equipped to create a strong bridge to my fellow brothers and sisters to know and appreciate God's love and purpose of creating/making us in his own image and likeness of peace which he gave us and not like the world gives us."

Why did you decide to join us in Kiptere this week?

"I am here to learn about peace."

"I am here to help unite this country so that we can all be one, whether or not we are Kisii, Luo or Kalenjin."

"I am here to socialize with different communities so as to become friends to create no room for conflicts."

"I am here to make people know that everything we did we did to ourselves. If we want to make peace, we have to make it ourselves, and if we make enemies, then this is our decision as well. So, I am here to make peace with my tribes to know ourselves better, and to know our nation and our universe. So, I guess I want to start with my country and then spread to other parts of the world because we belong to one nation as a whole so there's no need to keep ourselves enemies. We are brothers and sisters, so let's all come together and make an oath to the next generation. I believe that we are the future so if we keep fighting with each other then there is no future we are just making the world hell. Every time I see people fighting I feel like the weight of the world is on my shoulders because most people only care about money making, let's come together like brothers and sisters living in one house, because we're the ones, we're the children, we're the ones who make a better day, so let's start giving and make peace."

"The reason of my participation here is to foster mutual coexistence between the ever warring communities. I want to prove to the world that there is strength and hope to eradicate the existing tribal differences between us. I also want to exercise the love of God that we are all brothers and sisters in Christ, and love and peace should always accompany our lives."

What do you hope to take back to your communities after this seminar?

"I hope to take back a recipe for how people can live together in peace."

"I hope to take back the ideals of peace to my community, and also the unity of youths so that they know about dangers and how we should overcome them to make Kenya better."

"I would like to go back to my community as a role model, and hope that other youths will want to participate in similar workshops in the future."

"I hope to teach them about the message of peace keeping and how important it is to live in harmony with each other."

"I would like to go back to my community to spread peace, love and harmony."

What is Peace?

"Peace means being one in a community."

"Peace is when there is joy and interaction within the communities."

"Peace is a free environment of movement, working, giving opinion and speech without any interference"

"Peace is anything which is good."

"Peace is the comfort of the mind."

"Peace is humanity."

"Peace is a mutual coexistence, all around togetherness and open love between people regardless of their race, country, blood, religion and culture."

It seemed as though we'd managed to find the right group of youths. Their message was spot on even though we had not yet actually said anything to them. They were acutely aware of what they had chosen to attend and they seemed eager to jump into the project and get their hands dirty. The ultimate purpose of writing down their answers to these four questions was to get them to reflect, from the start, about what they wanted to get out of their participation in the workshop on a personal and team-oriented level, but they were already saying all the key words that I had written down in my notebook. They all wanted to be leaders, they wanted to be able to take back positive messages and programming to their respective communities, and the word "ambassador" was already being thrown around. We only read these pieces of paper later in the evening on the first day, but based on what we had spoken about previously, we were thrilled that our hopes and endeavours were already aligned in some way with theirs.

When each participant arrived we supplied them with a notebook, pen, a variety of other items they would need for the week, and a letter outlining our purpose of coming to Kiptere, and what we hoped to accomplish throughout the week. As a way of introduction, we started the letter with the following:

> Peacebuilding is a long process that requires patience, creativity, compassion, and social empathy. It is not an easy task and requires every high ideal that you possess. There are many peace initiatives on the ground in Kenya, as there are many in this country who dream of a peaceful Kenya. What these projects require is dedication

and persistence in order to succeed, and we believe that this week is only the beginning of a process that will bring a better understanding of conflict in general, as well as the problems in Kenya, to your respective communities.

We wanted the group to begin to think like peace builders. However, the truth was that we ourselves had difficulty defining peacebuilding and peace makers. So, instead of using definitions to shape the content of our program, we thought that it would be more appropriate to determine what emotions and values are associated with war, peace and coexistence projects, and from those emotions we could develop our own definitions and methods. As a starting point, we were fortunate that one of the participants had brought with him a peacebuilding tool which we found hilarious, as well as motivating and creative.

The tool was a piece of paper with a picture of an awkward looking white man on it, titled "Attributes of a Peace Builder." The black and white picture showed the man with abnormally large ears, a big stomach, bulging arms with huge hands, massive calves and misshaped feet, wearing shorts and a polo t-shirt. Around the picture were lines pointing to each body part, each symbolizing an attribute that this picture termed the necessary attributes of a peace builder.

The big ears were required to hear and comprehend everything that the other people in the group were saying, while the hard head (symbolized by a helmet) demonstrated the need to absorb as much knowledge as possible without the head breaking. The thoughtful-looking eyes, or "cleaver" (should be "clever") eyes, were required to see both verbal and non-verbal communication, while a small mouth was needed so one speaks less, but nevertheless exudes confidence. A big heart, illustrated by a large heart drawn on the outside of the shirt, symbolized empathy, while the large hands were capable hands, required to build a lasting peace. In one of this man's hands he held a large glass jar; this was called the 'ego container', which demonstrated self-awareness, and a line pointing to the man's groin was labeled "big bladder", which stood for endurance. Finally, the abnormally large feet represented "big feet firmly on the ground," which showed that our ideal peace builder was determined and principled, and was not to be manipulated by leaders or other people. This fantastic drawing would be the basis of our first conversation, as well as the start of many laughs that we shared together as a group.

Once we all had a chance to consider this drawing, as a way of introduction we thought we would lay out some groundwork for the workshop and speak to the youths about why we were there. I spoke to them about my perceptions of tribalism and youth idleness in Kenya, and spoke about our dream of having them become ambassadors, on their own accord, to both their own and each others' communities. My first words however, were "This is history." Based on what I had been told by others in the community, this was to be the first time that the Kisii, Kalenjin and Luo communities came together in any official and significant manner to try and sort out some of the outstanding issues among them. It was one of the first times that youths had been engaged in a grassroots manner in this region to try to erode those negative societal elements.

I had in my mind a line from an Israeli song called *Avshalom* written by the famed Israeli folk singer Arik Einstein. One of the main lines of the chorus of this song is '*Lamah loh achshav mah she'betach yavo machar?*' which means "Why not now, what we will inevitably have tomorrow?" As a kind of philosophy, this line and its message has often been a factor in my decision-making process. I find it helpful when thinking about taking advantage of opportunities and have it in mind when contemplating some of the things that are happening in the world. When things seem inevitable, as peace must be, I think that there should be no delay, and that not knowing what will happen tomorrow, it is necessary to get started with these actions right now.

If not now, when?

Peace is inevitable. It must be, otherwise our world will collapse in on itself. Despite the mess that we may find ourselves in at the moment, I believe that with the goodness of individuals and the power that many good people are able to wield, peace is something that will inevitably be achieved. It is with this mindset that I said today we are going to make history, so that what is inevitable in the future can become a reality today.

I was told that Kiptere and nearby Sondu were indeed hotspots for tribal violence and clashes, and so it was required from the start to explain why we felt it was important that this gathering was taking place here. I spoke of our desire to confront stereotypes and prejudice among the communities, and mentioned the idea that diversity must unite everyone. From this introduction I thought it would be good to get a feel for people's attitudes, and tried to spark a conversation about the notion of strength.

This idea of strength had been on my mind for some time, and the reason is because I had noticed some African tribal traditions that became traditions particularly so that people were able to demonstrate their own strength. The Kalenjin community practices circumcision at the age of 18 as a rite of passage and to demonstrate the strength of their teenage boys. Some members of the Luo tribe, when they are older, remove a number of their lower teeth also as a feat of strength and their ability to deal with pain, and members of the Maasai tribe make big holes in their ear lobes, also as a feat of strength. I saw that many tribes in Kenya, and all over the world, have their own traditions and ways to show their own sheer strength and what they are physically able to deal with, and these demonstrations certainly make sense in an archaic society where tribes would size each other up before they went to battle. The applicability of such traditions in modern days however seems anachronistic, but tradition is tradition, and these practices are still found all over the country, continent and world. I wanted to hear from the youths what they thought about the idea of strength, and how they believed this notion was perceived in modern Kenya.

One of the most animated participants of the workshop was named Geoffrey. Being an older youth (as Kenyans are considered youths to the age of 40) and leader in the community, Geoffrey was about 35 years old and extremely eager, always putting his hand up to offer his opinion and point of view. He very much wanted to take part in controlling the direction of any debate as well as the overall workshop, and though many of the youths came dressed in jeans and t-shirts each morning, Geoffrey always showed up in a pair of dress pants, black shoes, and a leather jacket. He was a phenomenal member of the group, and his eagerness was always accompanied by a sense of formalism, as he put his hand up first, stood to speak, and ended each assertion with "Thank you very much Sir and Madam."

The first time that Geoffrey spoke he made the point that strength is actually entirely neutral. "Strength," he said, "is a neutral concept and is merely a matter of whether one's arms are large or whether that person has enough influence to tell others what to do. It is what is done with that strength that is either positive or negative. Thank you very much Sir and Madam." I smiled and thought this was an acute observation by someone who had witnessed so much negative strength in recent years, and it made me think about how strength was actually interpreted and used. The tribal practices noted earlier are merely a demonstration of strength, but strength itself is irrelevant until one determines how they are going to use it.

A youth who spoke after Geoffrey said that strength is also displayed differently between men and women. She said that men display strength in the physical sense, or by demonstrating their wealth and influence in the community. Women, on the other hand, display their strength, she said, by waking up early, making food for the family, working, taking care of the children, and helping to take care of the home. Many of my feminist friends would perhaps have problems with this definition of strength, but to an observer in Kenya, specifically in a particular community where women are often subjugated into the role of housewife, it was, in a way, refreshing to hear that the women perceive themselves as strong in a certain way, and believe that they can wield that strength when required over their husband or family. Or maybe I'm wrong.

The message that the group seemed to pick up on was the way that one used their strength was how to best determine whether or not it was good or bad strength. The conversation therefore ultimately, and quickly, turned to politics and politicians in Kenya, and another participant talked about the way that politicians use their strength in Kenya. He mentioned that President Kibaki had misused his strength, and said that Kibaki essentially said, "I am not moving out of this office because my knowledge of the office gives me strength, and since I am stronger than you, I can command anything." Kibaki used his strength in a negative way, and the stubbornness and selfishness that many say he portrayed up to and during the 2007 election was a demonstration of negative strength. The post-election violence itself was a further demonstration of that strength, whereby he used his influence and power with the police and army to turn on his own people, and essentially give life to a tribal conflict that was, at the beginning, constrained to only a small number of cities and towns. This was a negative display of strength.

It was at this point that Charlie, who throughout the workshops would stand up and speak about messages from the Bible, brought up the story of Samson who was at his time one of the strongest men in the world. Samson though, had a weakness, which was his hair, and he used this analogy to show that although politicians and others may use their strength in a negative, sometimes fatal manner, that they were hardly invincible. Their desire to use overwhelming force is sometimes just a way to cover up their shortcomings. This is maybe why all the great legends of heroes with seemingly infinite strength show some way that they can be crippled and brought down to their knees. A lesson learned is that strength can be achieved, but it cannot always be maintained if not used appropriately.

Ibrahim brought up the point that strength is not only determined by what you do, but by what you don't do. "Restraint," he said rolling the first R, "is the most powerful sort of strength, since it requires you to hold back on your instinct and act in a way that is perhaps unnatural. It is difficult because it is a mental restraint that leads to a physical restraint, and this is sometimes the hardest kind." And he was right! His thoughts echoed the words of Cesar Chavez who said, "Nonviolence is not inaction. It is not discussion. It is not for the timid or weak. Nonviolence is hard work." The examples that Ibrahim used to illustrate this idea were Nelson Mandela and Mahatma Gandhi. Both of them had the perfect opportunity to use violence and force for their cause, both in different ways.

Mandela, upon being released from prison and ultimately becoming President of South Africa, could have let loose on the white South African population as his followers would have done anything he had said and the white population arguably deserved a bit of retribution, yet he preached tolerance, restraint and peace. What resulted in South Africa was a transition into peace and the prevention of an all out slaughter and future of tension.

Gandhi as well could have used force against the British and could have attempted to bring about independence in India the same way that many countries fought off the British and other colonialists throughout Africa and Asia. He insisted on non-violence however, and it was this restraint and determination that his way was the right way that ensured Indian independence, as well as his spot in history as one of the true heroes of the 20th century. Using your strength when you are urged to use it is easy, however keeping your cool and maintaining that restraint is a demonstration of strength, a good type of strength, and it can make all the difference in the world. Gandhi once said, "Nonviolence is a power which can be wielded equally by all—children, young men and women or grown-up people—provided they have a living faith in the God of Love and have, therefore, equal love for all mankind."

After more discussion, Charlie stood up again to conclude that there is strength in peace. "It is only by eradicating the experience of politics and harmonizing togetherness that we are able to find this peace, but once it is found we will be able to instill more fundamental values into each other and those around us." He spoke about the people in society who are the most weak, specifically mentioning those diagnosed with HIV/AIDS, and said that their strength has been taken from them and so they feel and have become extremely vulnerable. Nevertheless they require the strength of others to aspire for a positive future, and it is that strength which is positive and used for good. He said that if strength will be used, then it should be used for righteous purposes only, using (Biblical as always) the example of David slaying Goliath.

"If one's strength is to be restrained then," he said, "they must be sure that the restraint may not cause the harm or suffering of others." For this example he used the UN and international community's ability to help save those being killed in places like Darfur and the Congo, where they could step in but don't, and the negative impact of that restraint of strength. Charlie ended his comments by stating that, "It is the result of the usage of strength that is relevant in the determination of whether one's use of strength was noble or cowardly and only history can be the judge of that strength. The post-election violence was a negative display of strength, and Kenya's highest politicians will not be judged favourably by the next generation of Kenyans. This is why we have come here together to make sure that we are not judged in the future the same way as they will be." As he concluded this perfectly, I thought that since we had now considered the idea of how one's strength may be exercised, it would be pertinent to discuss the results of that strength and in particular the effects of both war and then peace.

This being the beginning of our program together, I had not yet thought about my role in conducting a discussion about the effects of war, peace and the experience of these youths during the post-election violence. Despite whatever knowledge I thought I had about the subject of conflict or political science, nothing of course compares to the actual knowledge you acquire from living through such a time personally, and so I knew that my role as facilitator when we got to these subjects would be complicated, to say the least. I was conscious of not responding to experiences that they told me about by saying things like "I know", or "I can imagine" because I didn't, and I couldn't, and at these times I found it important to merely suggest the subject, and then have them speak to each other. My life is and has always been conflict free (using conflict in the strictest sense) and as the purpose of this project was to help build bridges and peace between these communities, the point of broaching the subject of the effects of war and their particular experiences during such war was so they could speak freely and hear what others went through on the other side of the proverbial tracks. Though I wanted to assist and help facilitate the program to the best of my ability and with whatever experience I had, I felt that it was important to take as much of a back seat as possible when it came to discussions of the conflict itself so it could be discussed by those who had personally experienced it themselves, and hopefully by those who could empathize with each other and the circumstances that at one point they all had to live through.

We discussed the consequences of war as they affected particular elements in Kenya. When it came to the topic of women, the group said that war leads primarily to rape, which in Africa means the spread of sexually transmitted infections and therefore an increase in the rates of HIV/AIDS. As a result of sheer desperation as well and the inability to make a living, women in these times also turn to prostitution in order to try eke out a living. The participants offered that the women may be left behind in IDP camps as the men go off to try finding work, and when things do not work out and the men and others in the community get frustrated, there is a high likelihood that domestic violence will arise, and lead to the injury and indignity of women. Loneliness was another effect of war when it came to women, since men were the ones doing both the fighting and the dying, and when this occurs women may lose both their husbands and also their sons. If this were to happen there is also a risk of insanity, because losing one's family serves a blow to one's mind that is understandably difficult to overcome. When there is a dearth of leadership in a community, the women may be forced to stand up and take a leading role, which is something that they may not be ready or willing to do. On the other hand, this could provide an opportunity for a woman to demonstrate her ability to lead and take charge in a setting that largely marginalizes women and the role they have the potential to play.

It was telling that the first element the group wanted to consider was women, and I was both happy and proud that so many of the girls spoke up to address these issues. They were here to become leaders themselves and by taking this opportunity to speak out in a large group, and hopefully gain some skills that will enable them to become more outgoing in their local communities, it is these women who the future generation of Kenyans will hopefully be looking to. They spoke with conviction, they were thoughtful, and they knew that there were issues facing the women of Africa and Kenya, and wanted to make sure that those concerns were addressed in this forum.

The next element affected by war of course is children, and as one of the most vulnerable sectors of society they are most affected by war and its consequences. Children suffering through war are at risk of becoming orphans or at least losing one parent, which forces them to grow up rather quickly. One of the youths, Betty, said that when a child loses one or both of their parents they lose their childhood, are forced to mature too quickly, and thereby skip some of the most important developmental milestones in their life. They lose the chance to be cared and provided for, and so they are easily susceptible to having their identity or sense of belonging ripped away from them when raised in an environment of war. This further leads to their lack of education, as they must suffer to simply live and find money for food, which leads to their exploitation and manipulation by others in society. Betty said that they miss out on love, and when there is no love then there is hatred, and this hatred can lead to paranoia and the child turning his or her back on society or those who simply wish to help. The effect of war on children is a critical element to take into account when considering the general scourge of conflict, as it has the potential to exacerbate a child's situation for the worse.

The issue of child soldiers is an international concern that flows directly from the scourge of war, and many of the approximately 300,000 child soldiers that inhabit the world today come from Africa. It is difficult to picture ranks of children who have been abducted, intimidated, scared, orphaned, drugged, raped and pressured into joining the ranks of corrupt militaries, militias and gangs. This involvement will scar all 300,000 of them for the rest of their lives and it is noteworthy to establish this as a direct result of conflict and war. The poverty that dominates third world countries and the heavy reliance on the military in these countries means that children are coerced into joining some kind of fighting force. They are enticed by incentives such as money, food and shelter, but these are often simply a way of getting the children into the military fold. Once there, the military inherently takes full control over the lives of these children. They intimidate them, desensitize them to war, show them how to kill, train them to use AK47s, and drug them heavily. One need only imagine the consequences of such actions. The children are trained to patrol the streets and territories of war-torn countries, shoot on sight, and if they disobey the command of a superior, they themselves are killed. This becomes a child's world.

This is the life of a child soldier. Naturally if there is no rescue, no rehabilitation, and no chance for them to re-enter society, they will simply drift from conflict to conflict as they know only how to fight. It is these children who may become the warlords of the future, or the corrupt politicians who we see taking control of Africa today.

At the Tate Modern Art Gallery in London, I once saw a display of African artwork. One vivid painting showed an African child soldier, surrounded by flowers and scenery. In full military attire, he holds a pistol in a hand behind him, an AK47 on his other side, and there was a phone on his belt. His hands are held up, in a surrender position. Cheri Samba, the artist, has written at his feet, "I am for peace, that is why I like weapons." This is what child soldiers are taught, and it is clearly a lesson that must be altered for a peaceful future. This painting so clearly captures why the responsibility to help these children lies in our hands. Our abilities influence our actions, and we therefore have the power to help. The nature of the deed may change, but the fact is unalterable that we must resume some of the responsibility for implementing such change.

It is in trying to prevent this unbelievable trend of creating child soldiers that we must use all our efforts because 300,000 is a number that can bring about peace in our time. When 300,000 children are given a second chance to thrive in their communities, they can generate goodness. Though child soldiers are not necessarily a problem in Kenya proper, the trend is certainly evident in places surrounding Kenya such as Uganda. It is consequently important to identify this trend as something that arises from war, and eradicate it before it crosses borders and further entrenches conflict on the continent. Children are incredibly susceptible to negative forces, but as one of the participants said, they are more susceptible to goodness than they are to evil.

A further element that is affected by war is the environment. I was surprised when one of the youths mentioned this, but looking at our surroundings and having the colours of the countryside flash through my mind every morning when I woke up in Kenya, I was glad that this was one of the elements offered as a victim of conflict. The hands that went up around the room said that war destroyed crops and sources of water, and that many turned to stealing animals when the owners were otherwise engaged during a conflict. They posited that water can be easily contaminated, especially since it is not so readily available in this part of the country, and that people go and purposely destroy the crops of the opposing tribe. There is vandalism to property as well as machinery used to harvest crops and the fields, and pollution in general affects much in a fragile ecosystem.

Geoffrey stood up again to suggest that war both causes and exacerbates poverty. He said that people can try to engage in war to get out of poverty, but in the end the situation inevitably gets worse. Instead of tackling the issue of hunger, people find themselves suffering from starvation especially during times of war, and employment opportunities take a downturn. People have lower motivation to go out and get involved since they believe that conflict will be all encompassing and therefore affect their ability to do anything productive, and so they stay home. This leads to a lack of manpower around the country's industries and agricultural operations, which in turn simply resets the cycle of poverty in the country. Education is also overlooked at times of war, and in longer, drawn out conflicts, lack of access to education will mean that a whole age group will grow up without the know-how required to earn a living as adults.

It was made quite clear to me through this conversation that the youths were acutely aware of the impacts of war and conflict in their country, and the examples and specificity of what they suggested led me to believe that they had experienced more of these elements than I could have imagined. Finally, Abdullah stood up and said, "War has an impact on many practical things in our lives, but what is most important is that it has a negative effect on our potential. War means that we cannot attempt to do what we do best, whatever that thing is, and it contributes to the idea of a negative strength, a strength that restricts rather than enables." The variety of impacts that war and conflict has led to one obvious and poignant conclusion: no one wins in conflict. The winning party will suffer as much as the party that has lost because what results from conflict is a country torn apart. This leads to the inevitable conclusion that there must be a permanent interest in peace.

The effects of peace led to a much more positive discussion, and were accompanied with both smiles and laughter. The youths affirmed their beliefs in a permanent interest in peace, and to develop that peace they wanted definitions for some of the terms that we had been throwing around. We defined peacebuilding as making bridges between groups of people where there previously were none. Peacemaking was the idea of strengthening bridges and connections where there was already some basis for connection, whereas peacekeeping (made famous by UN forces in their blue helmets) was the act of ensuring that war does not break out again and that peace sticks once it has been signed. These are of course extremely simplistic descriptions of these three approaches to the world of peace making, but they helped us conceptualize what we would be attempting over the next few days.

We were peacebuilding, and trying to establish connections between communities and their members to ensure that there was a foundation for peaceful relations, and something to adhere to when and if violence once again reared its ugly head.

What could be done to help shape a future peace then? We wanted to hear some suggestions and get all of our brains geared towards creating practical solutions for the future. Keeping in mind what we had just discussed about the negativity of war and conflict, the youths proposed a wide range of programs such as sports activities, which they believed were extremely useful and appealed to everyone in the country. Ibrahim said that "peace means being close with each other," and there is nowhere that people feel closer to each other than when they are on a soccer field together. Gordon suggested using music to bring people together, and said that everyone loves music and has their own talents. Music has the ability to disseminate different messages and ideas, and people's ears open up when they hear a tune or melody that is catchy or touching. "It is very hard to resist the sound and power of music," Gordon said, and he was absolutely right. He also proved to be quite the musician himself as throughout subsequent work that we did following the workshop, he would often lead the group in song, whether it was a popular Kenyan folk song or a gospel song that managed to unite people from a variety of ages.

Geoffrey suggested that we create peace communities bridging the Kisii, Luo and Kalenjin communities, and that offices built right along the borders of these communities should be erected as soon as possible. I had no idea that there were actual borders between communities, but I would later be shown where they were and how skirmishes often broke out along these unofficial and difficult-to-determine boundaries that often consisted of a simple dirt-path. He said, "Peace is something that you cannot do without, and that it is something that you should think about and talk about every day. It is therefore the best idea to make sure that any of our programs are situated on the borders, and in clear sight for people to see. When they see our efforts, they will consider their own potential for peace, and this will make us succeed. Thank you Sir and Madam."

Kepha spoke up and said that peace is difficult when we are faced with challenges and so it is important to figure out how to keep people focused. He said that the best way to ensure that focus is to use humour, since people appreciate and love funny things, and pay the most attention to those sorts of tendencies. He said there should be entertainment in every forum in which we discuss peace, and said that we need to develop good ways to do it. He stressed that we also need to focus on convincing the youths of the word of peace, and not necessarily the elders since the youths have the greatest potential to spread a positive message throughout the country. It is also more difficult to shape the minds of the elders, and so if we are able to motivate the younger generation to believe in peace, then they could hopefully be encouraged to pay it forward throughout the country. It is this mobilization and motivation that is difficult however, and there was the need to create new techniques to get people excited and moving about these ideas. We had to get the attention of the younger generation in any variety of ways.

Geoffrey summed up Kepha's ideas by saying that "Peace is not hard because there is nothing hard in this world if you have motivation. Thank you Sir and Madam." Motivation can come from different sources, but it was suggested that nothing could be as motivating as seeing a member of another tribal group come to a village he or she would not normally frequent. This visit should be viewed not as a provocation, but rather as the extension of his or her hand outward, hoping that someone reciprocates the gesture. Whether they are looking for companionship, assistance, or even just company, seeing a member of the Kisii community on Kalenjin territory should encourage coexistence and feelings of comfort between each tribe. Jescah said how difficult it was to even get people from different communities to sit and eat together, but that tribes who sit together have the chance to speak to each other and spark the curiosity and dialogue required for a peaceful coexistence. Eating together is simple, yet it could have wide and endless positive repercussions.

Those who comment on peacemaking and negotiations talk about the importance of compromise. Many negotiators, including Uri Savir, say that compromise should be viewed not as a weakness but rather as strength, since it takes an immense amount of strength to demonstrate your willingness to compromise on an issue that you previously strictly adhered to. The youths believed that if they could learn to make compromises, that they could create peace, and that it might be important to begin scrutinizing their habits to decide how best to make those compromises. They considered their values and suggested that in Kenya they had many different values, values that were shared amongst communities. They all valued things like culture, tradition, religion, life, identity, family, sports, and education, and believed that these values should be used to unite rather than divide.

Ibrahim said that, "The different values that we have must be respected. This is the only way to promote peace. When we respect each other, we spice up life." He followed this up with the point that differences should be used to unite them, and asked why there are different colours in the world. "Each colour," he said, "represents something unique." He noted that no two snowflakes ever look the same (which was funny coming from someone who had never seen snow), and said that people require differences to grow and adapt. He said that external differences are unimportant since the values that all Kenyans hold near to their hearts are internal, and even if they are different, it is differences that people crave. He said that every colour and every unique trait has its own significance, so we should never crave to be the same as everyone else.

These ideas of what programs to develop, what values to work with, and how to utilize all the differences that came with 25 different youths from different backgrounds, would set the framework and foundation for the next few days. At the very end of our discussion on this first day we quickly brainstormed a few more qualities of a peacemaker, and without looking at the goofy picture of an ideal peacemaker, we came up with a few more qualities that we would seek to emulate starting this week.

Peace builders require compassion, and must be neutral. They should be able to take control of a situation and use the gift of both sympathy and empathy, while being patient and willing to look beyond immediate obstacles. They must be persistent and loving in their attempts, while developing the ability to help influence others and teach them about peaceful relations. They should have self-control coupled with confidence, as well as a good personality and ability to internalize what they learn and apply it to a situation that they may face, whether good or bad. A peace builder should be hypnotized by the future. We hoped that after this intense discussion on the first day about so many aspects of peacebuilding that we had been able to hypnotize them in some way to want to learn more, and see how they could address the issues that confront them both as a group as well as individuals.

This whole peacebuilding thing seemed like a daunting task. Courtney and I were exhausted after the first day of conversations, and were worried about the difficulties of keeping the group interested for three more days (and hopefully get them to commit to further projects after that), but we tried to stay positive and optimistic. The next day they wanted to discuss the post-election violence and get down to the practical discussions of how tribalism affected them, and show each other how important they believed peacemaking was in their own lives. This was all the motivation that we needed to push on, but the day's events and the expectations that they had set for the group, while inspirational, made me nervous.

I was nervous because I was worried that I was raising their expectations too high and grew concerned about the fact that perhaps I did not really have any way to support such expectations. I was nervous because I had promised them a fulfilling experience, and was worried about boring them or making our mission out to be more important that it actually was. I was nervous that we would run out of things to talk about, or that I would not be able to understand and show empathy when we discussed things like the post-election violence or other issues that I could not possibly understand. I grew worried that I was in over my head. I maintained a positive outlook however because I kept reminding myself that no matter what happened, this was only the first step, and I like to think that I usually see the cup as half full.

The first words we said that day in the workshop were "this is history", and I have those words written nice and big on the first line of my notes from that day of the workshop. It was history, and by setting this precedent it did not really matter what we did, whether it was productive or not so productive. After one day, it was already not a waste of time, since we had a good day, a fascinating conversation, and began to consider what we could do post-workshop. We had planted some seeds and did not have to live up to successes of preceding projects, as there were none with these three communities in this part of the country. We had the chance to pave a new way forward, be creative, and even if it involved failing a little bit, it meant we would just learn how to do it better next time. These thoughts put my mind at rest as I lay down in my hot-dog bed that night and wrapped the mosquito net around me, making sure that there were no cracks in the net so that I wasn't woken in the middle of the night by a mosquito going for my forehead.

As I got comfortable in my sleeping bag, a departure from the usual comforts of home, I looked over to the other bed in the room where one of the participants would be sleeping for the next few nights. Geverson, a Kalenjin, who usually slept there before we began the workshop, gave up his bed so that one of the Kisii participants had a comfortable place to stay while a guest at our workshop. As my new roommate got ready for bed he told me about how his house had been burned down during the conflict and how he had spent many months sleeping in a UN tent in an IDP camp. He had slept on a thin blanket on the ground outside, and said he was glad to finally have a comfortable mattress to sleep on. Here, sleeping a few feet away from me, this Kisii youth was given his bed by a Kalenjin who was trying to be a good host on his first visit to a Kalenjin village since the post-election violence had subsided. He was also able to finally have a comfortable night sleep because of this goodwill of another, while giving a week of his time to help create a peacebuilding project.

His very circumstances that very night gave me all the comfort and motivation I subsequently needed to continue this workshop, and as he told me how thankful he was of the comfort of something as simple as a mattress and thin blanket, any nerves or hesitation I had about the workshop quickly disappeared. We had made history, even if just for a day, and with the help of others we had at least made a difference in the life of one person, and that was the least we could ask for. The goal over the next few days then would be to make a difference in all of our lives, and despite the obstacles and the enormity of this task, we had the motivation. Motivation, in any case, is all that is really needed to start changing the world.

DAY TWO — CONFRONTING THE PAST

The tea fields in the Rift Valley Province are beautiful beyond words. Often when I'm at home in Toronto in the winter, I close my eyes and think about days when the sun is shining in Kenya, with only a few clouds above in the sky. Imagine looking out onto field after field of short green bushes, planted in perfect rows stretching as far as you can see. Because of the climate in this particular part of the country and the fact that it rains at least an hour every single afternoon, the green is a vivid and bright green which is starkly contrasted with the dark green of the grass and trees intermingling with the bushes. Mixed with some yellow and the brown of the mud underneath the plants, set against the clouds and the blue sky, this scene dissipates any gloom that may be felt on a cold and miserable Sunday.

Walking in between these rows of bushes are workers, men and women, spread out, walking with large bags hanging from their backs. They spend days in the field picking tea leaves in a very specific manner, picking two leaves and a bud each time, and throwing it into the bag behind them. They walk along the rows of bushes as they sing either gospel or traditional tribal songs to themselves, and repeat this action, day after day. When their bag is full they walk over to a tractor or truck parked nearby, empty their bags and then head back to work. Off in the distance are small round buildings made of either concrete or mud, with tin roofs on top. This is where these tea field workers live with their families, and even further in the distance is the large tea factory itself with a wide brown and dusty road leading to the front gate.

During my first visit to Kenya one of the community leaders organized a tour for me to see a tea farm. Though upon our arrival the main gate remained shut as a result of poor planning (or no planning at all on the part of this individual), we were able to take a walk to the part of the farm where the workers themselves lived. As we neared the houses of this community, I distinctly remember hearing the sound of children laughing and playing, and this being set against the backdrop of some of the most beautiful scenery I had ever seen, it is now difficult to imagine that this day was the first day that I learned about the post-election violence in Kenya from those who experienced it.

Walking amongst the homes I noticed that they were tiny for the size of the families that lived in them. At this particular farm, the houses (which were provided for free by the tea company) were round with tin roofs, and each building probably had a diameter of about 25-feet. Inside the house I found a wall that split it in half, and on the one side was the living quarters where a family of about 5-6 would sleep all together in one room, while in the other half was found a table, a bench, some chairs, a stove, and all the cooking utensils and food that the family required. I was impressed by how much room there was in this small and unassuming house, but with a poster of Obama on the wall, some children's toys on the floor, and the smell of freshly cooked *chapatis* in the air, it gave me a comfortable feeling of being inside someone's home.

The house was set amongst some tall trees under which children were playing, chasing each other from tree to tree until they caught sight of me, the *mzungu*. They stopped a safe distance away from me, and a few seconds later the youngest child burst into tears and started pointing at me in fear. From behind one of the other houses his mother walked over and picked him up, and brought him over to meet me so that he could see that there was nothing to fear. After this encounter, she shared some words with one of the locals who had accompanied me on this trip, and he then told me that this woman had been deeply affected by the post-election violence and was willing to share some of her story with me.

I sat with my back against one of the trees, and she sat cross-legged in front of me, holding her child in her arms, and told me that she had been scared. The beginning of January 2008, when the post-election violence began to spread throughout the Kenyan countryside, she felt the tension mounting in this small village on the outskirts of the tea farms. She told me that her husband worked in a village that was an hour's commute away, and as a result of the *matatu* drivers being too scared to drive long distances, he was unable to get home when she needed him. The reason for the drivers' fears was a result of an incident that occurred near the beginning of the violence in the very same region, where a *matatu* was forced to stop by a group of thugs, who pulled out all the passengers, checked what tribe they were from, and physically beat all those from the tribes they opposed. A picture of this incident shows the *matatus* stopped in front of an electricity pole with its front window smashed and the route number '46' hanging crookedly from the windshield. As one man has his hand reaching inside the window, two others stand next to the van's sliding door holding machetes in their hands, while a lifeless body lies in front of the vehicle, one leg under the car. This incident instantly spread fear amongst Kenya's taxi drivers, and so commuting between villages became a challenge faced by many.

This woman told me that it was not long before those perpetrating the violence came near to her community, sneaking through the nearby forest to evade the watch of police and members of Kenya's army who were on the lookout for violent thugs and gangs. She was hardly safe in her living condition, and having three young children limited her mobility and ability to hide for lengthy periods of time. She told me that when the gangs had reached the community, it was not long before she was found. She was soon raped by members of this mob who had come armed, ready to fight and kill those with whom they disagreed. She was subsequently beaten and left for dead, although her husband had later managed to find his way back to their home, find his wife, and nurse her back to health. She was thankful that her house itself had not been destroyed, although it had been ransacked, and her children had been left alone. Pointing her eyes at the ground she thanked God that what she had suffered was not as terrible as what had been suffered by so many others throughout Kenya, and held her son close to her chest as she lamented about what had happened to her beautiful country. She told me that in those few months Kenya had become paradise in hell, as she felt that she lived in a country that had its humanity stolen away, and wondered out loud whether there would ever really be peace in Kenya.

This story and experience of speaking to this woman and mother was my first encounter with the post-election violence in Kenya. Until this point I had not been able to place a human face on the suffering that I had heard about in passing, and the way in which she briefly described the fact that she was raped and beaten shattered my heart into pieces. Never had I met anyone who had spoken so honestly and openly about such a personal and debilitating attack, and my mind began to wonder about all those other people in Kenya who had stories like hers. There were 1500 people killed in the violence, and though the number itself is quite high, we must always remember those who were not killed, but who were wounded and injured who survived and must now live with the memory of what they did or had done to them during those few months in 2008. It pained me deeply that I did not know enough about it, and so I set my mind to learning about what dynamics actually led to the post-election violence in Kenya, and whether there was actually a chance of combating the hatred that leads people to do such terrifying things to each other.

Making our way back to Kiptere I had a lot on my mind and I was saddened, to say the least, by what I had heard. We actually got back to Kiptere by hitchhiking on a truck, and sitting inside the main cab of the truck with the driver we had another conversation that opened my eyes to some of the issues in Kenya. As we started driving he said to me, "So, what are you doing here in Kenya?" To which I responded that I was participating in a peacebuilding project and hoping to learn a bit more about the post-election violence. He shook his head, said that it was very good that I came, and then offered his advice for how the conflicts in Kenya could be resolved. "I think that if there is to be peace in Kenya . . . then all the Kikuyus should be killed. This is the only way we can have peace."

Shocked into silence by both the content of what he said and the ignorance with which he said it, I bit my tongue and remained silent for the remainder of the drive to Kiptere. Upon getting back to my room I opened up my journal to write about what I had heard and thought that day, and about my pessimism with regard to finding peace in Kenya. I wrote that there seemed to be many issues in Kenya that led to the post-election violence actually breaking out, and tried to define tribalism for myself. Most importantly however I realized that although I had now spoken to some people about the post-election violence, it had seemed that many people acted as if it had not in fact happened. Perhaps a coping mechanism was simply to ignore the fact that it had actually occurred. Maybe this was a result of embarrassment they felt for the fact that the country let itself get to the point of civil war, or whether people simply did not want to talk about the death and destruction that they themselves witnessed. I wrote that ignoring the issues that led to the violence and ignoring the past only exacerbates the problems and that there should be grassroots and government initiated programs to make people aware of what happened and why it cannot happen again. The last line that I wrote before going to sleep was, "Peace is always possible, but not in a constant state of ignorance." That line alone spoke volumes to me as to how I internalized what I felt was wrong with Kenya, and my subsequent trip to Kenya and the initiation of the peace project was targeting that exact ignorance that I thought needed to be combated.

Day two of the peace workshop was dedicated entirely to confronting the post-election violence directly and figuring out how to speak about it and bring it out into the open, so that we would be able to learn some lessons from history as a group.

The story that I heard from that woman at the tea farm was devastating, but was also, unfortunately, hardly unique. Though we had chosen youths from many different backgrounds, they had stories similar to those of this one woman on a tea farm, and we thought that getting them to speak would enable them to confront the devils in the past with forward thinking momentum. As I'm sure most people would imagine, this exercise proved more difficult than we thought it would be and though we had hoped, perhaps with some naiveté, that the participants would share their stories of what happened to them during that tumultuous period, many of them preferred to either stay silent, or share their stories with both Courtney and I personally at a later time. We were thankful nevertheless that they were willing to open up to us about it, and after speaking with them we learned that they had not shared their experiences with anyone at all since the conflict had ended. If anything, we could provide an outlet for them to reflect on their experiences and to let their emotions and feelings out, as internalizing such intense experiences could be unhealthy and difficult to struggle through alone. The conversation that we were able to have as a group however was both thought provoking and meaningful for anyone who happened to be in the room that afternoon.

Though the beginning of the violence was staggered throughout the country, by the middle of January 2008 there was widespread violence because of tribal tensions and suspicions of electoral fraud. For the first time since Kenya's independence, violence was felt right across the country from Kisumu on Lake Victoria to Mombasa on the Indian Ocean, and Nairobi and the slums surrounding it were particularly hard hit by the confrontations. Its widespread nature necessarily meant that many felt the pressures of the violence and began to fear for their lives. The youths in attendance at this peacebuilding workshop were living in villages surrounding the town of Sondu, which had always been a hotspot for violence, and so were particularly concerned that the violence would and could reach their homes and change their lives.

When I was in Nairobi I had gone to a photography exhibit about the post-election violence, and purchased the official book of the exhibit on the way out. It was a photography book and had inside the pictures that made up the exhibit. I thought that the best way to get the conversation going about the post-election violence was to get the book out there, let the youths take a look at it throughout the morning in a casual manner, and then show some specific photos while we were all sitting as a group, and ask the youths themselves what they thought or how they felt when they saw these images of inhumanity. As I flipped the pages and everyone got a chance to look at the photos that displayed the election campaign, the events that sparked the violence, the violence itself, and the aftermath and funerals, I asked what they thought led to the outbreak of violence. They told me that three prominent factors that led to the violence were corruption, poverty, and illiteracy.

Corruption was clear, as it appeared that the election results had been tampered with and that the overarching corruption of politicians dictated Kenya's political landscape. Poverty meant that the populace was vulnerable to manipulation by politicians and leaders who were willing to offer handouts of cash and other benefits for doing their dirty work and stirring up an atmosphere of violence and fear. Illiteracy was an interesting factor to consider, and one of the participants told me that because many youths in Kenya are illiterate, they are unable to inform themselves of the political situation or improve their knowledge of what is right or wrong in the circumstances. This was an acute observation that further verified how many elements, far more than just these three, played a role in the outbreak of war in Kenya.

Abdullah put his hand up and told me that the notion of hope was both used and abused during the events leading to the post-election violence. He said that the ODM, Odinga's party, promised things like increased youth employment opportunities and a new constitution, and this, he said, demonstrated an "unattainable hope." Though these ideas, coupled with other election promises, provided a good vision for the future and helped create unity especially amongst Kenya's youths, the people soon became despondent. They were dejected when they realized that not only would the promises not be achieved by the party offering them, but that when the falsified election results were announced, the party promising these new developments would be shut out of Kenya's government entirely anyway. Election day made people lose that little spark of hope that they thought would change the circumstances of so many from the smallest villages to cities like Nairobi and Mombasa, and without hope, people feel omitted from the process and cheated, yet again, by their politicians. Hope has powerful causes and effects, and it was an idea that continued to surface throughout the discussion about the post-election violence.

As we continued to look through the photos, the youths spoke about the violence that they witnessed. I was told that at the very beginning of the violence, on New Years' Day 2008, 38 vulnerable citizens were killed while seeking refuge inside the Kenya Assemblies of God Church in the small village of Kiambaa, not too far from Kiptere.

Assuming the church would be safe, the victims, 17 of whom were children, hid inside to escape the violence encompassing the village. In a short time, a mob of almost

1000 youths had surrounded the church, locked the victims inside, and set fire to the building. Most of those who hid inside were burned alive, making this event the most horrific incident of the post-election violence. A woman who survived the attack told a reporter later that she tried to save her baby by throwing him out the window, but that the attackers found the baby, picked him up, and threw him back into the burning building. Other victims who were not able to make it into the church were hacked to death by machetes outside the church by the mob that continued to terrorize the surrounding villages. The participant who described this event to me related that "there is still a scar on my heart," when she remembers this incident of appalling brutality. She expressed her fear of lawlessness, and said that at the time there was no security or police who were able to perform the most basic tasks of protecting human life and decency. In the months following this particular act of brutality, four youths were charged with perpetrating this heinous crime, but they were soon acquitted for lack of evidence. Having always lived in countries where the rule of law has reigned supreme, it is difficult to comprehend how out of control human nature can become when law enforcement is crippled or unwilling to assist.

"We felt thirsty for peace," Ibrahim said, as he noted that the violence continued for much longer than they had expected. The people in the small communities, who were feeling increasingly suffocated from the violence, were prevented from traveling too far from their home villages both as a result of the stoppage of *matatus* as well as the crippling fear they felt of being too far away from their families in the event that something happened. People were unable to make phone calls to each other since it was difficult to purchase credit for cell phones, and families wanted to stay together to share whatever resources they had. Geoffrey related that for three months he felt scared and frightened. "When I tried to picture the people of my dear country Kenya living together as brothers," he said, "it seemed like it was impossible now, that everything we had worked for in fifty years of independence was falling apart." Ibrahim nodded his head in agreement, and said that he remembered talking to his family about the fact that only a man of intense power and strength, a *shujaa*, would be able to make Kenya the country that it used to be.

Charlie said that he remembered feeling so depressed during the conflict that he had difficulty believing that it would ever be possible for things to go back to normal. "Without peace, there can never be life," he stated, and continued that "it is our duty to learn how to forgive and how to forget." He had seen bodies lying in the street, and as a member of the Kalenjin community, a warrior tribe that fights with bows and arrows, he remembered seeing a man lying dead on the side of a road with an arrow sticking out of his face. He told us that it was difficult to survive an attack from a bow and arrow. This is because despite the fact that it is a rather crude weapon, the Kalenjins used poison to tip the ends of their arrows. Even when the military squared off against Kalenjin militias, Kalenjins in the army knew to be wary since the arrows pointed at them were poison-tipped. Charlie said that it was a traumatizing experience and that although the future seemed increasingly bleak, instead of yearning for a return to normalcy he slowly began to reconcile himself to the fact that this is what the future of Kenya would be, and tried to adjust accordingly.

Three members of our group had their houses burned down, though thankfully none of their family members were inside at the time. One girl had rocks thrown at her while on her way home one day, and only by hiding in the dark corner of a barn was she able to evade those who persisted in attempting to knock her off her feet. She cried as she remembered seeing how people's animal instincts surfaced at a time when it was simple humanity that was most required, and scowled when she noted that hatred had become the dominant Kenyan emotion in those few months.

Writing this chapter is difficult. It is hard to try to convey the sense of despair felt by so many who were sitting in the room with us that day, and it is difficult to write it from the perspective of someone who has always known peace. Despite my knowledge and awareness of conflict zones and those who live in them, I know that no amount of knowledge on conflict zones can compare to seeing violence unfold in front of your eyes, and witnessing death and destruction in this way is hard to write about, not necessarily from an emotional point of view, but in the sense that I worry I am not doing those who were pouring their hearts out to me justice. Only a few times in my life, at very random and weird moments, have I witnessed death. I once saw someone jump off a building to their death, and once saw the aftermath of a drunken accident when someone had darted out in front of a moving car. These experiences alone left me feeling devastated, and these were people whom I had no relationship with, any knowledge about, and they had done this to themselves.

Few people in the developed world have ever witnessed death first hand, in front of their eyes, and even when they have it is likely not the result of circumstances that could possibly mirror what these youths sitting in front of me in Kenya had seen. They saw death that had been inflicted not by people to themselves, but they had seen people killing other people. Those 'other' people however had been people who looked just like them, and they were their neighbours, their friends, their parents and their siblings. This is a sort of experience that I could not even begin to fathom, nor am I sure that the way I went about broaching the subject with these particular youths was the most productive or sensitive way. It is this difficulty that I struggled with then as I struggle with writing about it now, but I also have the overwhelming sense that not enough is known about this subject, and so something, no matter how it is written, is better than nothing.

What I have felt is that since that violence came to an end in Kenya in March 2008, people worldwide think that things have gone back to normal there, and have stopped worrying about it. I feel like having been privy to so much information and so many personal accounts of those terrifying few months in Kenya that it is important that the information is offered, in any form, so that people are somehow aware that violence and its aftermath, no matter where it is perpetrated, does not cease to have an effect when the actual physical violence ends. An act of violence can scar a bystander for eternity, and it is therefore important and relevant to at least get down on paper the emotions and reactions of those who saw firsthand as youths what others around the world will be fortunate to never experience or see in their lives.

Violence begets violence, and my theme throughout both the workshop and this book is that only by confronting the past are we able to ensure a peaceful future.

Hatred was a word used by so many of those sitting around in that circle. They told me that they hated the politicians who ran Kenya, that they hated the President and Prime Minister, and that they sometimes hated the older generation for clinging to the idea of tribal differences. They told me that they hated suddenly being scared, as the emotion of fear made many of them vulnerable and unable to be themselves or help those who needed help the most. In particular, a number of them said that they hated that your friend could suddenly turn against you and become your enemy, and that the feeling of a forsaken trust created the most heartfelt and intense resentment imaginable.

One of the youths who was also one of the young leaders of the community had devoted all his time during the post-election violence to finding bodies, either alive or dead, and taking them to the hospital. "Those we found alive still had a chance to be treated and healed, while those we found dead deserved an afterlife that did not begin in a muddy ditch on the side of a road," he said. His work was admirable when many other youths from his community were gearing up to fight, and he was able to convince a number of his friends that the violence would end soon, and that when it did they would find solace in the knowledge that they acted to maintain human life, not destroy it through hatred. Hatred breeds hatred which breeds violence, and by going to at least one of the sources of that terrible atmosphere, he said it was possible to try prevent their world from sinking further into hell.

The word "psychological" was mentioned a number of times, and Kepha explained that people do not think rationally at times of conflict. He said that when people are acting with their instincts instead of reason they act in a way that is detrimental to either themselves or others near to them, and that this action could result in immense harm. Mob psychology was considered by many of the youths, and they noticed, as many psychologists have, that groupthink or large mobs acting together tend to defy reason and rationale, and act as a sort of herd of animals moving together. In a crowd those who may well be correct in their assessment of a situation may not be too loud or assertive, and so their voice is drowned out by the voices of those who are leading the charge with machete in hand. Groupthink means that critical evaluation of a situation is abandoned and this is precisely what occurred in places like Kiambaa when someone suggested that a church filled with scared women and children ought to be set on fire. People often feel safe surrounded by a strong group of their peers or supporters, and so individuality and reason is substituted with considering what is best for the group and how to get it done fastest, and this often meant that the larger the group, the more destruction was left in its wake.

Nonetheless, a suggestion was offered that positive elements also come out of a group and that was the benefit of sitting in a group today. This one young man, I believe the youngest participant of the workshop, said that he thought that was why we were gathered there today. Groups may act haphazardly and set aside reason and critical analysis, but they can also be used for good, and that strength in numbers means that we are able to unite under the banner of a certain idea and take that message out to a wide variety of others to ensure that we are heard. He acknowledged that he had seen some terrible violence, and said that he knew that there were people sitting in the room with us who had done some terrible things themselves during the conflict. He reiterated however that we had all come together to unite under the banner of peace and ensure that it was possible to use group dynamics in a positive and influential manner to affect real and lasting peace in the region. He later spoke to me in confidence about his own story during the post-election violence, during which time both his parents were killed. He said that having very little left to hope for in the world, he was attending this workshop to find similar minded youths who wanted to unite and work towards a common goal, and that he hoped and prayed most days that change was coming, because life in any other circumstances is not worth living.

There was talk of moral decay. The youths turned their minds to certain actions that they witnessed; things that they did not believe people were capable of doing. They witnessed murder, youths threatening women, children and elderly people, and the burning of homes. Throughout Kibera, the largest slum in Africa on the outskirts of Nairobi, houses and belongings were torched which was accompanied by mass incidents of rape. The use of rape in conflict cannot be understated (or entirely understood) and gangs of men throughout the country raped fragile women and young girls. This is the true face of moral decay.

Throughout history rape has been used in warfare to terrorize native populations, but recently, in particular with conflicts in Sudan and the Congo, rape has become a tool of war, a way to terrorize, dehumanize and scar in the most monstrous of ways a country's female population. In the recent revolution in Libya, it was reported that rape became such a widespread practice that the military and police were given tablets of Viagra to take in order to make the raping more widespread and common. On New Years' Day 2011, it was reported that Congolese rebels had raped 33 people, and that the victims' age range was from one-month-old infant to a 110-year-old woman. In Darfur, rape is used as a way to terrorize and impregnate forcefully, in order to literally alter the future ethnic makeup of the Darfuri people. Aside from a war crime, in Darfur rape is being used as an act of genocide. This potential for human evil actually makes me shudder, but it is precisely this sort of inhumanity that looms large and is so unimaginable during times of conflict all over the world.

I turned the page of the photography book to a photo that showed a green hill stretching out in front of the camera. Spread out around the hill were at least one hundred men standing, hunched forward, holding bows and arrows all moving in the same direction. It appeared that they were slowly advancing toward a target, and when I saw this image, the first thought that flashed through my mind was that they were on the way to the tea farm to attack the woman with whom I had spoken sitting under the shade of a tree. Silence fell over the room as someone asked me to turn the page so they could see more, but the next two images made people place their hands over their open mouths and gasp in both horror and sadness.

On the next two pages were photos of death. On the left hand page was a photograph of a field, which could have been any field like the ones we currently sat overlooking in the community center in Kiptere. On the outskirts of the field lay a body of what could have easily been a young man based on the clothing he was wearing. The man was wearing white shoes and navy track pants, also wearing a black t-shirt that had red along the sides and bottom of it. Adding to this already horrific image was the fact that the man had been decapitated, and instead of a head at the top of his neck, the photo clearly showed marks that his head had been hacked off and removed on purpose, and not simply eaten away by birds or other wild animals. A caption accompanied the photo, which said, "We didn't know who the body belonged to till we saw the face, the head, separate from the rest of the body. Unfortunately for us, the young children in our family also saw it and are still traumatized. It is difficult for them to see someone that they knew so well turn into a heap of flesh and bones."

The photograph on the adjoining page showed further carnage, as the body of a young man also lay in the grass below some trees, as he wore only a pair of navy blue pants and a black t-shirt. His right hand was outstretched next to his body, while his left was bent, his left hand touching the side of his face. Standing over his body were two youths: one who was looking on while the other was lifting over his head a boulder the size of a football, about to bring it down onto the head of the lifeless boy lying in the shaded grass. If he was not already dead when this photograph was taken, then he had likely taken his last breath by the time the shutter of the camera clicked back into place. Page after page showed photographs of violence that had engrossed the countryside, and one of the youths uttered the word "euthanasia."

I asked why she had just said that, and she explained that in the process of euthanasia there were two things that you could do: either actively end someone's life to end their suffering by giving them a lethal injection or performing other medical processes or you could let them die by simply not resuscitating them. She believed that both were a form of murder, one active and the other passive, and she equated these forms of murder with the situation in Kenya both during and after the post-election violence.

During the violence she believed that the youth were taking an active role in the destruction of Kenya, whereas the politicians were doing nothing to stop the youth, or by encouraging them quietly and discreetly to continue the violence. After the post-election violence had ended, she said, the elders of the country, who maintained their views about different tribes and the prejudice that accompanied such views were the ones who were actively wearing away at the goodness of Kenya. All this while the new unity government and the politicians in Nairobi were passively allowing their country to fall back into violence by not tackling the real issues that led to the post-election violence in the first place. She said, "It was not only the election results that made us fight each other, but it was a history of issues boiling within each of us that made us react so harshly. Kofi Annan's peace accord that was signed only ended the violence, but it did nothing to ensure that there would not be violence again."

And she was right. There was nothing that was being done by the country itself to ensure that the violence would not erupt again, and it was this apathy by the government and continued corruption by its ministers that inflamed and angered these youths who sat there. It was these young Kenyans after all who bore the brunt of the violence and who were used as both perpetrators and victims. They were furious at those politicians who encouraged the fighting and the violence, and the culture of impunity in the aftermath of the violence. Whether it was Kibaki or Odinga or any other member of the Kenyan government, accountability was not something that was to be considered when the violence came to a close. The only thing that Kofi Annan did in his role as mediator of the negotiations was create a government where the two individuals whom the youths viewed as the source of instability and violence, became the President and Prime Minister of the newly formed Kenyan unity government. They asked me how they are to understand the concept of accountability in a culture of impunity: the two people they blamed most were put in charge of the country while the rest of Kenya's ministers today sit in Nairobi as the highest paid politicians in the world, making a salary of approximately US$212,000 a year (significantly more than their American counterparts). Frustration and anger began to settle into the minds of these youths as we reached the end of the photography book that showed images of coffins and mourning Kenyans who, at the close of the violence, set to work burying the dead.

As the group grew increasingly quiet it appeared that it was time to wrap up this discussion. During a break many of them had come to speak to either Courtney or me to ask if they could speak in private later in the evening and tell us about their stories, and recounting such horrific memories was no doubt a tiring task for all those present. Their silence did not mean that they were no longer interested in this topic, but perhaps what was required now was more a time of silent reflection and memorial as opposed to a group debate. When we ended the workshop for the day and told them to head over to the nearby restaurant for afternoon tea, many of them just stood around speaking and waiting to get a chance to look through the book of conflict photography on their own. They wanted to see what the country had become and wanted to see if they could spot anyone they knew in the photographs.

We knew that this evening would be quiet and a time when the participants would be thinking about their families and all those affected by the violence. We knew they had stories that they would not want to share with either us personally or the group, and statistically speaking there were likely a number of participants who had done things that they would never speak of again. Despite whatever it was however, this was the purpose for our coming together in Kiptere this week. There is always a process required to confront the devils of our past, yet this demonic confrontation takes time.

What the youths themselves had decided to do was first learn about each other, as they did yesterday, and then learn about the violence that divided them. Once we had crossed the threshold as we had done today, we would be able to move forward and discuss practical ways to build peace in the region tomorrow, brainstorm ideas of how best to utilize the lessons learned from this week together, and then finally put a plan into place to ensure that what we discussed remains a discussion about the past, and not preparation for the future. The majority of Kenya's population is youths, and it was youths who resembled in every way the group we had in front of us who perpetrated the violence and made up the victims of the recent conflict. Instead of waging war however, these youths had come together to wage peace, and it was the plan for such a peace that we would try to put into motion in the next few days we had together.

The book of photography is scattered with both images of war and devastation, as well as small testimonials from those who lived through this nightmare. Near the end of the book there is a brief statement from Mwangi Njoroge, an IDP who was returning to his village after the violence. He said, "I am 80 years old now. I have been living in the Rift Valley since 1944. If we fail to forgive them, then what? In life, there never really is a need to carry anger and hurt towards the other person in your heart. We have to forgive them, and we will." These are the words of an elderly man who has seen not only the post-election violence, but also the Mau Mau Uprising that resulted in the creation of the independent nation of Kenya. He has now seen devastation and destruction as well as the founding of a nation and the hope that the people of Kenya would be able to pave their own way into the post-colonial world, which they did. Under his watch Kenya became the nation long considered one of the most stable and reliable countries on a continent riddled with trouble and corruption, and despite his displacement and potential for hatred and anger, he continues to hope for forgiveness. To Mwangi, forgiveness is perhaps the only way to ensure that Kenyans return to the way of life that he once knew, and it is this forgiveness that was sought by so many in Kenya following the post-election violence. He knew that as one of the most vulnerable of Kenya's citizens, if he were able to forgive those who perpetrated the crimes he witnessed, then perhaps others would have that same audacity to forgive. And when forgiveness spreads, the potential for change is created.

Forgetting is not an option, as it is neither helpful nor possible to forget what many of these young Kenyans saw. Forgiveness is however feasible, and perhaps the only option for a bleeding country to start to tend its wounds. Forgiveness leads to understanding which leads to introspection which leads to healing, and it is a particular form of healing that we were looking for together as a group that week. For Kenya to be healed its people needed to say proudly that the country was at peace, knowing full well that the elements that led to the post-election violence had been vanquished, and that even manipulated elections would never again hurl the country into such deep seated hatred. It was this healing that we would spend the rest of the program working on, and whether it would come in the form of a bandage or a miraculous total recovery would be up to the commitment and passion of these youths who were now leading the way forward.

Day Three — I Want it That Way

"*Moja, mbili, tatu, nne, tano, sita, saba, nane, tisa, kumi.*"

"Very good, that is how you count to ten in Swahili. Now, what other words do you know?"

"Well, I know from the *Lion King* that *simba* means lion, *rafiki* means friend, and *pumbaa* means careless. I also know that *hakuna matata* means no worries! Wait, is that actually true?"

"Yes, *hakuna matata* means no worries Mr. Adam. Now, is there any other Swahili that you have learned on your visit so far?"

"Well *kiboko* is a hippo, and *twiga* is a giraffe. And I believe *chai* means tea, and *kahawa* means coffee. Correct?

"Yes Mr. Adam, this is very good work. Anything else before we continue?"

"Uhhh, yes! Actually, I have learned how to say *nataka nyama choma na pombe baridi na supu yamatumbu!*"

This elicited an eruption of laughter from all those present. I had just told them, in my very rough Swahili, that I want warm meat, cold beer, and intestine soup (a word you never really forget once you learn it). I subsequently learned that by saying this basic demand for food, I can make anyone in Kenya burst into a fit of laughter, even when skyping with them 12,000 kilometres away.

This quick Swahili lesson over breakfast on the morning of day three helped us get our spirits up and get excited for the day to come as we were finally getting into the swing of things. We had spent the first days getting to know each other and learning about the objectives of this workshop. I learned their names, where they had come from, what they believed was possible to accomplish in our short time together, and what they wanted from their country. From speaking to them in both the group setting and in private I had learned many intimate details about them. Specifically, I learned about their experiences during the post-election violence, and how they believed that time in Kenya's history shaped them both in terms of their personal growth, and in how they came to see the only country that they had ever lived in and known. I learned what upset them, what made them proud, and I learned how to make them smile and most importantly, laugh. I felt that although it had only been a few days together, we had quickly grown into a cohesive group that could assemble and try to solve some pressing local challenges. The experience and expertise of many of those present meant that they had creative suggestions and an ability to see issues from a variety of perspectives. Courtney and I were both there to make sure that the ideas kept flowing.

Today we wanted to finish off discussing some final ideas about peacebuilding and peacemaking, and to spend time teaching the participants about other conflicts occurring around the world. We wanted them to know that although the post-election violence they experienced was obviously unique to Kenya, there are many conflicts raging in the world and that there are people in each conflict who are working to resolve it. Peacebuilding occurs on a regular basis around the world. To get the best results, it helps to acknowledge that there are others out there doing the same as you, as this provides the strength and motivation required to go on.

After the intense conversation the day before about the post-election violence, we wanted to lighten the mood today and make sure that we could grow together as a group by acknowledging our similarities, rather than by discussing that which divides us. The day before, one of the youths, Kepha, had come to tell me that he was a member of a drama club that did peace work through reciting poetry, performing skits, and singing songs about peace. He asked whether his group could perform during our workshop, and I told him that we definitely had some time in the morning.

Our third day started off with a phenomenal performance by this talented group, but I will reserve my comments about the group, their message, and their motivation for a later chapter.

The performance by the drama club elicited much conversation about pertinent issues in Kenya. One particularly lengthy conversation had to do with the desire for a new constitution in Kenya. For years politicians had been talking about drafting a new Kenyan constitution. Although some of their promises for a new constitution were met with skepticism throughout the country, in August of 2010 a referendum was held to decide whether to adopt a new constitution. The referendum results showed that the country was eager to endorse a new foundation for their body of laws, and soon after, a new constitution was in fact adopted. I found it interesting during this day of our workshop to hear about how the youths felt about the adoption of a new legal and organizational regime in their country, and what it meant to them.

They had high hopes for this amendment to their country's legislative and judicial structure. During the drama performance one of the youths stated that "law is the child of a constitution," and I thought this was actually a pretty succinct way to phrase it. They thought that a new constitution was needed to modernize the laws of Kenya, and that a new constitution could be used as a vehicle to modernize Kenyans' relations with each other, in particular amongst ethnic groups. They wanted the new constitution to address issues such as land reform, admissible police and judicial actions, electoral reform, as well as the balance of power between individuals and the head of state. The new constitution would introduce a huge overhaul to Kenya's domestic political structures too.

"The new constitution is like a baby waiting to be born but reluctant to come out. We are waiting for the ninth month," said Geverson.

Though not really having much of an idea as to the content of the proposed new constitution, these youths felt that a new constitution would free them of many of the problems that loomed large over modern Kenyan society. They spoke of the constitution bringing additional procedural transparency in Kenya's politics. They expressed hope saying that "we will know how things are being done while being confident in the possibility of peace." One of the biggest issues they were concerned with, and rightfully so, was the independence of Kenya's electoral commission, which was believed to have been meddled with by President Kibaki leading up to the most recent election debacle.

Reiterating their desire for lawfulness and the dominance of the rule of law (and edging into my law field finally), they told me with their basic knowledge of the legal system that a constitution is important when considering the context that it will be set in: Africa. They believed that a new constitution would help consolidate the prevalence of the rule of law in Kenya, and as one of them said, it "would help regulate what is right and wrong." It reminded me of a notable point once made by Irwin Cotler, Canada's former Minister of Justice, who said that the true test of the rule of law is not its application in the easy cases, but rather its retention in the most challenging of cases. Velma stood up and said that there were so many evils, so much negativity surrounding the lives of the majority of Kenyans, like poverty, corruption, and starvation, that the constitution would help regulate the country and ensure that the rights of the people were not overlooked by making sure there was an effective rule of law. These are the sorts of lessons you don't even learn in law school.

Their opinions with respect to the new constitution were telling in particular because no one really knew what a new constitution would bring. All they understood was that it was something new. Instantly new was equated with being different, and different with better. There were high hopes in the room and around the country at that time. The improvements brought about by the new constitution are yet to be seen. Currently there has just been bickering over when the next general elections can legally be held. What seemed to be important however was changing the past, and getting rid of those negative aspects of Kenya that had led to the post-election violence, and doing whatever they could to ensure that it would not happen again. These youths believed that an overhaul of Kenya's legislative system would bring about the improvements they craved in the country. Their opinions showed that they had been thinking about this issue and discussing it for a long time before today. Their craving for change was apparent as ever, and it made me hopeful.

The acknowledgement by many of the participants that they lacked civic education was important, as they stated that they wanted to learn more about politics and government. They wanted to change the situation from the inside. For the rest of the day, as well as in following days, they stressed this idea of civic education and learning about the various governmental systems of Kenya. I wished that I knew more about this particular area than I did so that I could contribute in some way to that knowledge, but the fact that they wanted it led to further suggestions that civic education should be included in any programs initiated by the government, if they were in fact to initiate any programs at all targeting the problems following the post-election violence. They learned very little about civics in school growing up. However, to get involved in the process, this education was something that they both wanted and needed at this point in their lives when they could actually consider making a wider impact in their country with the ability to bring about change.

At this point I had noticed that there were some new people in the group who had joined us from the beginning of the day. During a break, I asked them who they were and where they had come from. They told me that they were from Kakamega, about an hour away, and were from the Luhya community. There were four of them, and they represented two groups that were quite active in the Kakamega region.

The first group worked in the area of HIV/AIDS prevention, and tried to address issues that they thought many NGOs did not address in their work on the ground in Kenya. These youths were active on the ground speaking to those who were most susceptible to the impact of the HIV/AIDS crisis, such as prostitutes, sex workers, homosexuals, as well as a number of others. Members of these groups are largely overlooked as victims in Kenya. There is a particularly large concern regarding homosexuals. Homosexuality is not welcome in this part of the world (understatement) as a result of intense religious fervor. Therefore, this segment of the population is often overlooked. In other parts of Africa this is an equally disturbing problem. In fact, we learned that in Uganda someone had published a list of homosexuals living in Kampala. The day after the list was published many of those named were brutally attacked, and some were forced into hiding. Even more disturbing is the fact that an anti-gay bill is in the process of being passed in Uganda's political system, further demonstrating the intense bias against homosexuals in this part of the world. This Anti-Homosexuality Bill further criminalizes gay activity and provides for the death penalty, as one of many punishments, for being openly gay and even HIV positive, in Uganda.

So, the purpose of this group was to ensure that those affected by HIV/AIDS were being looked after and considered, and the woman speaking on behalf of the group, Jane, impressed many of the youths in the group who were listening to her speak about her work. They held seminars for those most affected in the region, tried to secure funding for anti-retroviral drugs, and attempted to change the narrative about this issue in Kenyan society in the hopes of trying to make it more appropriate to talk about these issues honestly and openly on a day-to-day basis.

The other group represented by these newcomers to our workshop told us that they were trying to make the government and politicians more accountable to the people. They said that their mission was to make the government transparent, and following our discussion about a revised constitution, their talking points really piqued the interest of those in the room. As they continued to speak about their objectives and desires for a new Kenya, their tone gradually changed however from reconciliation to anger. They began to talk about demands that they would like to make of the government, exposing its corruption and holding politicians accountable. They kept using the word 'blame'. It suddenly, and without me really noticing, became rather inflammatory, and I began to worry that our message of reconciliation and responsibility had been hijacked by the word 'blame'. They continued to speak, and some of the other participants offered up their hands saying how much they hated the politicians, how they felt used, and how they blamed the politicians for the violence and killing of the post-election violence. It was at this point where I became concerned that we had gotten way off-track, and feared the unraveling of a lot of the good work we had done in the past few days together.

I quickly suggested that we take a break, during which time I addressed the members of this particular group and expressed to them my concerns with their message. I was hardly one to intercede in what these youths wanted, nor was my intent to make the other participants of our workshop believe only a certain message. However, the message of this new group was simply drawing on the vulnerabilities and emotions of those youths I had been working with for three days now, and I could feel the atmosphere in the room change instantly. They were actually pretty apologetic about it and admitted that they did not really know what we had been doing or what our goal was. After explaining our goals to them, they became understanding, and for the remainder of the day sat in the back and kept quiet. Though I can hardly admit to knowing about the situation in Kenya better than Kenyans themselves or those who have lived through the last few crazy years there, I do know that progress is not made by blaming others. The only way to ensure that progress and peace is achieved is by ensuring that people understand their own potential for affecting change, and pursuing that potential with positive intentions. This is what we were trying to do. We took our time completing the discussion about the constitution and the role of politicians, and tried to bring the conversation back to encouraging positive action on behalf of the youths.

The early afternoon was spent teaching the group about some of the other conflicts in the world. Courtney and I decided to teach them about the conflict in the Middle East, the conflict and genocide in Darfur, and we even spent some time teaching them about both the 1994 genocide in Rwanda as well as the Holocaust.

During both my trips to Kenya I dubbed myself the walking Google. Throughout my collective two months in Kenya, I noticed that people saw me as someone coming from the 'civilized' North America, and so they therefore thought that I knew everything about everything. Now, luckily for me I can boast a pretty expansive general knowledge, and so I was able to impress them with some decent information about a plethora of subjects, but there was obviously much that I was not able to answer and I in turn learned much from them as well. I first referred to myself as the walking Google one day, when we were heading back to Kiptere after a weekend-long hike. One of the local youths came over to me, tapped me on the shoulder and simply said, "Mr. Adam, please tell me about Osama Bin Laden." I laughed out loud, joked in my head that him tapping me on the shoulder was like him clicking "I'm feeling lucky" on the Google site, and proceeded to tell him anything I possibly had in my head about Osama, which wasn't too extensive but did the trick nonetheless.

Anyway, after finding out that we were Jewish, a few of the youths had asked about the conflict in the Middle East as well as the Holocaust which only few of them had heard of, and Courtney and I both thought that we should take some time to teach the group about some important current and historical events.

The purpose of teaching about these conflicts was to tell them that they are not alone. They of course know that conflict grips the world, but there are always small groups that have come together to try to confront issues that affect them the most. We talked about the roots of the Middle East conflict, about the Holocaust, and about the fact that despite the numerous attempts throughout history to eradicate the Jewish people, they continue to thrive as a community and desire peace. We talked about the people on the ground in both Israel and the Palestinian Territories. Courtney and I both related our experiences talking to the actual people on both sides of the conflict, and how they had related to us their desire for peace. A year before our trip to Kenya we had both been to Israel and met with a group of Palestinian and Israeli youths in Jerusalem who worked together in very much the same way as our group in Kenya, to try find real solutions to the problems on the ground. In Israel and the Palestinian Territories people also have difficulty trusting their politicians, also allege corruption, and have difficulty being heard in a culture that gives priority to the voice of the elders. The difference was that the conflict of the Middle East is arguably the most publicized conflict in the world, one about which almost everyone is forced to have an opinion, whereas the conflict in Kenya is known almost exclusively to those in Kenya, and perhaps elsewhere in Africa, and so their problems are not taken up by the international community.

They did not know the roots of the conflict, and in our attempt at providing a balanced approach to the history of the conflict and how it stands today, they learned about the issue of self-determination, grassroots movements for independence and peace, and how religion and in a sense tribalism plays a role in this conflict. There were many similarities that one could draw on despite the glaring differences between these conflicts, and I was pleased to answer their questions and listen to their comments indicating that they both understood and appreciated what was happening in a conflict that was extremely important and close to both mine and Courtney's hearts.

Despite their proximity to Rwanda, we were surprised at their lack of knowledge about the genocide in Rwanda in 1994, and we tried to inform them about what had occurred. That particular genocide, after all, perfectly exemplifies both the way that tribalism can get out of control, as well as the epic failures of the international community to prevent mass murder. Rwanda was a good illustration of the way that tribalism, and tribal hatred, can lead to violence, and it helped accentuate the positive aspects of Kenya's post-election violence, namely that in three months 1500 people were killed, whereas in Rwanda, 800,000 people were killed in almost the same amount of time. OK, maybe not that positive. We discussed attempts at reconciliation in Rwanda, and we appreciated hearing the input of the youths and their impressions of what unfolded in Rwanda when they were only children.

Finally, our discussion of the genocide in Darfur, and reference to the conflict in the Congo, was to illustrate how diverse the problems in Africa truly are. They were familiar with many of the elements contributing to the crisis in the Sudan and were truly thankful that the same hatred that exists in Sudan, the kind that can lead people to attempt to actually exterminate an entire ethnic group based on land, politics and religion, did not exist to the same extent in Kenya. We taught them about the advocacy done for Darfur around the world, and they were impressed that there were so many international players who had tried to take up the plight and struggle of the Darfuris. People are always impressed when you mention George Clooney right? We taught them about the history of the conflict, the players involved, and asked them for their suggestions as to how to resolve such an endless cycle of violence and death.

This discussion about other conflicts was telling, and it was very clear that they had a thirst for knowledge. Their living situation did not always make it easy for them to acquire the information that they wanted about what was going on in the world, and what had happened in the world. Although they were taught much in school and read the newspaper thoroughly every day, they wanted more. They were limited in terms of their access to the internet, and so much more that we take for granted in the developed world.

It was for this reason that they saw me as a walking Google, or more aptly a connection to the outside world, and wanted to learn as much as they could about everything. This thirst for knowledge was admirable. It is often dismaying to see how friends and colleagues of mine are unaware of world events, and how we take for granted the access that we have to so much education and information right at our fingertips all the time. Access to education should never be taken for granted. Living through the period of the so-called Arab Spring, when people in the Middle East and North Africa are realizing with the advent of social media and internet that they do not have to continue living suppressed lives under dictators, we should be increasingly thankful for the access to the information that we have.

I was thrilled to hear the youths' interest in these subjects and to try answer the many questions that they had. It was important to us to try to teach them what we could about these conflicts that they could use to both have a greater understanding of history, as well as take lessons from which they could apply to their very own situation here in Kenya. The history lesson lasted longer than we had intended it to, but it ended up fitting in perfectly to the theme and flow of the overall workshop, as it meant that they could place their own situation in a global context and learn that they were not alone in the quest for peace and reconciliation.

The end of the afternoon was spent discussing some other attributes of peace-builders, and we made the point that every member of society has the ability to contribute to a peaceful future. Drawing on some of the points I had picked up on from the book *Peace First* and others, I noted that a peace-builder required vision, character, courage and integrative capacities. I stressed the point that a peace-builder must be hypnotized by the future, and that the future they are striving for goes beyond the next election. Uri Savir and other peace analysts talk about the notion that modern peace is about the hearts and minds of the people, and that in order to be a peace-builder, social empathy is therefore an important characteristic. They say that the best leaders are filled with a passion for peace and the patience to realize it, and even though they should approach any obstacles and challenges with rationality and logic, they should be able to consider even those ideas that appear to be totally half-baked. Many of the best discoveries and ideas in world history began as half-baked and ridiculous proposals, but giving them a chance and pushing past any initial hesitation may lead these crazy suggestions to be the most useful of solutions.

The most important point however, is that based on the above qualities of a peace-builder, it is often difficult for a single person to demonstrate all these attributes, and so the most practical approach is for a group to lead the process. A group can blend in the collective experiences and expertise of many and unite those who may not always assert themselves in an otherwise meaningful way. We should never underestimate the ability of even the most soft-spoken person, for passion is not demonstrated in the volume of one's voice or the tenacity of their personality. A group is an important vehicle for the combination of the best traits and personalities to come together and lead an effective peace process. This was the type of group that we felt forming in front of our eyes.

Having created a group, it now required a name. We stuck a piece of easel paper up on the wall and thought that the most democratic way to choose a name was to take suggestions and then vote on them. We heard a few options thrown out, but the name that was ultimately selected, and voted on unanimously, was Youth Ambassadors for Peace. This simple name succinctly described the role and mission of these youths, and it would be this name that would be adopted as the name of the organization and all its subsequent projects.

That night Courtney and I had a truly unique Kenyan experience. After dinner, some of the youths went to find a generator, a TV, and a DVD player, and set it up in the room we used to hold our discussions. Courtney and I took our time finishing dinner, and by the time we made it up to the room where all the youths had already gathered, we found something that just thinking about still makes me smile nice and wide to this day. The TV and DVD player were hooked up to the generator, and 25 youths sat in front of the screen, in a darkened room in the middle of a small agricultural community in Kenya, watching a Backstreet Boys music videos DVD. They knew every single word to every song, and as they sang they sat together, put their arms around each other, while Courtney and I watched this scene unfold in front of us. It wasn't long however before Courtney was pulled into the crowd by some of her loving fans, and encouraged to sing along to "I want it that way."

Three nights ago we sat in this exact room, an awkward group that was quiet and separated along tribal lines and unsure of what they had come to participate in. Tonight we sat singing together, smiling, laughing and teasing as old friends do, and it seemed that there were no boundaries, no restrictions, and nothing blocking the kinship and closeness felt in the room. If someone had described this scene to me three days before I would have laughed and described it as both optimistic and idealistic, though hardly possible. Tonight however I sat and watched (and yes, I even sang a little bit) as a group of youths ripped apart by conflict only one year ago came together in the context of a peacebuilding initiative, and swore that they would "quit playing games with my heart." We were now a cohesive group. A group that sings together can make peace together. Tomorrow we would attempt to put down our thoughts on paper and try to draft an agreement that would codify the expectations, desires and dreams of an entire generation that swore that they would never again resort to violence and bloodshed—only peace.

Day Four – A Draft of Tomorrow

On Friday morning I woke up much earlier than usual. It was one of those nights of sleep where you're both nervous and excited, and because of that pure anticipation and adrenaline my subconscious mind just felt like sleeping was a waste of time. I woke up thinking about the stories I had heard from the youths the night before, those who told me about their dead relatives, burned houses and shattered ideals. I didn't remember what I had dreamt about, but I woke up feeling startled. As soon as my eyes were open though, I was wide awake. I threw off the mosquito net, opened the door and managed to just catch the sun coming up over the horizon. The colours of my now too familiar view were just a little bit different at this time of morning, and the sound of the roosters crowing to wake up the village and the fact that I did not have to look over and see a cow being slaughtered gave me a sense of warped relaxation. With all these mixed emotions and butterflies in my stomach, I wasn't entirely sure where the day was going to lead.

I realized that we were being quite ambitious on this last day, but there were a few things that had to get done. I had thought the night before that perhaps it was a good idea to try draft a peace treaty with the youths involved in the workshop. Official or not, and whether or not it would find the requisite attention of government or any local officials, I felt in my gut that putting words to paper that idealized the desires of the participants was the only way to create a thorough mission statement, from which we would be able to develop other programs, activities and ideas. It was to be a framework, a basis for the workshop that was coming to an end, and it was the culmination of a week of intense discussion, collaboration, analysis, and thought. The goal was to get the input of every participant of the workshop, get their thoughts, ideas, feelings and desires, and put the treaty together in a clear and concise way to present to anyone who was curious about who the Youth Ambassadors for Peace were and what we stood for. Looking back, this task, though rushed in some aspects, is one of my proudest achievements and came together in a way that made every single participant of this workshop proud to be involved.

The idea and format for the peace treaty came from Uri Savir's *Peace First*. At the end of the book, a book described as the ideas that would bring about a modern peace in an increasingly hostile world, Mr. Savir presented a template of what a modern peace treaty should look like. The treaty was to be divided into different sections so that ideas within each section could be consistent, and so there was no overlooking or ignoring some issues while putting too much thought or emphasis onto others. The treaty would be divided into seven sections, and these sections were:

- Goals and Visions;
- Definition of Peaceful Relations;
- Regional Framework;
- Rehabilitation;
- Peacebuilding;
- Creating a Culture of Peace; and
- Security and Implementation.

The division into sections ensured that necessary attention was paid to the substance, procedure and symbols associated with our desires for change, and also ensured that I, a rookie peace-builder, had some sort of template to follow.

After a quick breakfast the group gathered in our usual meeting room, and before we began, I hung seven pieces of easel paper along the front wall. On the top of each sheet I wrote the name of each section of our soon-to-be-created peace treaty, and turned to the participants and said simply, "Let's go." Over the next four hours, we sat, with only a 15-minute break in between, had some last minute discussions, and listed all the issues that we wanted to include into our peace treaty. At the end of this time, we had 11 pieces of paper hanging on the wall all filled with writing, a room full of enthusiastic peacemakers, and the basis of the first peace treaty between the Luo, Kisii and Kalenjin communities.

This activity naturally fell at the end of our time together. The content of the treaty was the culmination of a week of discussions and thoughts, and many of the ideas that were provided to be included in the treaty were shaped in some form over the last few days, so they weren't exactly new. The difference was that this was going to be a foundation for how to conduct programs and activities, so what was included in this treaty was now going to govern what we did in the future, and with this air of permanence, there was some serious reflection and intensity that I heard when each participant put up their hand to offer their suggestion as to what should be included. The idea of permanence and finality also became clear when a number of participants who either rarely spoke or had not spoken at all throughout the workshop raised their hands to offer their advice for what should be included. Some of them, it seemed, saw this as a last opportunity to get involved in the process, and not wanting to be left out, those who were among the most silent (and more frequently the girls involved) offered some of the most touching and contemplative suggestions we had heard. We made sure to have feedback from every single participant, and after the four hours were up we had accomplished our goal. The participants had offered the substance of the treaty, and all that was then required was to clean it up, put the thoughts into sentences, and type it. When the discussion was complete, the newly formed Youth Ambassadors for Peace applauded, and then each walked around the room shaking each other's hands or hugging each other, congratulating themselves on a job extremely well done.

I had one free day between the workshop and the finals of the soccer tournament, and though I wanted to take some time for myself, I really needed to get this treaty typed up in a proper format and get a number of copies printed so that it could be signed and distributed at the soccer finals on Sunday. That Saturday, Courtney and I had planned with our local friend Robins to go to the town of Kisumu on the shore of Lake Victoria. We wanted a change of scenery, we wanted to eat some fresh tilapia, and perhaps see some hippos in Lake Victoria as well. I asked Robins if he would take us, which he eagerly agreed to, but I told him that before we got started with our Kisumu activities that I had to spend a bit of time at an internet café typing up our newly drafted treaty and getting some copies made.

When we arrived in Kisumu I ran into the first Internet café we could find, opened up Microsoft Word, pulled out my notebook into which I had transcribed everything from the easel paper from the day before, and started typing as fast as I could. Had I not actually thought of some of the language I would use in the *matatu* on the way there, and had I not paid attention in my international law class the previous semester, then it would have taken much longer to write. Though the language was far from polished as it was written in my notebook, I took out a red pen and set to work typing our peace treaty. It took just one hour to get a first draft.

Admittedly, I'm pretty impatient when it comes to writing. I love writing, but I try to be content with my first draft, and I find proofreading to be a tedious exercise. When I do edit however, I like to print it out, take a blue or red pen, and go through the draft thoroughly, crossing out words and adding in whatever notations are needed. With a lack of time however, and with my desire to make the treaty as perfect as possible, editing on the computer was one thing that I could not avoid. As Courtney and I both sat editing and scrutinizing our newly drafted document, we would shout things out loud at each other to see what sounded better, whether we would use a certain kind of wording, and once in a while we would propose the idea that we should one day run for elected office together, because hey, we were on fire. After another 45 minutes of editing, formatting, and Robins getting increasingly antsy waiting for us to get on with our outing in Kisumu, it was complete. The only thing left to do was add some lines at the end for people to sign along, and we had to name it. After throwing out a plethora of suggestions we sort of just took a look at what we were trying to achieve through this project and the treaty itself, and the name eventually just presented itself: *The Youth Treaty of Hope, Reconciliation and Peace*. This name embodied both the goal of the project and what we had been able to accomplish in those few short days, and we were happy with the result (the treaty itself can be found in the appendix of this book).

Having completed the more serious task of the day, we departed the internet café content with our progress and headed for lunch: freshly fried tilapia straight out of Lake Victoria. Lunch was followed by a brief boat trip into the lake where we spotted rare varieties of birds and chased a family of hippos. We then headed to a hotel to take a swim in their pool, and finished off the day trip with some beers outside the local supermarket. Heading back to Kiptere I had in my backpack a wet bathing suit, some souvenirs that I had purchased from a young artisan on the side of Lake Victoria, my camera, and eight copies of our newly drafted peace treaty in a manila envelope wrapped in a plastic bag. The next day we would present these copies to the Youth Ambassadors for Peace to sign, and those copies would be distributed to local VIPs, while a community copy would be held in the office for anyone who was interested in reading what their local youths had decided the future of the country should look like.

Returning to the previous day however, the last day of our workshop, once we had finished drafting this treaty we were told to rush to a nearby church as a closing ceremony for the workshop had been organized by the local pastor and some other gathered elders. As the youths got up to make their ways over to the church, Courtney and I sat to debrief and ensure that we had everything written down. Once we had got down everything we needed for the next day, we walked outside to find Sister Lucy waiting to give us a ride to the church in her handy Rav 4.

This closing ceremony was the one part of the workshop that I had had no part in planning and was only actually told about it the morning of the last day. Those who had put it together were not too forthcoming with me about what they planned, and told me only to prepare some words to say when they called me up to speak. As a result of the rushed peace treaty and last minute work I hadn't had time to prepare anything for the closing ceremony, so in the short car trip to the church and while I sat watching and listening to the others, I racked my brain thinking about one last message that I could share. As we made our way to the garden in front of the church, Courtney and I sort of just walked in anticipated silence to see what awaited us. Although we expected to enter the church grounds seeing everyone waiting inside the building, we found the group gathered in a circle outside in the garden of the church with the pastor, the District Officer, and a few other community members. In a pile next to them sat some saplings and we were told that our first activity was going to be planting peace trees!

Thrilled by this impromptu little donation to the environment and the grounds of the church, we got right to work. A few of us 'VIPs' were given the first trees to plant, and the first went to the District Officer. As he was handed the tree to plant, one of the youth started singing a song which basically went, "Panda panda, pandaaa pandaaa," and then some other Swahili words after that. I was told that "panda" means "plant!", so we were singing the planting song (well, not we, but them, as Courtney and I smiled and swayed along awkwardly to the beat). As each of us was given a turn to plant a tree, the song was sung, we planted the trees in the pre-dug holes, covered it up with dirt, and shook the hand of the person who helped us plant it. After a few of us were given the special honour of planting the main trees throughout the center of the garden, the remaining youths then each grabbed their own sapling and went to the edges of the garden to plant what was left. As they were humming the song under their breath, Courtney and I just laughed and watched this spontaneous occurrence that meant so much to us, the pastor of the church and all those doing the planting.

As the rest of the youths and others streamed into the church to get started, Courtney and I stood outside speaking to Sister Lucy, trying to spend just a bit of time outside relaxing before the sun went down and we began the closing ceremonies. After a few minutes, having decided it was bad form to hold up the event, we walked in through the wooden doorway to see what awaited us inside.

At the front of the building was a small stage behind which was a draped white curtain, in the middle of which was hanging a giant crucifix. Whoever had organized the event had procured a generator to provide power to the microphone, speakers, DJ equipment, and a few light bulbs that were placed strategically around the church, and we found the participants had quickly made themselves comfortable in their seats. As we walked in, two of the participants were already up on stage leading the group in a number of gospel songs, which included the ever popular "If you're happy and you know it say amen!" and some other wonderful religious Swahili songs.

I was seated at the very front of the church with Courtney, Sister Lucy, the District Officer, and the pastor of the church. As the crowd settled down and a number of local elders and youths joined us to celebrate the close of this part of the peace project, Weldon, one of the organizers of this event, stood up to start the ceremony. He spoke about why we were gathered here, what we had spoken about during the previous week, and asked that we spend the beginning of the ceremony memorializing all those who had lost their lives in the post-election violence. He distributed candles to each of the youths who had participated in the workshop, and asked them to line up down the centre of the church with candles in hand. One by one they would each come up to a table set up in the middle of the church, and put their lit candle on the table that was covered in the day's newspaper.

As they all started to stand up, Weldon asked the young man who was acting as DJ to try put on some music that was fitting to the mood of a memorial ceremony. Now, I have to be clear that the music that was being played was basically elevator music or those midi songs that old cell phones would have as their ring tones. Though I don't remember what was being played before the change of music was sought, I remember being curious as to what song would be used to best fit the mood for a ceremony remembering the 1500 lives lost during the post-election violence. The DJ put on one song that was quickly vetoed by Weldon, but the next choice was determined to be the song most suitable for this somber event. After a few seconds of listening, Courtney and I both burst into laughter (which we were both forced to quickly muffle with our hands), as the song they had chosen was the 1999 favourite . . . *Livin' La Vida Loca*. Though we could hardly contain our laughter, and had a difficult time doing so, this music was chosen to set the tone of the next few minutes, and the memorial procession began. One by one, each youth approached the table, lit their candle, and placed it standing on the table in the middle of the church. For the remainder of the closing ceremonies these candles would stay lit in the middle of the building, and would actually provide the majority of the light for us as the sun continued to set.

After this short memorial service the pastor and Sister Lucy each led the group in a prayer, and we were then given the chance to hear from some of the participants. I was happy to see some of the more quiet participants stand up to talk about how proud they were to be a part of the group that we had established, and was proud myself to see in front of me what we had been able to accomplish in such a short time. It was the first time that I actually felt truly calm and relaxed over the last week. This is not to say that the week overwhelmed me with stress, or that there was that much effort really required ensuring that it worked thanks to the cooperation of everyone. But, five days before this, when the youths had initially arrived in Kiptere to begin the workshop, it sort of hit me that I was going to be monopolizing a week of their time, without paying them, and that thought alone really weighed down on me. Even though each day went smoothly and we were thrilled with the contributions and support we had received by these youths and their communities, there was still that underlying thought at the end of each day that we're going to have to do this again, and that we were not entirely sure how to approach the next day's subject matter. It had somehow come together though, and the relaxation I felt at this point lasted only a short while until I realized where this project inevitably had to lead.

Putting the idea of the workshop into motion was a thought that I had a long time before coming back to Kenya. Thinking back I remember mentioning it to a few people as a very minor thought about what I would possibly do if I were to return to Kenya, and even when I had come back I only had a very short amount of time to put parts of the project together. My thoughts at that point were then solely focused on the workshop, a daunting task on its own, and whether it was foolishness or simply just trying to get the task at hand completed successfully, I had not really thought until then what would happen now that the workshop was done. The successes we had were solely a result of the commitment of those who attended, and anything we had accomplished was because of them.

I have mentioned that the group had come up with some plans, such as putting into place a program for September 21, the UN International Day of Peace, and we spoke about initiating some high school peace clubs; but aside from those projects that they would be involved in, I had not really conceived of what I personally had now created and invested in this project. Sitting in that church I began to think what the next few months would be like and I wondered what we would be able to accomplish going forward. I thought about the development of the program, how I would support it once I got back home, and whether I would find the requisite support. Sitting at the front of the church I wondered if I should seek support from religious or secular sources, whether I should put any particular spin on the project, and whether I could find other people to help support me in the running and organization of the project. These were only some of my thoughts as I listened to the District Officer, some of the village elders, and the youths themselves, as they addressed the crowd gathered before them on this Friday afternoon.

When the District Officer stood up and spoke I realized that I had met him many times before but that this was the first time I would hear him speak publicly. He was easily six-feet tall, very thin, and wore glasses, a green pair of pants, and a button down shirt with a blue tie. He had an extremely warm aura about him, and I had always appreciated the fact that he had remembered me from the first time I had visited Kiptere. Despite his quiet appearance he spoke well and his passion seemed to excite all those in the room. He had clearly been quite shaken by the eruption of the post-election violence, and shared some of his own experiences from that time. The substance of his speech was committed and determined, and it was clear that when he spoke the youths related to him on some level. He mentioned that youths in Kenya are youths until the age of 40, and said that he too, therefore, was still technically a youth. Perhaps this enabled him to better connect with the younger participants.

He told the youths that starting a peace movement first requires you to find peace within yourself. He said, "The first step to making peace, is finding that peace deep within your soul. Once you attain that peace in yourself, and it is a good peace, then you must start speaking to your friends. Then your friends will find their own peace and speak to their friends, and from this first step, peace will continue to spread." He thanked me for coming and helping facilitate the workshop over the past week, and told the youths that despite the fact that they had just participated in this program, that "you do not need funds to talk about peace. All you need," he said, "is belief in your fellow countrymen." He followed this statement with "We are going to make an army. An army of peace, and unlike all the other armies in the world, this one needs young men and women." I sat watching and listening to him as he spoke from his heart, addressing the youths he knew had witnessed bloodshed and strife just like many others in Africa had, but he was clearly encouraged by the fact that Kenya is a country that is not like every other African country. It has a history of peace and understanding, and by relying on those most important elements of Kenyan society, the youths, he promised that Kenya would one day rediscover the peace that it was currently lacking.

While writing this account and looking back at the time that has passed since the facilitation of this project, it has not exactly been what I expected. I don't really know what I was thinking facilitating a peace project, and though the projects have been successful (as I will highlight in chapters to come) my own personal commitment has been challenged often, and the Youth Ambassadors for Peace are people who I think about on a daily basis. I love doing the 'field work', on the ground in Kenya, meeting and speaking to the youths, and brainstorming with them about what to do next and how peace affects culture in Kenya. What I do not always love however, is the organizational work, the fundraising, the publicity, the website design, the social media, and everything else that goes into running a peace project, or any project for that matter. I look back at what I was thinking and doing for those few days in May 2009 and wonder if I had a plan in place for what the organization would become, and the truth is that I did not. We were taking this project one step at a time, and I would say that the successes of the project rest solely on the shoulders of those youths who are working so hard in the villages to promote the idea of peace, and that the failures of the project perhaps fall on my shoulders, as I could have always worked harder to fundraise, find partners for the organization, and try to inspire others to get directly involved in this particular project.

The solace that I find in this sentiment is that it is ongoing however, and that there is always room for development. The fact that the organization's structure is not set in stone and the fact that it is a project and organization that involves just me on the ground in Canada and all these youths on the ground in Kenya means that there is always a chance for someone else to get involved, whether it is someone who wants to help fundraise, someone who wants to get their name on a project of their own, or whether it is someone simply advising me how to structure the organizational aspects to create the most successful framework. The ability to change is important, and my hope is that by the time the next elections in Kenya in March 2013 come around, the Youth Ambassadors for Peace will be a solid organization with funds and resources, with the power to inspire more youth on the ground to turn to peace when some politicians may encourage them to turn to corruption or war. These thoughts were not with me that day sitting in the church watching the closing ceremonies unfold, but to be honest if I had known then what I know now, I don't think I would have done things much differently.

The week that we had just completed was a blessing. It was a blessing because those who chose to participate actually chose to participate and take a week out of their lives to assist in the development of this half-baked idea to bring ideals of peace to a small community in the Rift Valley Province of Kenya. It was a blessing because of the support I received from the community in Kiptere, and because of the quality of the youths who were involved. As I sat watching them sing and speak about what they learned the past week, I thought about how naïve we were, and how naïve others continue to be, about the intelligence, commitment and passion of the people of Africa. I was so thrilled with the feedback that I had received from the youth, the comments that they made during the most intense of discussions, and how we were able to laugh and sing with each other each evening. Never before would I have imagined the experience that I was able to share with these youths, and the thoughtfulness and sincerity that they espoused each time I spoke with them made me proud to now be associated with them. Whether or not they would stay involved, and despite what they got out of this workshop, I knew that I had learned plenty from them, and I hoped that they got out of the workshop at least a fraction of what I myself did.

All these thoughts were swirling around my mind as I stood up to speak to the youths at the end of the closing ceremony that evening. I wasn't entirely sure what to say as I approached the podium in the church and tried to piece together a speech that would not simply be lost under the shadow of the District Officer's. On a scrap piece of paper I had written down six things that I wanted to make sure I mentioned when I got up there. The points, as I wrote them down that night, were: the Golden Rule, donors, Mandela, Semisonic, save a life, and I learned a lot. Those assembled had heard me speak plenty over the past few days, but what I had written down on this scrap piece of paper were some very random thoughts that I wanted to make sure I mentioned while I still had them listening to me at least for a few more minutes.

The Golden Rule, as mentioned a few times throughout this book, states that one should treat others the way they themselves would like to be treated. The rule is also referred to as the *ethic of reciprocity*, and I related to them a story that is common in Judaism. In Rabbinic times, someone once approached Rabbi Hillel and asked him to explain the entirety of Judaism while standing on one foot. Without hesitation, Rabbi Hillel balanced on one foot and recited the Golden Rule. I thought this an appropriate message for this gathering since the entire week had been spent talking about issues that confront people in their day-to-day interactions with each other. Aside from the post-election violence, the purpose of our discussions was to promote coexistence, brotherhood and camaraderie, and I believe that the Golden Rule is a maxim by which to attain those high ideals.

I mentioned donors because I had always noticed in my time in Kenya the assumption held by those in the villages that all white people are rich. It was an assumption that I just had to deal with because it was so widely held and because it was difficult to talk them out of this misconception when

I came to Kenya equipped with a digital camera, iPod and Ray-Ban sunglasses. It still irked me nonetheless, though I suppose we all have different ideas of what is considered 'rich'. I wanted to make sure that I mentioned the donors who had provided me with the funds to make this trip possible because I wanted not only to acknowledge the generosity of others, but I wanted to make sure that they knew that it was not me personally who had funded the entire program. I further wanted to ensure that all those involved were aware that strangers abroad also cared for them, even though they had obviously never met them and likely never would. It is clear, looking at the clothing and the goods that are found in Kenya, that much of what the people there live off of is in fact charity, like clothing from Goodwill for example, but it was important for me to give a shout out to all those who assisted with the project in perhaps one of the most important ways possible.

Nelson Mandela is the quote-king, and a book I once purchased in South Africa has hundreds and hundreds of quotes by Mandela on every possible subject, including even jelly beans (on which he is quoted saying, "What are jellybeans? Are they something that is eaten?"). I had of course spoken of Mandela highly and frequently over the past few days, but the quote I chose to reiterate again was "I dream of an Africa at peace with itself." I mentioned this quote and said that I believed we had ignited a spark that would lead to a peaceful Africa one day. I told them of my dream that one day the Youth Ambassadors for Peace would breach the boundaries of Kiptere, spread past the borders of the Rift Valley Province, reach the coast in Mombasa, and then continue to spread into neighbouring countries like Ethiopia, Somalia, Sudan, Uganda and Tanzania, other countries that are also desperately in need of peace. I told them that I hoped they would be able to assist in this goal of spreading peace throughout the country and the continent in order to ensure that Mandela's dream of an Africa at peace with itself would find a practical existence within our lifetimes.

I have no idea how the next point came to mind, but I had written down Semisonic because the song "Closing Time" had popped into my head (a distant memory from my days in junior high school). The very last line of that song is, "Every new beginning comes from some other beginning's end," and I thought this was a great thing to throw in not only to give Semisonic a shout out in East Africa, but it also just fit with what we were in the midst of doing. The workshop had just ended, but in ending it had creating new opportunities and ideas that our newly formed group could be involved in, and what we were embarking on together was indeed a beginning that came about as a result of the end of another beginning. Think what you will . . . I liked where I was going with this.

The next thing I had written down on my scrap piece of paper was "save a life", and not remembering exactly why I had written it, and after broaching the topic of popular music, I instantly thought that I had somehow brought in the Fray's music to my speech as well. After searching the lyrics for anything meaningful, I now remember that the mention I made of "save a life" was the universal message, found in the teachings of many religions and cultures, that "When you save a life, you save the world entire." It was not the workshop or the work we had done together that I was referring to, but much that we had discussed together over those few days, in particular pertaining to the post-election violence, was that the only way violence spreads in Kenya is through the willingness of the youth to pick up a weapon and succumb to the manipulation and corruption of their politicians. In saving a life, I only reiterated what is said in the teachings of Christianity, Judaism and Islam, where the decision to save a life means that you have done something good in the world, and that instead of turning to violence or hatred, rejecting such elements will only result in good. People do not always consider their own potential to affect the world, and since I have started this project I've been labeled as the one who wants to change the world. As flattering as this characterization is, I think that everyone has the potential to change the world, and that it all truly begins with small acts of kindness and goodness. Whether it is something like paying it forward, or just doing some random good deed, changing the world does not imply grandiose plans or the brokering of a peace accord between ancient enemies. On the contrary, the only way to change the world is through little acts of goodness and kindness, and it was precisely this idea that I wanted to offer to those who were listening to me that evening. Margaret Mead, the renowned anthropologist, once said, "Never doubt that a small group of thoughtful, committed people can change the world. Indeed, it is the only thing that ever has."

Finally, I ended my speech with the mention that I had learned a lot, and this is something that I have already written about above. Despite some of the discussions that were held where I taught the group about specific issues like the conflict in the Middle East or some random history lesson, the workshop was first and foremost a forum for discussion and introspection. What I learned, both from what I heard and what I saw, will never leave my mind and has shaped my outlook on the world since. What I learned in those few short days have shaped my opinions, my worldview, previously held beliefs about the African continent and its people, and has affected me in more ways than I can imagine. It was difficult to get all of these thoughts out so all I said to those in the church that night was essentially thank you for giving me the opportunity to learn from you, and thank you for teaching me more than I would have ever gained in any other setting.

As I got off the stage and resumed my spot next to Sister Lucy, my mind suddenly turned to "What's next?" and I began to think about how the upcoming weekend and following week would turn out. The next day Courtney and I had scheduled a day trip to Lake Victoria, but two days from now we would be holding the signing of the Peace Treaty and the final day of the soccer tournament. After that, it would be entirely up to those who had participated in the conference to decide where this project would go. What follows are the developments in the days, weeks, months and years since the closing ceremonies came to an end on that Friday evening.

As the ceremony ended we made our way back to the community centre in Kiptere where we would all be having dinner together. Before joining the others at dinner Courtney and I went up to our rooms, retrieved two candles and a prayer book, and stood out on the balcony on a crisp African Friday night to light the Sabbath candles. After figuring out a way to shelter the candles from the wind, we lit them with the traditional blessing, a blessing on both the candles and a glass of whiskey (since we had been unable to locate the required bottle of red wine), and sat quietly looking at the moon while the candles flickered between us.

I recall both of us being emotional as well as exhausted after the week's events, and in not wanting to get up and go anywhere, we were missing dinner. Opting to forgo eating with the group we were soon visited by Jessica who came to reprimand us, in her nicest-motherly tone, for skipping dinner with the group as people were wondering where we were. Seeing the candles, she asked what we were doing, and then sat down with us to ask about our Friday night traditions. When we were done talking and there were a few moments of silence, Jess asked us if we were able to teach her a song in Hebrew. At the same time, both Courtney and I offered the one song that was the most fitting for the theme of the past week, which is called in Hebrew *Od Yavo Shalom* (Peace is Still Coming).

The lyrics in Hebrew are: *Od yavo shalom aleinu, od yavo shalom aleinu ve'al kulam. Salaam, aleinu ve'al kol ha'olam, salaam.* Translated, the song means, "Still peace will come upon us, still peace will come upon us and everyone. Peace . . . to us and to the whole world, peace." Teaching Jess some of the lyrics, and sitting in the darkened evening lit only by candlelight provided the ideal moment for reflection on what we had accomplished that week. As the flames of the candles slowly made their way down to the dusty floor, and we sang a song of peace, I realized that the first step of initiating my very own peace project was coming to an end. What started as a week of disorganization and nerves had ended with the formation of a youth group, the drafting of a peace treaty, and the commitment of 25 young Kenyans to try to change their communities for the better. It was the first step, and in realizing that every new beginning comes from some other beginning's end, I felt that what we had collectively done is set the stage for a tomorrow that would hopefully inspire first a village, then a country, and eventually bring, as the song goes, peace to us and to the whole world.

SHUJAA: A PERSON OF GREAT BRAVERY

"Our children may learn about the heroes of the past.
Our task is to make ourselves the architects of the future"
—Jomo Kenyatta, father of Kenyan nationalism

As a young former South African, I always grew up learning about Nelson Mandela. When I was probably around ten years old I tried to read his autobiography *Long Walk to Freedom*. It had been published in 1995 following his release from prison February 11, 1990, after 27 years. It's a huge book, 656 pages long, and I remember taking it to elementary school for a few days and telling people that I was reading that book. My classmates didn't care that I was reading it, and my teachers didn't really believe me. I remember in subsequent years doing a presentation about Nelson Mandela's life based on another biography written about him, and I remember that when I was younger, my parents had always spoken positively about him.

It was only in the last few years however that I started to think about Mandela for who he was, who he is, and what he did. As a young professional in the Jewish community I thought it would be a good idea to start a project that focused on heroes, trying to create heroes, trying to make young people in the community more outspoken and listened to more than they usually were. I looked around at society and everything I then wrote about this idea of heroes enunciated my position that there are not really any heroes anymore. The likes of Winston Churchill, Anwar Sadat, Yitzchak Rabin, Mahatma Gandhi, Franklin Delano Roosevelt, were no longer around. The people in charge are increasingly making errors, brought to their knees by corruption charges and other similar embarrassing occurrences and extra-marital affairs, and do not always fight for what they believe in anymore. Politics is all encompassing, and the dreaded coalition government means that people seeking power are content setting aside some of their ideals, for which they came to power, in order to ensure another four to five years in office.

It hit me as quite sad and I realized that all those whom I admired, all those whose personality traits and characteristics I craved to emulate, were long gone. Their successors have been left without the ability to affect serious or permanent change, leaving my peers and me with few people to truly look up to.

The lack of role models can have a dreadful impact on those who desire someone to look up to. Celebrities today, as an example, have to frequently get ahead by using sex appeal. The new, young stars, though they may be very nice people, have shown that you have to be attractive to get ahead, that you must often sell out or break with your true ideals to get a certain contract or position, and money is the real thrust behind a lot of decision making. This is not to generalize that it is always the case, but it seems true that very few of those stars who stick to their original, pure passions, become as big as some others who have to make sacrifices if they want to make it in the demanding entertainment world today.

225

I do not want to totally discredit all the people in charge today and I think that there are certainly people left who have exhibited phenomenal abilities. I think that there is of course allure and personality and that if you were to search for someone who exhibited confidence or charisma, those traits would not be hard to find. I just think that it is difficult to find someone who is the entire package these days. Someone who gives you the ability to say: "I would love to be like them, because of who they are, what they have done, and what they believe in."

For these reasons, I believe that Nelson Mandela has been elevated to the person that he is today. At the time of writing this he is 93 years old, and his life story is the story of South Africa. I am thankful for Mandela because of what he did to his country, and without him, without his extreme physical and emotional strength, the country would be very different than it is today. Today Mandela is one of, if not the most, venerated political personalities alive. Look at him and you see qualities that you just wish others would emulate. In him you see the potential for people who have fallen far from what they could achieve. Look at Robert Mugabe, the President of Zimbabwe. Also a political activist who struggled with white domination in his country, he came to power amid fanfare and hopes that he would make things better for the people of Zimbabwe. Rather than become the leader people had hoped he would become, he became a tyrant, a dictator of sorts, that turned on the white population of the country, taking their land, scaring them away, and absolutely devastating everything that Zimbabwe has to offer. Today Zimbabwe is rocked with inflation, political corruption, and there is little hope for sanctions since although the goal of sanctions would be to harm Mugabe, the ultimate victims are the people of Zimbabwe. And, as is a continuous message throughout this book, Africa and Zimbabwe are far down on the list of the international community's priorities.

There are countless other examples of places in the world where people have come to power with the highest of hopes, yet they have turned out to harm the people they self-admittedly came to power to help. Everyone understands how pressure can play a role and drastically change results and events either for better or worse. The first thought that comes to mind when thinking about pressure is a hockey player shooting penalty shots after the overtime of a tie-game has just ended. Pressure can mean a pitcher throwing one more strike over home plate to finish up a World Series game, or the final kick in a soccer game like the World Cup Final between the Netherlands and Spain that we recently witnessed. Everyone has their own way that they react to pressure. It is like playing tennis. Some people like to get out on a court and practice their forehands and backhands and feel like volleying the ball a bit will make them really demonstrate their best shots. They aren't interested in playing a game just yet because they don't want the pressure to get to them. There are others however who are dying for the game to start, because they know that they perform best when the pressure is on, when all eyes are on them, and when they don't just want to succeed, but have to.

This is the sort of leader that Mandela turned out to be. Years and years of pressure were on his shoulders. The expectations that the people of South Africa and the people of the world had of this one man were unlike expectations that have been seen in recent history. This man was expected to change a system of Apartheid, of brutal racial discrimination, rooted in decades of hatred and segregation, and try to make people live together and love each other. It was something that the people of South Africa had slowly started to believe in, and it was something that they soon realized was necessary, but to put all that weight on one man's shoulders seemed a goal perhaps even outside of the ability of Nelson Mandela. This however was not the case.

The South African writer Alan Paton wrote his landmark book *Cry, the Beloved Country* in 1948 at the nascent stages of South African racial discrimination. In the book he details in beautiful prose the relationship between white and black South Africans, and the way they were expected to behave, and how they impacted each other's lives. The line that stood out the most from this book to me is a line of fear spoken by one of the black characters in the book who says, "I have one great fear in my heart, that one day, when they are turned to loving, they will find we are turned to hating." This simple line, that characterizes human nature, human dignity, and human expectation all in but a few words, stands out as the legacy of Nelson Mandela, a man who emerged from prison determined to turn everything around.

Mandela is considered a hero because of his ability to make love out of hatred. Despite the fears that drove people from the country, despite the concern that the fall of Apartheid would result in revenge against the white population of South Africa, the country did not fall apart. Though there are of course many problems with South Africa as a country today, whether it is crime, illegal immigration, poverty, government corruption, or any of the other ills that seem all too common to an African country, Mandela ensured that people did not turn to hating. His smile, his voice, and his never-ending optimism have created a country that has waged an uphill battle against its tumultuous past and has overcome the obstacles thrown in its way. His characteristics will place him as a hero at a time when there were no heroes, and as someone who was able to overlook any personal gain or advantage in order to make sure that his people and his country would survive. He embodies the Mishnaic maxim by Rabbi Hillel that says, "In a place where there are no men, endeavour to be a man." Mandela's heroism is demonstrated in so many ways, and the 27 years that he spent in prison must be understood as contributing to the way he was willing to sacrifice everything for the good of his country. On trial in 1964 before receiving his life sentence, Mandela famously stated,

> I have cherished the ideal of a democratic and free society in which all people live together in harmony and with equal opportunities. It is an ideal which I hope to live for, and to see realized. But, my Lord, if it needs be, it is an ideal for which I am prepared to die.

Fortunately for all of us, this ideal that he struggled for was realized within his lifetime.

There are any number of ways that South African history could have been different, but it is purely thanks to this man, today a demi-god in South African society, who made sure that freedom reigned supreme and that the past would not be forgotten but rather used as a lesson to construct a positive future. It is this idea that Mandela personified, and it is this idea that Jomo Kenyatta, the founding father of Kenya, also alluded to when he said that "Our children may learn about the heroes of the past. Our task is to make ourselves the architects of the future."

Though I don't want to overdo the quotations of others, there are so many powerful words that have been spoken about the impact of heroes. This very fact alone means that people have recognized the ability of individuals to change the world, and the words of these great authors and leaders are ones that I feel must be brought to peoples' attention. This ability of one man to stand up and make a difference is well embodied in the words of Robert F. Kennedy, spoken in an address at the University of Cape Town on June 6, 1966. In his profoundly moving speech, spoken at a time of the height of Apartheid in South Africa, Kennedy said,

> Each time a man stands up for an ideal or acts to improve the lot of others, or strikes out against injustice, he sends forth a tiny ripple of hope, and crossing each other from a million different centers of energy and daring, those ripples build a current which can sweep down the mightiest walls of oppression and resistance.

These words, powerful on their own, are even more powerful when placed into the context of speaking to a massive group of students in Cape Town, South Africa. Kennedy was acutely aware of the political circumstances at the time in South Africa, and spoke these words as a way to empower and inspire a group of students whom he knew would soon be in charge of dictating the future of their own country. He understood both his own influence and the potential influence of these youths, and these words enable these youths to understand the power that one possesses when they simply stand up for their beliefs.

It was with these ideas of Mandela, Kenyatta and Kennedy, and embodying the ideals of heroism and leadership that I approached my own youth project. Youths are, as we know, particularly susceptible to manipulation and political games and so it is important that they understand not only their weaknesses, but also primarily their strengths.

A weakness is easy to manipulate. A weakness exposes fragility, insecurity, and can bring someone to their knees quite quickly. People often hide their weaknesses because they fear that any weakness means that they will be taken advantage of or used. They automatically believe that if one person knows of another's weakness then they will use it against them. They see weakness not as an asset but as a hindrance to their ultimate success, and fear that if others only knew about their weakness, that it would essentially be their demise.

Strength however, as mentioned in other parts of this book, is understood as ability, and to most people, strengths overcome weaknesses.

Weaknesses are therefore important to understand because even the strongest of people have weaknesses. Great historic epics talk about even the strongest men of their times having weaknesses, such as Achilles' heel or Samson's hair. These stories from our collective past are meant to teach us that everyone has weaknesses, and that this understanding means that everyone has a breaking point. People are not to be perceived as supermen, and those true heroes are willing to admit that despite their achievements and strengths at overcoming adversity, they have weaknesses that have taught them abundant lessons that have contributed to their overwhelming success in life.

It is for this reason that weakness is something to be controlled and accepted, and understood as being present in others whether they are your friend or your foe. A thought that was enunciated by one of the youths in Kenya essentially is that there is no inherently good or bad strength or weakness: it is the consequences of that strength or weakness which is inherently good or bad, and it is how it is used.

In affluent western societies, youths are often engaged politically and are considered to be 'the future'. I think that often youths are not given enough credit for what they are capable of believing, writing, thinking, doing, or perceiving. It is nice for politicians to talk about the youths, talk about the future, and what they want to leave for the youths to inherit, but they are not always willing to engage the youths and entrust them with any significant power until they have somehow proved themselves. I have noticed this in a variety of ways in my lifetime, and know that newspapers only want to hear from older people, various media outlets only speak to youths for special segments or under unusual circumstances, and politics is only a point of discussion for the older generation. Youths are often perceived as weak for reasons that they are young, that they have not yet decided what they are doing with their lives, or simply because they do not have the requisite experience that older generations may feel is important to have before they are to be called on for their opinions.

I have always felt that my generation, a generation that is particularly and increasingly connected to the world, and a generation that is able, unlike generations in the past, to shape the future of the world, are still left out of the discourse and dialogue that can make all the difference. Our age is perceived by the older generation as our weakness, and we in turn see their inability to either trust or use us as their weakness. Both generations certainly have weaknesses, but again looking at the historical record, age has never necessarily been a factor of weakness that should be taken seriously.

Throughout this book I have remarked about the state of the world, and am always reminded of a cartoon I saw in a newspaper in the days immediately following 9/11. It was a simple cartoon but it stuck out in my mind, even at the age of 16, and today I believe that this little piece of commentary was far ahead of its time. The cartoon was simply a map of the world drawn upside-down, with Antarctica on the top of the map, and Canada, Russia and the Arctic on the bottom. This was one of the ways that people saw the world after the 9/11 attacks rocked New York City and drastically shaped the world after that day, and that is the way that I have seen things since. The world does seem upside down, and events that take place around the world that people would once never have imagined to have occurred, are now taking place. The world is indeed upside down, and decisions that are made today by those in charge have the profound ability to change the future. This is not only with regard to war, but also with regard to the environment like global warming and oil spills, social trends like gay-marriage and abortion, and other issues of the same ilk. These decisions will impact the future, and though they may be made thinking only about the immediate impact, it is the responsibility of my generation, of the younger generation, to be the voice of reason and to object where objection will be practical, and to insist when it is critical to insist on something that we know must be done.

My friends and I have referred to this requirement as *Generational Fortitude*. What the older generation has done has worked for them, but they must never forget who will come next, and the ability that the future generation can play right now. The most fitting definition of fortitude that we could find for this phrase is "the strength of mind that allows one to endure pain or adversity with courage." Let me repeat this for dramatic effect, and to make sure how generational fortitude is tied into the idea of strength and weakness.

Generational Fortitude is the strength of mind that our generation has that will allow us to endure pain or adversity, strength or weakness, success or failure, with courage. We have seen destruction, and unlike the older generation who saw wars that lasted years and social movements that took decades to develop, we saw a radical shift in the world that took place immediately after we witnessed with our own eyes two planes flying into two towers that changed everything. We saw the catalyst, we saw the immediate result, and we know what can and what must be done. It is important therefore for youths to understand both what are our strengths and weaknesses to ensure that we are not just used to achieve the political objectives of those in our western nations who wish to achieve whatever goal may please them now.

Youth empowerment and youth responsibility in Kenya is however profoundly different than it is in most affluent western countries. Youth are considered and relied on in different ways than are the youths in countries like Canada or the United States, and perhaps this reliance is the reason why in Kenya someone up until the age of 40 is considered a "youth", and you get a card and everything. I do not believe it has anything to do with maturity or ability, but with demographics. The population of Kenya in general is quite young, and though there are many elderly members of Kenyan society, the vast majority of Kenyans are youths. For this reason they are relied on for a number of different tasks, and one of the most blatant ways that politicians have used these youths in recent memory is to incite violence and drive forward their political messages and goals.

As an aware Canadian citizen, politics is something that I am aware of, but Canadian politics is by no means interesting, stimulating, or sexy to me. Elections are called, some would say, far too often. Politicians here literally all look the same, with the necessary bilingualism and ability to flirt with people of both English and French backgrounds. As someone who loves politics and wishes he could make himself more interested in Canadian politics, I believe the reason why people in Canada are not too interested in politics here is because it's just, well, a little boring (apologies to my friends at the Prime Minister's Office).

During World War Two, Winston Churchill once referred to Canada as "the linchpin of the English speaking world." At the time, it was true: Canada was a world player, had a profound impact on the direction of the war, and was able to make significant changes on the world stage. Today however, Canada's status has changed ever so slightly. This is by no means meant to be a criticism of Canada, as I believe, especially in terms of politics, no news is good news. The very fact that trying to engage in Canadian politics is somewhat boring is I guess a good thing, because it means that this is just one less thing to worry about. This is not to say that Canada isn't a fantastic place to live nor is it intended to ignore all the positive aspects of Canada as a country and home.

It reminds me actually of another comic that I saw in the newspaper in October 2008, when federal elections were being held in Canada. There was a comic of the Prime Minister, Stephen Harper, standing in front of a press conference announcing the election, while all the press and all the cameras had their backs to him, watching a television showing Barack Obama and the American elections unfolding. Canadian politics are important for a number of different reasons, but in terms of sexiness and immediate impact on its citizens, especially the kind of politics that can get youth engaged and involved, there is just not too much there (unless you love campaigning, because we've got plenty of elections to campaign for). This is significantly different to politics in countries like America, the United Kingdom, Israel, and Kenya, where politics is real, where decisions are made that influence the rights and the realities of its citizens in the immediate time frame. It is for this reason that the youths in Kenya are engaged and involved, and all know something about their party, their Member of Parliament, and their policies and views.

When politics is real, when a decision in the parliament that day has the ability to make you act a little differently tomorrow, then you live in a country where the youth become engaged, and can be called into action.

Politics in Kenya is, of course, still extremely tribal. Support the leader that your tribal community supports, not necessarily the leader that has the best foreign policy platform or best ideas for the economy or taxes. Support the party that is made up of members from your community, and policies that affect specific practices of tribes will gain the support of those groups. Why would the economy be important in a country where poverty is rife? And why is foreign policy that relevant when you have no real sway on the world stage and your neighbours are South Sudan and Somalia? What *is* real are tribes and tribal allegiances, and politicians are well aware of this. They come from these tribes, they grew up in these villages, and they know what they can get. So how do Kenyan leaders engage their youthful constituencies? They use them.

So many times throughout the workshops and program, and just speaking to Kenyans in general, we heard about the idea of being used by politicians. People express their frustration and anger at being used, manipulated, tricked, and negatively influenced. They understand what is happening and all the synonyms associated with the concept, yet it continues. They know not only the Prime Minister and President, but also ministers who are in essence riling up the population to get involved when issues start to get out of hand, be it a general election or constitutional referendum. The civil conflict that broke out after the December 2007 general election was a prime example of being used by members of the government, and everyone in Kenya has a story to tell about what was done to them.

During that post-election violence, the youths were pushed to fight. Politicians would show up in villages, say what they had to say about Kenyan unity and their feelings about the opposing party, and they told their supporters that to be loyal supporters they had to show the opposition why they were right. It also always helped when they handed out fistfuls of cash to the youths who had nothing. It was this demonstration of correctness, of political strength, of corruption and greed and determination that turned into violence. Though the bait was not always taken before the election, the post-election debacle and results were enough to push it over the edge. And how do you tell a 22-year old with nothing not to take a wad of cash from a politician only to be used for getting "politically engaged?"

Youths in Kenya are manipulated because of their age and their social standing. The majority of Kenya's population is disenfranchised living in poverty in small villages. Many of them live idle lives in poor rural communities, where they come from farming families and spend the nights drunk or getting into trouble because there is basically not much to do when the sun goes down. Idleness is a factor of Kenyan society that is manipulated without end, and it is a factor that must be eradicated.

Many projects from abroad have been initiated to target youth idleness. These projects include various income generating projects like bringing solar power to villages, starting up small independent farming projects, and getting youths to build some kind of infrastructure in their villages. Other projects, like the one I helped start in Kiptere, try to eradicate youth idleness by giving them a particular type of training that enables them to speak to others, get involved and teach other youths about issues like peace, politics and conflict resolution, and in a way come together to shape their own future. Though this is not necessarily physical work, it gets them thinking about the future more than they usually would and aims at preventing them from going down a path of self-destruction.

In the village I stayed in there was a young man named Charlie. Charlie was a native of Kiptere, again a small rural farming village, and was fortunate to be able to leave Kiptere to attend the University of Nairobi. Charlie seemed to understand the issues that affected Kenya, was acutely aware of the politicians' desire to manipulate the youth, and spoke about it regularly. As a Kalenjin as well, a member of a community that is often pressured about land rights, he knew that land was a big issue when it came to tribalism in Kenya. He said, "We have peaceful coexistence, but the leaders try to bring division to us, and we listen. The issue of land is very divisive and the ministry associated with land is trying to bring reforms. This causes many more issues. We need to address these land issues to achieve peace." Further focusing on the problem of leaders, he said at the end of our peace workshop, "The leaders use us: they gain, and we lose. We must resist being used. Let us have harmony to each of us. We can now sleep in one room, and we are like brothers." Here was a Kenyan youth, in his early 20s, fully aware of the role that leaders play in the trials and tribulations that have made Kenya what it is today. Another member of the group proclaimed that, "We have corruption in our blood!" and went on to talk about how the youths of Kenya had been desensitized to corruption, as a result of growing up with it being so predominant. Another talked about 'moral decay', and lamented, as others often did, of Kenya becoming like the rest of Africa. These are the opinions of the youths, and they are progressive and thoughtful ideas that must be heard by those at the upper echelons of power in Kenya. These ideas are important, they are advanced, and they are cries of help from young people who feel that they have no voice in a country where their voice should mean everything, as they are the majority.

It is these voices, and the ideas that they regularly pronounce, that must become the future heroes of Kenya. One day during a seminar on strength and weakness, a particularly enthusiastic member of the group stood up and proclaimed, "Let us make our own tribe called the youths, and this tribe shall encompass all the other tribes that are strangling progress in Kenya." This is the empowerment and the idealism that I am referring to when it comes to creating heroes. It is these ideas that will pave the way forward to a better future in Kenya, and it means that these youths, in a place where there are no men, are endeavouring to be those men and women.

This workshop and this project were designed to provide these youths with the ability to learn skills required to become leaders in their community. My approach to this workshop was not to come in and impose on them what I wanted to see, but rather my idea was to help facilitate whatever the youths had in mind, whatever they believed would be able to improve their own lives. They decided to participate in a workshop that looked at the issues that affected their lives, and they spoke about what they wanted to see in their own futures. The interesting and dramatic transformation that I witnessed however from the start of the workshop to the end, was the way that some of these youths were able to stand up and proclaim what they saw as problems, and the way that their opinions, regardless of the fact that they came from different communities, were united and clear: "We know that we were manipulated, and we do not want it to happen again!" they seemed to say with one voice. By simply participating in this program they were taking the first steps to becoming the heroes they wished to see in their lifetimes in Kenya.

Despite the controversial and troubled history of Jomo Kenyatta's presidency (which I know to many is an understatement) he was still a revolutionary leader and first president of Kenya, and so is thus admired to a certain extent by many. Referred to as the *Mzee* or "old man", he was the one who took the future of his country into his own hands. By leading the Mau Mau Uprising against the British and ensuring that the people of the colony of Kenya would have their own state, he was a hero for many who dreamed of self-determination and shaping their own futures. Often with such leaders and heroes, it is a common trend to look to their children to emulate the actions of their parents, and many in this sense have looked to Uhuru Kenyatta, Jomo's son.

Uhuru has had an interesting career in politics, and is currently the Deputy Prime Minister of Kenya. His supporters have hailed him as a visionary leader, while those who are not his fans have characterized him as a corrupt politician, like many others in Nairobi. He has said, "Growing up in the Kenyatta household taught us many things. My father taught us to treat everyone fairly. He taught us the essence of justice and fairness, he told us to learn from history but not to live in history." Nice quote, but now contextualize how Uhuru has put his father's lessons and legacy into action. In December 2010, Uhuru Kenyatta was indicted by the International Criminal Court (ICC), along with a number of other Kenyan politicians, for inciting violence in Kenya and running a group of bandits following the election, whose role was to intimidate detractors and stir the violence around the country. On January 23, 2012, the ICC confirmed that they would be formally charging Uhuru Kenyatta for perpetrating war crimes and crimes against humanity, along with three other high ranking Kenyan officials. There could not be a clearer example of dissuasion that is felt by people who wanted to look up to the son of a national hero for guidance and belief. Uhuru of course has denied any wrongdoing and hopes to run in the next Presidential election in March 2013, and this is of course a problem for any number of reasons.

The reason for picking on Uhuru however (Uhuru is a Swahili word for "freedom") is to come back to my original thought that heroes today are scarce, and many times even those we hope will emerge as leaders are unable to at a time of instability, incompetence, impunity, and corruption. It is precisely for this reason that the youths in Kenya are disillusioned, but are beginning to realize that the future of their country will land squarely in their own laps. With movement at the ICC as well, they see support in the fight to refine Kenya's political landscape and culture of political impunity. If the current generation of leaders is unable to change things for the better, something that must inevitably happen, then it will be the role of these young future leaders to do just that.

Mo Ibrahim is a telecommunications philanthropist originally from Sudan who is today considered to be worth approximately $2.5 billion. He has earned his money as a businessman working in the telecommunications industry, and he founded the company Celtel, an African cell phone company.

In 2007, Ibrahim created the *Mo Ibrahim Foundation*, and soon afterwards inaugurated the *Mo Ibrahim Prize for Achievement in African Leadership*. The purpose of this prize is to encourage the recognition of positive leadership in Africa, and to heighten awareness of African developments and the individuals who are active in African politics and society. It is presented to former African heads of state who encouraged developments in security, health, economics and education, and who transferred power democratically to their successors. Further criteria are leaders that have governed democratically and within the limits set by their country's constitution. The prize awarded is an initial payment of $5 million, with an additional $200,000 a year for life, making it the largest financial award in the world, far exceeding the financial remuneration given with the Nobel Prize. In 2007 the award went to Joaquim Chissano, the former President of Mozambique. In 2008, the former President of Botswana, Festus Mogae, was given the prize, and in 2007 Nelson Mandela was also made an honorary laureate of the award.

The purpose of the prize is simple: promote leadership and good governance. In both 2009 and 2010, the foundation announced that it would not be presenting the award to anyone, stating that they were unable to find any leaders in Africa at this time who fit the criteria of the award. I accept that some of the criteria for the award are quite specific, and so perhaps this is why no one has been chosen recently to accept the award. However, consider the fact that there are 53 countries in Africa, and 53 leaders of these countries. 53 people and they were not able to find *anyone* who represented the concepts of leadership and good governance? Oy.

Not wanting to get into a large scale criticism of every African leader, I will simply state that I hope that this award can actually encourage leaders to lead effectively and heroically. It is still a young award and perhaps has not yet permeated the mindset of many African leaders who today are considering what direction they will take in their approach to their country's future and their own legacy. Many African leaders speak of the challenges that they face governing African countries, and one would hope that this award itself is some form of encouragement to lead responsibly. Anyone has the ability to be swayed by a large amount (and constant flow) of money like the amount offered in this prize. Consider what I said before about Kenyan youths being paid small amounts of money to risk their lives. In contrast this is African leaders being paid fortunes to just be good leaders! And yet they were unable to find these sorts of leaders in the last two years.

Mo Ibrahim created this award to encourage leaders to lead, and said that, "whether there is a winner or not, the purpose of the Foundation is to challenge those in Africa and across the world to debate what constitutes excellence in leadership." Awareness of the issues, and the momentum fostered from previous winners will hopefully induce the current leaders of Africa to be those heroes, and become the role models that the youths of their countries so desperately crave. Often all that is required is for a discussion to be held, and an idea to be planted, in order for it to become a small act of resistance against the status quo.

Absolute power corrupts absolutely, and so we find ourselves looking at a continent with too many Mugabes, Gbagbos, Gadhafis and al-Bashirs. There are however also leaders like Liberia's Ellen Johnson Sirleaf, Ghana's John Atta Mills, Rwanda's Paul Kagame, and of course Nelson Mandela. These leaders demonstrate the qualities required to overcome adversity and become heroes, and will hopefully inspire the youths in their countries to aspire to become leaders themselves. In the words of Ledmark, one of the youths I worked with in Kiptere, "We aspire to inspire before we expire."

In keeping with Kennedy's theme of the power of a rushing stream, Nadezhda Mandelstam, a Russian writer and educator, wrote that, "A person with inner freedom, memory, and fear is that reed, that twig that changes the direction of a rushing river." This is the sort of power that the youths in Kenya have been encouraged to pursue. The inner strength and ability to overcome adversity in order to rise to greatness, know when to reject violence and manipulation, and be persistent in their search for justice and peace.

When it came to putting a human face on a modern hero in Kenya however, I seemed to be in a fortunate position since Barack Obama had only recently been inaugurated as the 44th President of the United States, and as we know, he has some Kenyan roots.

THE KENYAN BOY WHO WOULD BECOME PRESIDENT

"Let's just go and see her! Kogelo is only two hours away, and it would be a great story to tell when I get home!"

"Mr. Adam, I don't think you know how much a celebrity Mama Sarah Obama is and the security forces that are currently occupying her village. Let's rather go to Kisumu on the shore of Lake Victoria. We can get some fresh tilapia and go see the hippos, and as always, you can pay."

It is one thing to try to inspire people to become leaders. It is another thing to do it when Barack Hussein Obama has just become the President of the United States.

Whether you like him or not, the effect that Obama had during his campaign for the presidency had an overwhelming effect on people everywhere. Young African American children in the projects were suddenly aspiring to do things far greater than they had previously imagined. Those who witnessed the civil rights movement come to life under the personalities of Dr. Martin Luther King Jr. and Malcolm X were seeing the culmination of a dream, and far away in Africa, boys, men, and village elders, saw a Kenyan tell a depressed world that there was hope.

Being in Kenya during the time of the Obama transition was an experience that will be difficult to forget. "Hope", "change", all the tag lines of his election campaign, quickly forgotten in the US soon after his inauguration, were still words spoken regularly by the people of Kenya. Of all the countries in the world besides America, Kenya identified with Obama the most as his father was of Kenyan descent, and was from the Luo community. Everyone knew this, and almost everywhere you traveled in the country, Obama was mentioned.

The mention of Obama was almost comical at times since no matter where you went, someone claimed a connection to him. Although members of various communities often attempted to associate with Obama, it was mainly members of the Luo tribe, again the tribe of his father, who tried to take possession of Obama. Whenever I met members of the Luo community as a result I would hear "you know

Obama? He is my cousin!" or "he is my brother!" or "he is my father" or "he is my nephew" or "he is my son!" As funny and impossible as some of these assertions were, the look on the faces of the people making these comments was what said the most. Although some of the claimants were just trying to make me laugh or trying to make a point of claiming ownership over Obama, they all had a look of pride on their faces and how they went out of their way to sometimes explain Obama's roots or connection to Kenya was really quite amazing to watch. Often I would also get the more tame "Did you know that Obama is a Luo?" or "Did you know that Obama is a Kenyan", and the look of pride that these youth had on their faces illustrated that to them, Obama was not simply a President but rather an icon.

Two months after Obama's inauguration as President, I went to Washington D.C. for a visit and was floored by the amount of Obama merchandise that was available. Besides the obvious pins, pens, blankets, posters, and framed pictures of the newly crowned President, there was the more unique stock of goods. These ranged from Obama mints called "Peppermints We Can Believe In", Obama pajamas covered with his face, and my personal favourite: shower products entitled "The Audacity of Soap", a pun on the title of his second book *The Audacity of Hope.* Though the products being sold in D.C. were of good quality, professionally made, and highly priced (who wouldn't want to pay $50 to sleep in a shirt with the President's face on it?!?), the goods to be found in Kenyan marketplaces were made with the two most important ingredients: love and inspiration.

Whether it was in the tourist market in the heart of Nairobi, the supermarket in the suburbs of the capital, or the stalls next to the food markets in the rural villages, Obama merchandise could be found everywhere. Unable to afford the more luxurious items like mints or pajamas, Kenyans had settled for adoration and imitation of Obama by purchasing Obama calendars, cheap Obama watches, Obama belt-buckles (which I myself bought), and strawberry flavored Obama bubble gum. There were posters, key chains, and even cardboard cutouts with a smiling Barack.

Knowing not only the Obama family history in Kenya but also the effect that Obama has had in inspiring the world in almost its entirety, I was not necessarily surprised by the goods I found. The only product that truly struck me as unique however was a book that I found while perusing a stationary store in the town of Kericho. As I walked into the store, I was faced with a shelf of children's books, many consisting of tribal African folklore, stories of Kenya's past, and even a book or two of some more modern Western stories. On the top shelf however was a book with a small African child on the cover standing behind a podium with the seal of the President of the United States on it. The book's title was, *The Kenyan Boy Who Grew Up to be an American President.* It was not until this point that I realized that the adoration and attachment that the Kenyan people had felt for Obama was not just because of the connection his father had with the country, but rather that they felt that he was one of them, a Kenyan boy who on his own became President. This simple cover made sense of all the hype in Kenya surrounding Barack Obama.

The Obama momentum could be felt everywhere at the time when he campaigned, and his messages of hope and change, though perhaps superficial at times, and perhaps merely campaign language, were successful precisely because that is what America and the world were craving at the time. As a somewhat idealistic person, I felt a connection to what was preached in town hall meetings and televised debates, and though I may not have had as many qualms with the previous US administration as some of my peers had, I did feel a sense that there needed to be change. As a Canadian, aware of how the world perceived America and President Bush, it was clear to me that change would be a welcomed current whether it was a simple paradigm shift or merely a new face for the White House. I was taken by this idea, and thought that perhaps if Obama could deliver what he was preaching then maybe we could see a radical shift in the international status quo. Despite the skepticism that people express about the ability of one man to make a difference, historical precedents speak otherwise and it is never outside the realm of possibility.

Though all the candidates throughout the 2008 election campaign used the concepts of hope and change interchangeably, I believe there is a distinct difference between the two.

Change is easy. Change is an alteration, a modification, a different present than what has just passed. Change is useful, it has a practical purpose, and it keeps things interesting. Though things may be working well one day, who knows what good (or bad) can come the next day with a bit of change? Change keeps things interesting because it either confirms of rejects predictions, it ensures that affairs, whether personal or international, remain dynamic and it leads to progress. Sir Isaac Newton famously stated, "If I have seen further it is only by standing on the shoulders of giants." In this, a change of personality meant a change of perspective, a change of attitude, and a change of the history that comes with that person. This alteration enabled whatever past progresses were made to continue to progress, and in sticking with this example, this change of personality, Newton taking the reins from his predecessors, enabled great leaps to be taken in the field of science and physics. It is from change however that the concept of hope draws its meaning.

Hope is a powerful idea that has both blessed and plagued humanity throughout its history. Hope has led people to greed in times of warfare, and has pushed people to the brink of disaster all in the name of what they hoped could be accomplished. One need only consider the hope that accompanied the aspirations of great military dictators or leaders that led to their swift demise. Napoleon's hope for conquering Europe led to greed, which resulted in his swift fall from grace, and King Henry VIII's hope for a male heir led to the prompt death of his third wife and his legacy as a womanizer rather than as one of the greater kings of British history. Hope can lead to greed, despair, and as was so aptly put by Red (Morgan Freeman) in *Shawshank Redemption*, "Hope is a dangerous thing. Hope can drive a man insane." When one is stuck, or one has ambitions too big for their means, it is hope that can make the difference between success and failure. It is this mistaken belief in hope that people feel has resulted in the failures that some perceive as emanating from the Obama administration today.

Despite the negative consequences that may accompany hope, there are indeed positives that cannot be overstated or misunderstood. At the conclusion of *Shawshank*

Redemption, Red is rebuked by Andy Dufresne (Tim Robbins) with, "Hope is a good thing, maybe the best of things. And no good thing ever dies." Hope propels people to act and hope enables people to last. There is the hope that prisoners in Auschwitz held onto that enabled them to survive the darkest period of human history. There is the hope that children feel when they step onto the bus on the first day of school, and when they hope they have the right answer they are empowered to raise their hand for the first time in class. It is this hope, this positive hope, which has enabled generations of human history to take risks, take chances, move forward, and progress into bolder more innovative times. With hope, people are empowered to see beyond their limits, ignore all obstacles, and imagine better more ideal times.

I would argue that one of the best TV shows ever made is the *West Wing*. Detailing the day-to-day life in the White House and other American political affairs, it shed light, however fictitiously, on political life in the United States. Towards the end of the series, Congressman Matthew Santos, a Latino from Texas, decides to run for President. At the time the show was airing, in the beginning of 2005, Senator Obama had only recently given a speech at the Democratic National Convention when John Kerry was running against George W. Bush. This speech turned many eyes towards the Junior Senator from Chicago and people became increasingly aware of his presence in American politics. It was later revealed that the Santos character was highly influenced by Barack Obama, and if you are able to watch the show, this will soon come into stark realization. The point of this *West Wing* tutorial is to introduce a speech that Santos made when he declared his candidacy for President of the United States which I think shares some powerful insight into the idea of hope:

> I wanted to start this journey in the place where it all started for me. Soon we will be inundated by the polls, and the punditry and the prognostications all the nonsense that goes with our national political campaigns. But none of that matters. This is the place that matters, because every day children walk into this schoolhouse to glimpse their futures, to ask for hope. They may not know they need it yet, but they do. And I am here to tell you that hope is real. In a life of trials in a world of challenges, hope is real. In a country where families go without health care, where some go without food, some don't even have a home to speak of, hope is real. In a time of global chaos and instability, where our faiths collide as often as our weapons, hope is real. Hope is what gives us the courage to take on our greatest challenges, to move forward together. We live in cynical times, I know that. But hope is not up for debate. There is such a thing as false science, there is such a thing as false promises, I am sure that I'll have my share of false starts in this campaign, but there is no such thing as false hope. There is only hope. And with your help and your hard work, and the hopes of good people all across this land, I hereby announce my candidacy for President of these United States.

Makes you feel good eh? Even without knowing that Jimmy Smits, who played Matt Santos in the show, decided to base part of his character on Obama, you can almost hear the crowds shouting "Yes we can!" by the time the speech is over.

It is this positive form of hope that transformed Obama from a candidate for the American Presidency to a Kenyan national symbol. To Americans, Obama symbolized a new era of leadership, a younger face, and the personification of the civil rights movement. In Kenya, and throughout Africa, Obama was far more. He symbolized the ability for someone from the depths of Africa, a continent often deemed hopeless and forgotten, to rise to the most powerful position on earth. He gave hope to mothers, fathers and grandparents in Kenya that their next generation perhaps had the chance of escaping all the possible negative consequences of being African. They hoped that their children would escape the grips of extreme poverty, would not be constantly threatened by the onslaught of HIV/AIDS, and would not have to worry about where their next meal would be coming from.

For this reason, for the potential to escape the woes that face Africans on a daily basis, Kenyans were willing to overlook the fact that Obama does not have as close a connection as they would like him to have, and that he is not exactly, as the title of the book describes, *The Kenyan Boy Who Grew Up to be an American President*. Anyone with a basic understanding of Obama's history would know that a more apt title would be *The Hawaiian Boy Whose American Mother Married a Kenyan Man Who Played a Minor Role in his Upbringing Who Grew Up to be an American President*. Despite Obama's father's roots in Kenya, he was estranged from his father, was born in Hawaii, lived in Indonesia as a youth, and is primarily American. These details of his life did not however deter those whose aim was to brand him as Kenyan. To them, he was a black man, from the Luo community, whose father was born in Kenya, who has a half brother who lives in a Kenyan slum, and whose grandmother lives like other Kenyans do in the small village of Kogelo. For all these reasons, Obama was just like any one of them. He had an African soul, an African look, and he had defied the odds and gone on to occupy the most powerful office in the world.

To add to this comparison to the new President, it helps that Obama has a half-brother who lives just outside of Nairobi in Kibera, one of Africa's largest slums.

In August 2008, a few months prior to the American election, *Vanity Fair* magazine announced that it has discovered Senator Obama's youngest half-brother living on the outskirts of Nairobi. His name is George Hussein Onyango Obama. Twenty-six at the time, George Obama claimed that no one knew who he was, and said that he lives in Kibera on less than 1-dollar a month. The interviews conducted with George Obama were particularly revealing because he showed that he lived like so many Kenyans do: in abject poverty, in a shack made of mud, wood and tin-roof, with few aspirations or dreams of leaving.

He says that when people question his relationship with Barack Obama because of their common surname, he tells them there is no relation. Why? He is ashamed. This shame is not reflective of any actions of his half-brother Barack, but rather an introspective shame that he was not able to become the kind of person that his half-brother became. He is ashamed of his poverty and ashamed of his life, and does not want to be compared to this brother that he has never known. Only meeting Barack twice, once in their youth, and once when Barack visited Kenya in 2006, they do not know each other and they are far more different than they are similar.

This distance, and the late acknowledgement of the connection between the two made for an interesting comparison between the two brothers, and people in Kenya acknowledged that here was a President who, despite his distance from Kenya, does have relatives who reside within this country. Being able to make this comparison eliminated the distance that was felt between the Harvard-educated candidate and the people who aspired to be like him, and this familial connection brought Obama to the level of most Africans. Though this comparison did little to help George Obama, there was now an Obama in their midst, and so the more important one could not be too far off.

The most promising relationship however that Obama shares with a Kenyan citizen is his grandmother, Sarah Obama.

Mama Sarah Obama was the reason I wanted to visit Kogelo near the end of my stay in the western region of Kenya. Kogelo, in the heart of Luo-land, has been her lifelong home, and the connection between her and her grandson was not simply discovered on the eve of his candidacy. Sarah Obama has known of her grandson his whole life, and in interviews conducted with her she speaks of her pride not only with his candidacy for president, but also the excitement she and her village felt when he was sworn in as an American Senator in 2004. In an article from the

Globe and Mail titled "Obama's ancestral village boosts its favourite son" (12/07/07) is detailed the adoration that Sarah has for her grandson. Speaking before his election to the Presidency, she said, "To be President of the U.S. is like being the president of the whole world. I am very happy." On the wall of her mud hut are photos of both her step-son and famous grandson, including a signed Senate campaign poster from him that says "Mama Sarah. Habari! And Love." (*Habari* is a Swahili greeting).

Admittedly, my motives for going to visit Sarah Obama were selfish and may or may not have included the idea of just being able to tell people that I had met Obama's bubbie. I did however also have some questions for her, and wanted to speak to her and know what her thoughts were on the image that Kenyans have created of her grandson. Here was a woman who in a sense had it pretty easy. She played no particular role in Obama's upbringing, is not even a blood-relative of the President (she was Obama's father's step-mother), but achieved stardom in her own country as a result. It was also interesting to make a comparison between Sarah and Obama's other grandmother, Madelyn Dunham, who played an extremely active and important role in Obama's upbringing and development.

It is hardly possible to make a comparison between these two women in Obama's life. Sarah Obama played her role from afar and was able to enjoy the pride that her grandson was able to bring her. Madelyn Dunham on the other hand played a critical role in Obama's upbringing and played a significant role in defining the type of person, and perhaps President, he would be. I have always found it interesting to consider the role that people play in the development of your life, opinions, thoughts and dreams. Some people, with only a simple comment or question can stick in your head forever, create a perception that is difficult to shake, and just stay put. There are of course others who play a constant role in your life who will no doubt shape who you are, such as your parents or siblings, but the comparison between these two types of influences is significant to reflect on. I am by no means one to speak for Obama, nor do I truly know the role that either of these women played in his life. What I do know however is that one gave him constant guidance throughout his life, while the other maintained a firm connection between Obama and his Kenyan father, and as is understood by anyone who reads Obama's reflections on his life, this aspect plays a huge role in the kind of person he is and wants to be. What they were able to give to him and what they are able to see as a result is also, in a way, tragic. Sarah Obama today continues to live her life tilling her fields and picking her papayas while her grandson leads the free world. In a tragic, almost cruel turn of events however, days before Obama was elected President his other grandmother Madelyn passed away.

Despite the distance between Sarah Obama and her grandson Barack, she has played a role, and her fellow countrymen want this role to be as real as possible. It is for this reason that they persist in their labeling of him as Kenyan, and it is for this reason that they despair when he, whether intentionally or unintentionally, acts against them.

On May 17, 2009, I woke up to my usual routine in Kiptere and went to buy a newspaper. As I paid my 40 shillings I was handed the newspaper and read the headline, "OBAMA SNUBS KENYA".

The headline certainly did the trick and piqued my interest. As I read on I discovered that President Obama had planned his first African trip as President and that he would be traveling to Ghana. The author of the article and the general comments about this particular visit stated that the choice of Ghana was prompted by the fact that there is actually progress occurring there. The United States considered Ghana a potentially powerful partner in Africa with a bright future. The Americans were eager about the progress being made in the country, and the democratic values that its president, John Atta Mills, was instilling in its people. To most this announcement passed without issue. In Kenya, there was outrage.

Remember what I have said though about their love of Barack Obama. This outrage was not directed against the President for ignoring his homeland: the outrage was entirely introspective and they looked to see how they had hurt him.

This story was followed for days with letters questioning how Kenya had let President Obama down. "What did we do to deserve a snub like this?", "What can we do better?", "How can Obama not make his first African visit to his homeland?" The decision to visit a different country in Africa left the people of Kenya wondering what they had done to upset the President. It prompted immediate self-reflection, calls for change, cries for hope, and a desire to please the American President.

Observing the reaction inside Kenya through the newspapers, and outside Kenya on the internet, was actually a somewhat amusing exercise. In their eyes, Obama, as a descendant of a Kenyan, had the obligation to visit his homeland first. Put politics aside, they said, this President's first visit should be personal and should show people the role that Kenya plays in his life. In truth, though hardly a political adviser myself, I would assume that a visit to Kenya would not have gone over so well in the American State Department. Aside from not having any real political reason for visiting Kenya and spending taxpayer money on such a trip, Kenya as a government is corrupt and is at the moment hardly a model of African development. Having suffered through a civil conflict and paying little attention to the needs of people who require the most assistance on the ground, the first trip of a newly elected American President should go to a country whose main reason for accepting an offer should be more than "He's Kenyan . . . duh!" Politics of course will always play a role, but in the emotionally heightened state of affairs that I've described, it does not surprise me that those with this opinion did not get their articles printed in the national newspapers. And so, the trip to Ghana progressed without a hitch and the people of Kenya were left wondering what they could do to better impress their prodigal son.

The Obama phenomenon certainly gripped the world. At the time of writing this, it is becoming clear to many that the standards President Obama set for himself in his campaign were too high to achieve. His approval rating is not what was envisaged, the last three-years of his Presidency attest to varying degrees of concrete progression or successes, and like many politicians Obama has proven to be perhaps a bit more-talk-less-action than people expected. He has also had the difficulty of being faced with a high level of partisan politics in Washington that has certainly played a role in halting the effect that Washington should have. The purpose of this is not to criticize but perhaps merely to reflect on what has the ability to happen when too much hope is created at a time of despair.

As a hardcore idealistic-realist I will never underestimate the power that hope has. Seeing it all over the world and witnessing it first hand in Kenya was a truly uplifting and inspirational experience that contributes to my persistent belief in hope. I went to a pub in Kiptere that was lit only with a kerosene lamp. When they wanted entertainment one night, they brought in a generator, found the necessary gasoline, powered it up, attached it to a TV and DVD player, and popped in a DVD that had only one video on it: a music video created about Senator Obama's visit to Kenya in 2006. This ridiculous 25-minute music video, seen in the middle of the night while drinking warm beer, showed me everything I wanted to know about hope. It showed me that patriotism and national pride is tied to hope, and it made me realize why, only 5 months after Obama's inauguration, there was already a *Barack Obama Road* leading to the Mombasa International Airport, a Senator Obama school in Kogelo, and a local beer called *Senator Beer* adopting the name "Obama".

In *The Audacity of Hope* Obama writes,

> It wasn't just the struggles of those men and women that had moved me. Rather, it was their determination, their self-reliance, a relentless optimism in the face of hardship: the audacity of hope. Having the audacity to believe despite all the evidence to the contrary that we could restore a

> sense of community to a nation torn by conflict.
> The gall to believe that . . . we had some control
> over our own fate.

The project that I helped build in Kenya is inherently tied to the ideas of hope and the influence that Obama was able to have over so many people. This is exactly the kind of determination that Obama talks about in the above-mentioned quote, and this is why a handwritten copy of this quote was hanging on the wall for the duration of the project.

Hope created now does not always have to be overshadowed by failures later or the ability to live up to that hope. Hope is a phenomenon that exists in its present form, and in Kenya in particular, it works. For the peace project that I had been working on, it was also practical to play off the momentum that had been created by Obama's swift rise to power and the inspiration that he gave to so many youths to be something more.

Oscar Wilde once said, "We are all in the gutter, but some of us are looking at the stars." No other words are required to put this in the Kenyan context and despite his political successes or failures, the role that Obama has played in lifting up the spirit of Kenya should not and cannot be overshadowed or denied. It was in this spirit of lifting ourselves up and elevating ourselves to the position of heroes that inspired many of the youths involved to try and create programs and experiences that would influence the future of the country, and the first project we would attempt was the creation of a drama group that preached the message of peace.

DRAMA IS LIFE, AN ESCAPE, HAPPINESS, AND SADNESS ALL ROLLED INTO ONE

I have never been one particularly interested in the field of dramatic arts. For the majority of my life I watched in awe as friends of mine were able to get up and perform, sing, or dance in front of large groups of their peers or total strangers. I did not understand what went on in drama class that could make someone go from being a shy introvert to an emotive and expressive actor. This whole idea of drama and training one to become 'dramatic' still eludes me for the most part, but I do have to say that I have come to understand and appreciate the field of drama a little more over the last few years, and understand what sort of role those involved in drama play in any number of different fields.

I can actually pinpoint the exact moment when I realized the role that drama can play in different aspects of one's life. After completing my undergraduate studies I moved to London for a year and found a job working as a tour guide for the Big Bus Company. This job was a dream come true, and I loved being able to learn all about my new surroundings, the history, the culture, the place, and combined with my love of teaching people, here I got to conduct tours for hundreds of tourists each day throughout the summer in London and ensure that they knew everything there was to know about London (that I could tell them in 2.5 hours).

Whether it was teaching them about the quirks of the Royal Family, teaching the history of the Tower of London or reciting to them my memorized list of all 42 monarchs reaching as far back as King William I who took the throne of England in the year 1066, I was trying primarily to educate and entertain the tourists on my bus. Conducting three tours a day, each one approximately two and a half hours long, people who asked me about this job often inquired whether or not it got boring. After all, doing this job for a year both full-time and part-time, I had in the end probably conducted around 250 tours, and I was confident (I even tried it once) that I could conduct a tour with my eyes closed. When I was first asked about whether the job gets boring I told my inquisitive friend that it did not, because I was simply trying to put on a show. In trying to make the tourists smile, laugh, and appreciate their surroundings, I was, in a sense, dramatizing to them this entire experience and I was able to work off of their positive energy. Only after these words came out of my mouth did I realize that I was, in some way, acting for the first time, in front of group of strangers, and although it was not singing or dancing, it was definitely putting on a show.

I suddenly became very proud of my abilities to do this, and in every subsequent tour I kept this idea at the front of my mind: you are putting on a show, make them enjoy it! Scripted jokes aside, I tried to make sure that my presentation was direct, that I spoke slowly, succinctly and clearly, and that the people leaving the bus now appreciated London to the same extent as I did. Of course I had received training with regard to learning the information for the tour, but my supervisors expected that we all put our own spin on the tour to ensure primarily that the information was out there, but how it is done was entirely up to us. I therefore made sure that I never sat down when conducting a tour (despite the numerous turns and swerves that the bus driver made on any given day) and I always stood facing the crowd, sometimes asking for a high-five or asking questions to see if they were actually listening to all my fun facts about London. Because of the fact that I suddenly realized that I was putting on a show, the only side-effect was that if the bus was less than full or only had a few people on it, I had to try extra-hard to make it fun for myself. Once, I must admit, I almost fell asleep giving a tour to a group of six people who were less than enthusiastic about the city (at one point I wanted to see if they were actually listening to me, so as we came off Tower Bridge, I pointed to the Tower of London on the left and said "On your left you can see the Tower of London, the birthplace . . . of Darth Vader." I got no reaction). I came to gain my energy from that of the tourists on the bus, and so we sort of had this give-and-take relationship throughout each tour. What I came to realize is that I was just an actor, with no formal training, but that I was picking up hints and seeing what worked and didn't work with each tour. I was lucky to have 250 chances to perfect my performance, and with the help of enthusiastic and encouraging tourists as well as my supervisors who were always willing to give tips as to how to make the tours more fun and effective, I have to say that I developed a pretty good two-and-a-half-hour tour of the greatest city in the world.

It was this experience as a tour guide that made me appreciate the idea of drama, but as someone who is largely impatient with theory and always eager to get onto practical experiences and trial-and-error, I still could not really comprehend the idea of a drama club. A club designed to simply work on the techniques of drama did not make much sense to me, and I guess in my own little ignorant way, I just assumed that if you had it you had it, and if you didn't you didn't. This attitude of mine was of course ignorant because I was someone who for most of my life did not have any potential to be a performer of any kind, but only through the experience of being a tour guide was I able to gain confidence in standing up in front of groups of random people and improve my skills with regard to public speaking, a fear that used to reduce me to nerves and made me quickly lose my words. After working in London and developing this understanding of drama in some way, I went to Kenya to start up a project where drama was the last thing on my mind.

In the midst of our peacebuilding workshop, one of the participants named Kepha came to speak to me one night over dinner to tell me about this drama club of which he was a part. He told me that he, along with a group of 14 others, are members of a drama club called *Tujipange*, which translated means "Preparing ourselves". He told me that the group was recently formed and that they got together to write songs, skits and poetry, and then perform these pieces at a variety of different venues. These venues would consist of school grounds when given permission, random marketplaces where they would set up in the corner, or really any other location from which they could reach a large number of people at a time. Kepha told me that they had support from a few community members and though this support was largely motivational and not exactly financial, he told me that with some of their connections they were able to travel to different areas and perform. They had also once received a grant from USAID, an American organization which provides grants for certain independent projects on the ground in third-world countries, and with that money they had been able to make some t-shirts and pay for performances.

Kepha was telling me about this project not just because he wanted me to be aware of the existence of the group, but because of the nature of their work he thought it would be fitting for them to perform for the group attending our peacebuilding workshop. He told me that his drama club has always focused on the idea of peace, and that many of the concepts that we were discussing in the context of our workshop fit directly into the pieces that they performed as a group. After some deliberating with him about the logistics of getting the group to Kiptere to perform, two days later they all showed up in the village, all wearing their white USAID t-shirts, and were ready to go.

I had no idea what to expect from them, and to be honest was not sure how much this performance would fit into what themes we were trying to explore in our workshop. I did appreciate the enthusiasm that Kepha and the others demonstrated however, and the decision to invite this group was made only after consulting with the other members of the workshop to see if this was something they would be interested in. Once we got the OK from the group and it seemed clear that they were looking for something a bit more than just participating in a discussion for a morning, we thought watching the group perform for a while would be a nice change in the itinerary.

The performance was of course meant to inspire and teach the youths involved. It had little to do with me, which was good, because 90% of the performance was done in Swahili and so I just sat and watched with a smile as I understood almost nothing of what I heard. I liked the tune though, and I liked the beat. Despite the language barrier I was impressed with the level of sophistication that the group displayed, and it became overwhelmingly clear that they spent time rehearsing, writing and choreographing these performances so that whenever they were called on to act, they were more than ready.

Their performance consisted of songs, poetry and short skits, most of which were accompanied by some choreography. I was most impressed when the poems were recited, as stanza by stanza the youths spoke all the words at the same time, in perfect synchronization. They knew every word and for the one poem that they performed in English, it was of a high quality and was recited with passion and deep emotion. They danced, they stomped, they were loud, and the looks on their faces and their conviction resonated with me, again, even though I only understood a minimal amount of what was being said.

Here is an example of one of their English pieces, which they were gracious to provide me with at the close of their performance:

"We Shall Never Go Back to War"

> They bought our rights,
> they cut our voices,
> and in counter reaction, we marched.
> To express our disappointment
> because this shouldn't have happened

and still should never happen.

Where did we go wrong?
That we decided to cut and slash each other.
Where did we take our humanity?
To start reasoning with inhumanity and carelessness.
Tell me to make amends,
so that our struggle to be one waved.

Most have heart for unlike Ochomba,
at least you have buried his head.
Though you loved him, God loved him most.
Though you wanted more time to make amends
for past mistakes,
he will be in peace and in faith.
He will be with you.

Families in agony,
children as orphans.
Adults without arms,
some legless,
was the result of our action
just in the name
Of a stolen election.

Yes we shall never go back to war!
Yes in pain!
Yes in happiness!

Together we stood.
In one voice we spoke.
Though in tongues we varied,

our aim was one,
our desire was the same:
that democracy was to prevail.

"Dust to dust" the priest said,
"Where you came from you shall return," he added,
as he laid to rest the remains of human parts with
the fallen families around the mass grave.

Besides the banana tree
the head laid.
Warm tears flowed down his innocent face,
and so just like that the child was gone.

We will never go back to war!
Yes we will never go back to war again!
This is a lesson the youths must learn.
Our differences might be great,
our opinions might not be the same,
but though it might stretch,
the stitch holding us together
must never break.

This poem was written following the post-election violence and expresses the emotions that many felt once the ceasefire took effect. It was clear that the authors of the poem were torn by what had occurred in their country and what they, as youths, had permitted to unfold. It was telling that they blamed themselves and asked where they had gone wrong, and this reflective tone and inquiry really seemed to penetrate deeply into their collective mindset. Echoing many comments that I had heard from others about how they had been manipulated and played by politicians and elders, this poem speaks to the feelings of frustration and resentment but also to the spirit of being able to take control of their ultimate fate to ensure that such an occurrence does not happen again.

The combination of this poem and getting to know so many youths on the ground in Kenya led me to perceive that people in Kenya were surprised by both what had happened in the post-election violence, and how it had happened. I came to realize that this was something truly out of the ordinary in this country. What the violence did however was bring to the surface many of the issues lingering just below for so long, and though the violence had by now subsided, these youths were aware of what had driven the country to its breaking point, and could identify the elements that could prompt this violent trend to occur again. Despite the fact that violence was not an ordinary incidence in Kenya, they saw peace as the exception rather than the rule, and one of them even told me that, "peace is like a volcano: it erupts, and then lays dormant until the next eruption." It was interesting hearing it put this way, and the frustration that became apparent in their writings and in their performance was uniquely telling with regard to what they expected and anticipated for the future.

Rebekah Adams once said, "Drama is theatre, life, an escape from life, happiness, and sadness all rolled into one", and this was precisely the definition that I would have given this activity myself if I had any clue at all. I know that much of what this drama club put together had to do with land issues, with peace, with conflict amongst brothers, and with all that has divided their country in the last few years. Still however, their poetry and their verse contained lines that made the audience react with laughter and with smiles, and it showed the power that drama can have, even if it is organized in a crudely built home with a tin roof in the middle of rural Kenya.

Despite the fact that I did not understand most of the performance as it was conducted in Swahili, I asked the group to perform a few more of their pieces while the other youths sat silently watching the show unfold. The noise the group had made throughout their performance, despite the fact that it was on the third floor of the only properly constructed building in the village, led a number of other community members to find their way upstairs to watch. They found the performance to be uplifting and insightful. There was time for the group to answer questions, and during the break that we took following their performance I had a chance to speak to them and get a translation of much of what they had been performing.

Before they left I spoke to the troupe again and they asked me for my support. To be perfectly honest, the support that I was able to offer them would have been in morale only as I had no additional funds to allocate to them, and fundraising in Toronto is hard enough when you are just focused on one or two other projects. I had not planned to incorporate this club into what I envisioned to be this peace project, but even though I made this perfectly clear to the members and told them that I would *try* but could not promise to find them any financial support from abroad, which was what they were looking for, I promised that I would always speak highly of them and do what I could.

Only after I said this did I realize one of their tactics. A few days later as I was walking through Sondu with a group of youths heading to one of the high schools that we would be targeting for our soon-to-be-formed high school peace clubs, Kepha approached me, put his arm around me, and said in his deep voice, "Mr. Adam, I have news from my drama troupe." (Kenyans always call me Mr. Adam, as a sign of respect, and it always makes me smile.) Just sort of nodding along, I asked what the news was. "We have decided to change the name of the group," he said to me, "and from now on it shall be called Adam's Youth Group."

Not again.

Like I said when I realized the soccer tournament was named after me, it was very touching and I really was thankful that they were going to honour me in this way. I will not however forget the feeling of discomfort that I felt standing on that football field with my name blowing in the wind of the trees as my name was plastered all over those signs. I did not want this sort of recognition for whatever was being done here, and in particular with the drama club, I hadn't even done anything! I felt uncomfortable seeing my name all over the signs for the tournament, and did not intend to loan out my name for any other projects that would arise as a result of this project. Nevertheless, there was no talking Kepha down.

"Please Kepha, do not change the name of the group, it was so nice the way it was!"

"No, I am sorry Mr. Adam, it is already done."

"What do you mean it's already done? It's a group of 15 of you, just meet again tomorrow and change it back to *Tujipange*! That was a waaaay nicer name!"

"No Mr. Adam, we have already submitted the paperwork! It is official."

(At this point you have to imagine the quizzical look on my face as I peered from side to side taking in my surroundings. Here I stood, wearing ripped jeans and a dirty t-shirt, big rain boots on my feet, haven't shaved in three weeks, and in the middle of a muddy dirt path which had run down wooden and mud-brick shops on either side of it. There were chickens, cows, and stray dogs running around, people walking with ripped clothes, few wearing shoes, and we stood outside the gate of a school that had as its security guard a woman who looked to be nearly 90 years old, holding in her hand nothing but a wooden stick which she was using to clean her teeth with, and Kepha tells me that the decision is "official" because they have already "submitted the paperwork." I laughed as he had used such formal language in what was clearly such an informal setting.)

"You've submitted the paperwork? Where? How? Where did you find paper?" (Excuse my condescension, but I was clearly taken a bit off guard as finding paper and standing in line waiting to file something in a rural area was not an easy task.)

"Please Mr. Adam, it is ok, we thank you for your support, and this is now the name of the group."

"Well, I don't know what else to do, but fine! Fine. Thank you, I appreciate that, but seriously, NOTHING

ELSE!" (He wouldn't listen to this directive either, as I will discuss later).

This was the tactic that I had discovered: Name things after Adam to guilt him into fundraising for it. Very clever I must say as well. How can I tell people there's a project named after me in Kenya and then follow it up with "and I don't care"? Although I have not yet brought this tactic up to them, I think they have made it abundantly clear from their actions and I have to hand it to them, it's worked. To their credit though, the work that Adam's Youth Group has done since their re-establishment has been phenomenal and I can truly say that without the work of both Kepha and the other members of the group, I fear that much of our efforts would have ground to a complete halt.

A few weeks after I returned to Canada from Kenya, I received an email from Kepha with some details about Adam's Youth Group. After deliberating whether or not to edit what he wrote to me in that email or not, I have decided to just include the whole thing so that you can get some sense of what our communications are like, and how well both Kepha and others have been able to articulate what their goals are with regard to this and other projects. Also just a note about technology: though many of the villages in the region do not have readily available electricity, some of the larger villages have internet cafes where internet usage is frequent. We therefore have been able to keep in touch through email, and, though I shouldn't necessarily be surprised, Facebook is a huge trend in Kenya and most of the youths with whom I work have Facebook accounts. Alright, so here it goes (and it is lengthy, but you will probably learn more from this email than anything I have written in this entire book—and the only thing I've corrected is the spelling):

Dear Mr. Adam,

Every society's development is enhanced by availability of information to its members. Relevant information always leads to positive development. On the other hand, misinformed society is always at war with itself. It is on this reasoning that Adams Youth Group was incepted. Our main aim is to spread message of peace, harmony and provide necessary information that will be important in advancing development agenda for across Kenya as a country and our villages in particular. As a group we do travel a lot across the country to promote peace and harmony. During these tours, we've come to learn that our nation, starting from the villages is a victim of misinformation and lack of avenues to attain relevant information while in a fairly informed society, information available is not enough to spearhead development. Take for example:

a) A person who is not aware of the most current entrepreneurship agenda and objectives of the society will most likely do nothing to advance the same.

b) A youth who is aware of youth entrepreneurship fund but lacks know how on how to be a beneficiary of the same, will always remain wishing.

c) A person who hardly accesses information will for instance not understand the benefit of any move by any shareholder to aid in advancing his or her development.

All these factors, added to the fact that we are living in a resigned society with no one willing to take leadership role of making this information easily available are among the driving force for forming Adams Youth Group. Consequently we are striving to do our part as best as we can. We have therefore set out project calendar of ensuring that by 2012 we will be better placed to spread relevant information to our peers and others alike to avoid 2007 occurrences. Major and immediate in our plans is to set fully equipped Youth centres. We plan to start with Omosaaria Centre for a case study to determine how much the locals will embrace this idea. We have however done necessary investigation and groundwork hence are very positive on the feasibility of this project. The centre in mind will be majoring on:-

i) Encourage youths to invest in their talents and abilities.
ii) Availing relevant information on HIV and AIDS
iii) Teaching the significance and importance of diversity
iv) Availing relevant development agenda to the youth
v) Spearheading computer literacy
vi) Involving other stakeholders to advance poverty eradication.

These can however not be achieved without external intervention from relevant stakeholders. It's obvious these auto suggestions cannot be realized without support/ we therefore, hope to bring the very stakeholders on board to jumpstart and realize the projects. This is where you (Adam) come in and why we find it very necessary to share our ambitions with you.

ABOUT US: ADAMS YOUTH GROUP is a group of like minded youths from KENYA objectively formed to preach peace and harmonize coexistence of diverse Kenyan society. Its inception and needs was propelled by the 2007/2008 post-election violence. It's aimed on capitalizing on individual creativity and artistic skills of its members to address pressing society needs and aim at updating the society on the truth and current issues by employing reasoning as opposed to accepting inflammatory remarks.

We as a result have been travelling across the country spreading this gospel of harmony.

Our objective is to:

Engage idle youths who would rather be wasting themselves in hopelessness and unproductive activities such as drug abuse, in becoming society's voice of reason

Learning different cultures as to preach their good value hence making cohesion and acceptance possible by those who would have been repellant to the same as a result of ignorance

To take centre stage in AIDS/HIV awareness projects and activities

To eventually become internationally known and recognized as youth ambassadors of peace through our creative presentation by engaging other relevant players

To start education centre where all youths from different tribes will be coming to discuss and share ideas.

To start business enterprises that will employ the locals thus help them earn a clean noble income. On top of that we are already having a project which is running (poultry keeping) whereby we do donate eggs to people who are suffering from HIV/AIDS.

All these have happened and others are underway and we acknowledge to the unending support from our sponsors Adam Hummel (Canada) and madam Courtney (USA).

BACKGROUND INFORMATION: Following the 2007/2008 post-election violence we realized that there was dire need to spread wide the values we hold together as a society. We realized that one major reason why such inhuman occurrence took place is ignorance and lack of what holds us together as Kenyans. This made it easy for ill minded leaders who utilized our diversity for political mileage to incite the innocent youths all over the country to turn against one another based on ethnic differences

Supporting their arguments, these leaders took advantage of stereotype reasoning minds into hostility. The very bad blood that exists between different ethnic groups is based on retrogressive past speeches and misinformation that was intentionally aimed at dividing Kenyans for easy ruling. We believe that the past mistakes can be amended by preaching a more unifying and harmonizing gospel. It is on this reasoning that we unveiled Adams Youth Group to the youth ambassadors for peace.

The group was initially Tujipange that collapsed but reemerged as Adams youth Group.

The group is based on accountability, proper consultations, oneness, honesty and focus and with this the group is more stable and has withstood many challenges.

To symbolize our new resolutions and way of running things, we changed our name from TUJIPANGE to ADAMS and was decided on by members with reasoning that Adam was God's most creative creation who succeeded in naming all God's creations. Nevertheless, Adam was a beginning of mankind hence our new beginning is properly symbolized by the name. It is also important to mention the fact that our mentor and advisor, Mr. Adam Hummel is coincidentally also Adam. The name therefore has better orientation and reasoning for its being the best members excitedly could think of and unanimously agree on.

With the new start, some of our projects to enhance and hasten peace initiatives are already underway. In line with this we are organizing tournaments to bring youths together so as to provide us with platforms for poems and share presentations as well as an avenue for bringing leaders from all sides together round table agreements

N/B. Most of these thing we are about to write about are what Courtney and Adam Hummel taught us and saw us through their implementations

The group started in the year 2008 with the aim of building peace and reconciliation after the 2007/2008 post-election violence. We first met with Adam during his visit to Kenya in 2009. Our group was invited at Kiptere Youth Center where we were performing about peace and reconciliation. After our performance, Adam was impressed with us and he wanted to know more about the group. Adam sponsored a peace tournament of the most affected three communities, namely, Kalenjin, Luo and Kisiis whereby we were invited as the Youth Ambassadors for Peace. Through Adam, we started mobilizing youths through forming youth clubs in schools where our group up to date is in charge of carrying out various exercises through poetry, drama, storytelling, singing and guidance and counseling. We have done shows at Chebirate (Kalenjin-Kisii boarder), Chabera (Luo-Kisii Boarder), Omosaaria Market, Nyamusi Market center, Magwagwa center and Ikonge. Adam has done a great job in sponsoring us in carrying out all these activities.

As if this is not enough, Adam has assisted us to open an office which has a youth center. He has also equipped the office with the following:-

a) A computer
b) 5 chairs

c) Stationeries like files and writing materials.

We started a poultry project and Adam has already promised to spearhead it. The aim of this was to donate some eggs to the HIV positive families in the three communities.

We are also waiting for the cameras he sent us which will assist us in taking photos to show the activities that we do perform.

We are requesting support in the following projects if possible:

1. Recording and producing our works.
2. Buying more office equipment.
3. To standardize our poultry project to reach out to interior pats of the country.
4. Costumes for the members ex. African traditional costumes for our songs and stories.
5. Public address system.
6. Means of communication amongst members and the forthcoming tournament.

We are praying that the Almighty Lord sustain Adam and other well wishers who are contributing to see our group a success.

Ok you have to be impressed by this. Aside from the fact that he used the word "retrogressive", the values and beliefs that are enshrined in this sort of mission statement for the group leaves no surprise that these are the sorts of youths writing the poetry that I provided above. When I received this I was also thrilled to read about the real reason for the rebranding of the drama group, specifically keeping in mind that in their mindset of this being a rebirth, they immediately used the name Adam, referring to the Biblical Adam, as the first man who made many decisions when the world was first created. Ladies and Gentlemen you have it there from a primary source that he did not name this project *only* after me, but that it was simply a coincidence (yes, a coincidence) that both I and Biblical Adam share a name and therefore have equal stake in the name of this newly formed group.

As was laid out in this mission statement, which included their vision for the future and what they plan to do throughout their existence, the members of this group have many goals. They have been critical in ensuring that the work we initiated in Kenya in May 2009 has continued and flourished. Every time I have been able to find a donation for the cause they have put it to good use, and in putting it all down in writing we both now have a reference point to which to look in order to discuss what to finish up, and what to do next.

One of the projects that Kepha touched on above is the founding of a poultry project, and to date this is one of the most popular accomplishments of the group. Prior to receiving the email above, I had fundraised a small amount of money to send to the group for them to buy some of the stationary and chairs that they listed as being part of their office. A few days after I sent the money to them I received an email which listed the budget, what they had spent the money on, and at the bottom of the list there was a small amount that had written next to it "poultry farm." Not having heard of this part of the project before and curious as to how this money was being spent, I replied to ask what on earth they were buying chickens for, and the response I received really warmed my heart.

I was told that the chicken project was designed to make part of the project that we had established focus on the HIV/AIDS crisis in Africa. What Adam's Youth Group would do is purchase chickens with whatever residual amount of money was available, keep them in a poultry farm, and they would take the eggs from these chickens to donate to people who have recently been diagnosed with HIV/AIDS. Eggs in this part of the country are a more expensive commodity and though eggs obviously do not improve the medical condition of those affected by both HIV or AIDS, they do provide some nutrients and more so, it is a way to ensure that those on the receiving end of these donations understand that the community of youths is looking out for them and has them in mind. People on the ground in Kenya are not necessarily able to assist HIV/AIDS victims with the medical treatment that they always require, which is the job of clinics, hospitals and VCT volunteers, but in providing these members of society with something small, something with a bit of value, they are telling them that they are not alone in their suffering. These donations include visits from the members of the group, and they have specifically targeted people in the three communities with whom we worked for the duration of our peace workshop. Today we have expanded to help members of five communities and we hope to continue to expand.

Many people when they hear about this actually laugh, especially when they hear the name of the project which is, of course, Adam's Poultry Project (I didn't even bother protesting this time, what's the point right? The name of the farm has however since been changed to *Nikki's Chikkies* to acknowledge a generous donation from my friend Nikki). To incorporate this project into all the others I had to find out the costs for the chickens and for actually building a chicken farm, and found out that each chicken costs only $5. Easy enough, so now I have to go and ask people if they want to buy a chicken! It is a bit ridiculous to make such a suggestion, so this has become one of my more enjoyable fundraising exercises, and to make it a bit more fun people can of course name the chicken they purchase. This is different to other poultry projects in that the purpose is to keep the chickens alive thereby using their eggs and not the chickens themselves as food, so it only makes sense to be able to name the chickens. It boosts investment in the project, and there is now a sign up outside the chicken farm that is updated regularly with the list of names of its feathered inhabitants.

The farm is a great success as both friends, family members, and total strangers who have heard about it have been more than generous when it comes to maintaining and finding the funds required ensuring its continued prosperity. Though you may not believe me writing this, I was hesitant about biting off more than I could chew when it came to this peace project, and although I knew that it would be adding too much to the work that I had already created for both myself and those involved, I had naturally wanted to include something in this project that had to do with HIV/AIDS awareness. I had thought however that this was something that I could work to incorporate at a much later time, and thought that the ultimate goal of peacebuilding was enough for the moment. The fact that the members of Adam's Youth Group proposed and got started on this farm entirely through their own initiative could not however be ignored, and despite the difficulties that often arise when it comes to fundraising I am blessed that this project is unique in its approach to assisting those most vulnerable in society who are afflicted with this condition. It is also important that we are able to fundraise for this effort with both a funny and meaningful slant, to guarantee that people are able to see directly where their money will end up.

The efforts and achievements of Adam's Youth Group are tremendous and today they have set up an office in Matongo, a village many of their members call home. They have made t-shirts, decorated the outside of the office with the name of the organization, have two computers, have stationary, have chairs, and their office is open for visitors all day long. They are committed, they are dedicated, and they above all dream about spreading a message of peace throughout their country. Now to bring it all back to the beginning of this chapter, this all began with drama, and who knew that it could go such a long way.

I suppose that those who participate in drama clubs have skills that go a long way in helping them become leaders and reach out to others. They are outgoing, confident, ambitious, carefree, and risk takers. Those who can put it all out there and act in front of others, sharing their emotions, their ideas and their creativity, will always be subjected to both the good and the bad, and will find that they have people who will be and will not be supportive, but that is simply a risk worth taking. For those who are able to overcome that initial step there is a chance of finding great accomplishment and a sense of achievement, and hope that those in front of whom they perform will embrace them. For others who are not willing to take that risk, then they may never know how valuable their own gifts and talents are, and will be left keeping it to themselves. I think I have always seen those members of drama or acting troupes as those willing to share a bit of themselves with their onlookers. They shed their vulnerabilities and insecurities, throw it out to the crowd, and see who latches on to what is offered. In being a constant source of entertainment to youths, elders in the market place, and even IDPs in some instances, the members of Adam's Youth Group are giving to others everything they've got.

Noted Freemason and American Civil War Confederate Officer Albert Pike once said, "What we have done for ourselves alone dies with us; what we have done for others and the world remains and is immortal." Those involved in drama, acting, and working to enlighten the lives of others give part of themselves to their community and to the continent. By sharing what they have, they ensure the provision of something wonderful to their greater community, and they may therefore leave something greater than themselves when they are gone. This drama club is an insightful and passionate group of youths who live in an unknown and misunderstood part of the world. They will not find themselves performing on a grand stage, and will likely not find themselves positioned in front of a news camera because of the good that they are doing. They do it all however because of what they perceive to be their mission: to improve the state of affairs in Kenya, and ensure that youths and those most vulnerable are not again swept up by negativity and led to war. These youths who have taken drama and personalized it to detail the unique Kenyan narrative have taken a step in the right direction and hope to change the world.

I cannot overstate the role this drama club has had in ensuring the success of this peacebuilding project. They have been dedicated and thorough with their planning and despite the fact that they are made up largely of members of one particular community, they have done excellent work in spreading out to different regions and including various individuals in all the work they do. The emails that they send and the messages they continuously post on Facebook make me laugh and give me a reason to breathe easy, as I feel that when the project is in their hands it will guide the way to future success. Though I often speak about the separate aspects of this peace project, whether it is the chicken farm, soccer tournament, drama club or high school peace clubs, I believe that in its entirety it is only successful when all these separate parts are each functioning effectively. It is for this reason that I am thrilled and proud to share the inspiration and the ambition that the members of Adam's Youth Group continue to exhibit, and I know that their continued work will help spread the word of peace throughout at least the Rift Valley Province of Kenya, if not more.

It was important to us as well to use the momentum felt by those youths assembled to spread the message to those most willing to listen, and with a poem in our minds and a vision driving our motions, we set our sights on Kenya's school system.

PEOPLE WHO PROMISE THINGS THEY DON'T FULFILL ARE LIKE CLOUDS THAT BRING NO RAIN

300 children swarmed me on my first visit to a school in Kenya. I honestly didn't really see it coming. Based on the looks and reactions that I got as the only white person walking around the village, I suppose it was to be expected. This swarming, and the subsequent touching of my arms, legs and whatever hair is to be found on my body quickly earned me the nickname "Obama". The one who gave me the nickname said, "Obama is a famous black politician amongst whites, and you are a famous white politician

amongst blacks!" Not quite famous, not quite a politician, and not quite used to all the touching, I didn't really have a choice, and so the swarming proceeded.

It was the day of our first attempt at a soccer tournament during my first visit to Kenya, and we were using the field of a local elementary school to hold the games. School respect and protocol are taken pretty seriously in Kenya, and any visit to the grounds of a school, especially from an eminent politician such as myself, requires the necessary visit to the headmaster's office for formal introductions, the obligatory signing of the guest book, and a tour of the school's facilities. When we arrived at this school just down the road from Kiptere, we walked through the gate and into the main dirt driveway. The buildings were laid out in a sort of L-shape, with rows of classrooms jutting out from a central hub area, which was where the main administrative offices were. This school was built of bricks, concrete and tin roofs. Because our first task was to go and meet with the headmaster, it meant that I had to literally cross through the centre of the school, where 300 schoolchildren just happened to look out of their classroom windows at the same time to see me: A white guy, wearing shorts and a t-shirt, showing as much whiteness as possible, before they jumped out of their desks and swarmed.

Before I knew it they were all around me. Everywhere. The faster kids had obviously reached me first, but they stopped short about a meter away, slowed down, and then approached slowly. To show respect to someone that they are meeting for the first time, a traditional Kenyan greeting is to extend their right hand to greet you, while they place their left hand on their right wrist as they shake your hand.

These children all did just this. Amidst their excitement, and after shaking my hand, they went on to then quickly cop a feel of my own wrist, then arms, then legs, and for the taller ones . . . the hair on my head. I had no idea what was going on with all the touching until I realized that, and please excuse my bluntness, I just had more body hair than anyone else there did! They did not have hair on their arms or legs and I would say 99% of the students, both male and female, had shaved heads, so I could understand why they wanted a feel. This whole experience made me burst into a sort of giddy giggle, and as we pushed our way through the swaths of students, I quickly tried to compose myself before we reached the headmaster's office. Once we arrived at his door he stepped outside and in an instant, the students were all back sitting at their desks. I should also mention that some of them must have been holding pieces of my leg hair when they got back to their classes, because I definitely felt them pulling it out as I forced my way through the crowd and remember thinking "OW! WHY ARE THEY STEALING MY LEG HAIR???"

As I arrived at this headmaster's office I went through a series of steps that would be repeated at every school that I subsequently visited throughout my project. I, along with what would become my posse of at least six others, would sit on the porch of the school while the headmaster was informed of our arrival. Then, after waiting the requisite ten minutes (which I am now sure was simply a display of some sort of power) I would be shown into the office. The headmaster would then get his staff to scramble and find us seven suitable chairs, despite the lack of space. After having some tea together and chatting about the weather (and watching his reaction when I told him how cold Canada can get in February), I would tell the headmaster why we were here. On this day we were here to play a soccer tournament, but attendance at other schools would involve both soccer and then later, the creation of high school peace clubs.

Visiting these schools was an experience that I came to increasingly enjoy at every opportunity. Though the experience of being rushed by all those students did not actually happen at every other school, visiting these first few gave me insight into yet another aspect of Kenyan society in these rural regions. Though many of the villages that I either stayed in or visited were not what one would call the most attractive of locations, the schools always made a great effort to ensure that the grounds were immaculate. For the most part, the grass was cut, there were flowers and plants around the entrance as well as a large engraved sign with the name of the school. The school's motto was emblazoned on the various paintings and murals throughout the school grounds. What they valued most in the education system was visible on all the walls of the buildings. Visiting these schools made clear to me the importance placed on education in these communities, and it made me value the opportunities and experiences available to me in my youth that much more.

The students at each school wore a uniform, and most were only able to each afford one. Their uniforms were bright and clean, and the amount and type of clothing that made up a uniform varied from elementary to high school. In the elementary schools, students usually wore a button down shirt with a sweater over it, and a pair of shorts that were either khaki or matched the colour of the sweater. I assume they did not always wear the sweater on hotter days. In the high schools, students wore white shirts with ties, and sweaters if it was cold, as well as grey pants for the boys, and skirts for the girls. The uniforms were almost always clean, and I was told that usually what happened was that students would get home and wash their uniforms immediately, so that by the time they had to get dressed in the morning, they were dry, clean and ready to be worn again. They would then get dressed and walk the necessary five to ten kilometers to school every morning and afternoon. The uniform colours, as I said, were vivid and bright, and some schools wore royal blue sweaters with yellow button down shirts; others wore hunter green sweaters and pale green shirts, purple shirts and white shirts, or burgundy and yellow uniforms which, yes, vaguely matched the uniform most often associated with Gryffindor House and Harry Potter. The cleanliness and order that these uniforms exuded added to how impressed I was with each visit to these schools.

Sometimes when one walked across the school grounds, there was a mural on the side of the main building. These paintings were also done with vivid colours and were by no means roughly done. Whether they were done by professional painters or gifted students is irrelevant, as the message conveyed by these paintings shows what kind of an institution one will find beyond that wall.

Many of these murals show either a map of Kenya itself, or a map of Africa as a whole. On one building at a school that I visited, there was on the right side of the wall a giant yellow map of Africa, with each country outlined and identified. It also included the location and name of each capital city. To the far left of the wall there was a mural of a Middle-Eastern looking man wearing the garb of a shepherd, holding a long staff in his right hand and a smaller stick in his left. Behind him were mountains and a herd of sheep following him, and I assume that this was either supposed to be a depiction of Moses or Jesus, as above him there was the phrase "The LORD is my Shepherd". Maybe it was God, but it was probably Jesus. Anyway, here was the always present religious imagery that many of these schools placed front and centre, and in the middle of these paintings was written, "School Motto, Mission and Vision: Motto—Simplicity High Learning; Mission—To promote individual development and self fulfillment in education; Vision—Provision of knowledge and holistic skills for the child." I loved this. I just thought it was so gratifying to see a description of the school written in plain (though quite advanced) English clearly on the front of the school. Maybe it's just me, but I find this is much more effective than the Latin mottos that so many schools in Europe and North America adopt and that the vast majority of the students likely do not understand at all. Here was the mission clearly enunciated in front of me, set clearly in the context of Africa (the map) and religion (the picture of Moses/Jesus . . . . Mosus?).

As a matter of fact I found this artwork at almost every school we visited, and found it not only at the entrances but also on buildings throughout the grounds of these institutions. Though the motto, mission and vision were directed at visitors or potential attendees of the institution, the messages varied on the paintings that were found within the school grounds. These messages focused more particularly on concepts such as the importance of knowledge, education and the ever-looming topic of safe sex.

At one school that we visited in Matongo I found a huge mural painted on the side of the library which was signed "By, Matongo Health Club", titled "Still a Youth? Education First, Sex to Wait Till Marriage." This mural was designed as a sort of cartoon strip, with four boxes arranged as a square. In the middle of the painting, in big red underlined letters, was the word "ABSTAIN."

In the top left box there was a painting of a teacher standing under a large tree speaking to a group of students sitting at her feet. There was a word bubble coming from her mouth that said, "Irresponsible sex leads to STIs, HIV and AIDS." The words STIs, HIV, and AIDS were painted in red while the rest of the text was black. In the box on the top right there was a picture of a man and a woman who were angry. The woman was walking ahead of the man. The man was saying "Upuuzi!" which translated roughly means "stupidity", while the woman was saying "Nonsense!" I read this as meaning that these adults did not believe in the dangers associated with irresponsible sex, and had turned their backs on these warnings. In the bottom left box there was a picture of a disgruntled man sitting at a table that had a water jug and a glass on it. He had his elbow on the table and his head resting in his hand, and he is saying, "I have AIDS, I have no future." Finally in the box on the bottom right there were two despairing adults who were thin and unhealthy, standing in front of two graves marked with bright red crosses. These two adults were saying in unison, "AIDS, I wish I knew!"

This was a striking painting and because it was placed in the middle of a high school it made me further realize the importance of educating students from the youngest of ages about this scourge of Africa. They clearly don't tip-toe around these issues the way we do in other parts of the world.

Other painted signs around the school spoke of knowledge and understanding. On the side of one building was painted the word LIBRARY, and underneath was a verse from Proverbs 2:6, which said, "For the Lord gives wisdom, and from His mouth comes knowledge and understanding." I found other signs with all sorts of messages, and these painted pictures and signs became a way for me to distinctly remember each individual school.

The first task for the newly formed Youth Ambassadors for Peace was to travel to a few different high schools in the area around Sondu and establish peace clubs. Thinking about what they were going to do in their newly established organization, this seemed like an obvious first step. It was a project that they could initiate on their own; it figured within the overall goals of youth empowerment and school clubs are somewhat easy to set up and maintain. What we needed to do was choose some high schools, visit them, speak to the students, and encourage them to volunteer to take charge. The role of the Youth Ambassadors was going to be to help facilitate these groups, give the students ideas, and offer guidance so that peace projects could be initiated and executed by younger Kenyans who could use their school as an instant support structure.

The visits to establish these high school peace clubs were different from other visits because I was attending with the group of youths with whom I had just shared the peace-training workshop, and there were many of us. Nonetheless these visits required the mandatory meeting with the headmaster who wanted us to meet both with him and then with his other staff who would be found in the school's staff room when they were not conducting lessons in their own classrooms.

I usually told the headmasters about the nature of the project that we had initiated and who the youths were that had accompanied me. I told them about our goals and the tribal makeup of the group, and for the most part they seemed impressed. These were small communities and some of the high schools we visited were chosen particularly because a participant of the group attended one of the schools, and so the headmaster liked the idea of promoting a project that included an alumnus of his. A number of them again insisted on taking me on a tour of the school and wanted to tell me about the curriculum, how the school operated, and the number of students from each tribe who attended the school. Many of the schools, located in central areas, had students attend from an array of different communities, and I was therefore curious to find out how these tribal tensions found expression in high schools. The headmaster at the school in Sondu ensured me that there were no visible tensions on school grounds, but that he could obviously not control what was done or said at home. At another school where we spoke however, the headmaster promised me that as a result of our visit, "From now on, our teachers will ensure that the students know that they are brothers and sisters."

At a school we visited in Chabera, in the midst of a region that was primarily Kisii, I was told that many families had stayed on the grounds of this school when their houses were burned down during the post-election violence. As attacks were not isolated to one community, it meant that families from a variety of tribes, now essentially refugees and IDPs, slept at a school, living together. It was difficult to imagine people living on the grounds of a school that was obviously a location with limited living resources, but this only added to my understanding of how quickly society fell apart both during and in the aftermath of the violence. The classrooms were used to house families, their kitchens were used to cook food for dozens, but most importantly, their grounds were used as a sort of way to unite people at a time when they would not have otherwise come together. On the fields of these schools, citizens were able to meet and realize that they had both become victims of a senseless hatred. I heard stories about those who learned much from members of other communities despite all the differences and prejudices that had previously kept them apart. This was an incredible thought: people brought together because of violence intended to tear them apart.

I visited the staff room at each school and was invited to meet and shake hands with every teacher in the four schools in which we were planning to work. Each staff room looked the same: A wooden building with a tin roof. Around the walls were motivational posters, similar to the kind you would find, for example, of a cat hanging from a branch saying "Hang in there!" There were other posters about reaching for success, planning for the future, and posters that talked about HIV/AIDS and how to prevent its spread. Each teacher's desk had piles of paper on it consisting of tests, essays and class exercises. There was little room left on these desks for the teachers to actually do their grading, but there they sat, working diligently. Also, they each had room on their desks for a mug of tea and perhaps a small fried pastry.

In this particular staff room, above the blackboard at the front, was a big banner that read, "People who promise things they don't fulfill are like clouds that bring no rain." I liked this message in its particular setting. Firstly, I liked the idea that here, clouds weren't a bad thing. At home if it's cloudy, it's considered miserable. Here, if it's cloudy, it means it is going to rain, and in an agricultural setting, that means food! At home we see clouds and hope they dissipate soon so that the sun can come back out. In Africa, they hope that the clouds are not just out to tease them, and they see clouds for their practical value, as potentially providing that which they require for their everyday life: water. The first part of this message was further important because it talked about making promises in the context of a school. I liked the idea that the teachers were, in essence, being told that they were making promises to their students. Whatever those promises were, the reality was that teachers are mandated to promise their students something, whatever that something is. I think this is an inspirational line to have hanging up in the room where teachers make their decisions about what they are going to impart to their students on any particular day.

Henry Brooks Adams, an early American journalist and academic, once wrote: "A teacher affects eternity; he can never tell where his influence stops." When I started high school I made the decision that I really wanted to become a teacher. I loved the idea of being able to teach others and join in their educational experience. As an historian at heart, I really looked up to my high school history teachers; I wanted to emulate them and inspire other students the way they had inspired me. I remember actually finding a few quotes about teachers and the above quote by Adams always stuck with me. To me, it illustrated the truth that teachers have the ability to shape their students in ways that others simply cannot. Teachers are not meant to give their students a particular outlook on life nor are they mandated to necessarily shape their students in any particular way. They are merely supposed to help their students develop the skills that are required for a successful future, and help foster in each of their pupils the ability to inquire, speak up, raise their hand, and be confident with their future decisions. It is in this context, of the power of the teacher and the importance of the school environment, that I found deep meaning in the idea that teachers are making a promise to their students.

Even, but perhaps especially, in these small wooden schoolhouses in rural Kenya, teachers are giving their students the skills required to become something in the world. These educators are supposed to inspire their students to ensure they have the confidence in their own capabilities so that they can graduate and go on to alter both their own and others' futures. In looking at the message hanging over a blackboard, the teacher is exactly like a cloud, and where a cloud gives rain, a teacher follows through on that promise to educate his or her students and prepares them to make decisions in the future. It was this idea of a promise that also encouraged me to incorporate these schools, and their youths, into our peacebuilding project. And yes, I may have made the career change to law, and no, I probably cannot find the same inspiring words to describe lawyers or the legal profession, but most of my friends today are teachers. Knowing who they are and what they do, I maintain that teachers are by far the most valuable assets in society (and they are not given nearly the amount of credit that they deserve).

When I walked into the staff room with the headmaster, many of the students were getting lunch at the school (food is provided for them at many of the schools in the region), the teachers were diligently sitting at their desks either marking, reading, or chatting with one another. The headmaster announced our entrance, at which point each teacher politely stood up, and I was asked to walk around and shake hands with each of them. I noticed that most of the teachers were middle aged. There was one younger female teacher, who was probably around my age, and I was surprised to find two male teachers as well. I had somehow just gotten the impression that in Kenya, it was mainly girls who went on to become teachers. I was later corrected and told that there were always a number of male teachers at every school.

I sat and spoke to these teachers for a few minutes about what I was doing in Kenya and why we had come to their school. I told them about the soccer tournament and about the workshop that had been held, and I told them that the purpose of our project was to bring people together and inspire peace. I told them that I wanted their students to play a role in our project. I shared my belief that I felt that students are never too young to learn about peace and that at any age, they can comprehend the simple message that people working together results in a more successful future than when citizens are divided along illogical and irrational lines. When I had finished speaking, the teachers each took turns expressing their enthusiasm for our project and asked me how they could help. This was a positive step in the right direction, and they invited us to speak to a few of their classes and establish these peace clubs.

We intended these clubs to be run by a group of student volunteers who would organize different programs on campus at various times. After speaking to some of the teachers, I discovered that there was actually a very strong club-presence in many of these schools, and though many were sports-related, there would probably be students interested in helping to run these peace clubs too. The teachers related stories to us about their students and how they had personally experienced the post-election violence. They told us that, as a result of these shared experiences, the students would be more than enthusiastic about getting involved in such an endeavour.

I personally went with the Youth Ambassadors for Peace to four different schools: Kiptere Primary, Ongera Primary, Crystal Hill School, and Sondu Primary School. In each school we met with students of varying ages, and in each school we met in a different type of setting. In the first school we spoke to the students while sitting in a shaded field under some trees where they all sat on the grass. In the second, we spoke to them in a classroom, standing at the board while each of them sat at their own desks. At the third school we met in an empty room which was suddenly filled with students who each had to bring their own chair to come and listen to us speak. In the fourth school we stood speaking to the students from the porch outside the administrative offices, while 700 students brought chairs from their classrooms, and sat lined up in front of us in their bright green uniforms. Although each school offered a different setting, a different combination of tribes present and differing goals and aspirations of students, the one element that these schools all shared was that, at the end of each presentation, we were able to find a solid group of eager students who were prepared to help spread the message of peace throughout their own school.

Another reason for setting up these clubs, aside from getting young students to help us in our mission, was to test the newly minted Youth Ambassadors for Peace. After spending a week training them and hearing what they had to say, I wanted them to get to work and start putting to use what they had learned.

Obviously, I have no credentials to run an actual peacebuilding workshop, and they knew that from the beginning. However, passion, creativity, and a few good books laid the groundwork for the workshop and we were all pretty happy with the results. When I asked them what they wanted to do after the workshop concluded, the youths themselves suggested these peace clubs. My intended role when we went to visit these schools was just to sit and watch the youths with whom I had worked engage these younger students and attempt to convey the message that we had crafted within our group.

The Youth Ambassadors for Peace were charged with spreading a peaceful message in their own and each other's communities, and these peace clubs would be their first opportunity. Each visit to a school was run by a smaller group, since we could not have all 25 of them speaking at every school. The way that each visit was structured was planned by the youths without any input or guidance from me. They spent time talking to large groups of students at each school and it is perhaps fitting here to share with you some of the insights that were shared by these young students. I believe this material is valuable because it shows a deep understanding of what is so wrong in Kenya that even these youngest of citizens can feel it. What we heard from these students, who went on to help form these high school youths clubs, exemplified the insight and passion that the youngest of any society possess, and demonstrates the "Generational Fortitude" that can be found even in schools made of nothing but wooden walls and tin roofs.

The first question that was asked whenever we met with a new group of students in any school was always "Is there peace in Kenya?" This entire project, of course, was premised on the idea that there was not. Being tasked with answering this specific question means defining peace, and identifying whether that particular brand of peace is present. The question was asked and we were always astounded by the thoughtful responses that we received. These are some of their thoughts:

No, there is not peace in Kenya because: there are political issues that divide the entire country such as disputes and rivalries; there is complaining about corruption; there is violence after elections that kills people; there is racism and tribalism; there is insecurity amongst people of different tribes; there are thugs that beat others up if they disagree with their politics; we do not love each other; we have enemies, like Kibaki and Raila.

A few students said that there was peace in Kenya, and they said that there was peace because there was not currently any violence and that tribes could get along. One student told us that there was peace because he was able to go and buy a chicken from his Kalenjin neighbour and that he did not have to be afraid, while another said, "Yes, there is peace, because we are together here today with you." This exercise was a useful way to gauge the viewpoints of many of the students, and it was a way for the youths running the actual sessions to get started with community service and leadership in a comfortable setting.

Gordon, one of the youth leaders, liked to ask the students to define peace. He would get up, wearing his brown suit and green tie that he wore each day of the workshop and to the school visit, and ask the students, "How, ladies and gentlemen, do you define peace?" This was the sort of question that would elicit a great response from the students involved, and each had their own perception of what peace was. It also shed light on the values and perspectives of the younger generation.

They said that peace is: when people live together in harmony with each other; taking care of the environment; something you cannot do without; something that needs to be owned by looking at yourself first; a condition that enables us to improve our own economic status; a trend that encourages unity and understanding; living together to be one. One student stood up and declared that, "When there is peace, we can build our country," while another told us that, "We have a right to education, a right to work in unity, and a right to live in peace." After asking this question, Gordon thanked them for their input and told them that each of their definitions was important because it gave peace many different meanings, and concluded by telling them that, "Like Americans, we must become one." I told you Obama had a ridiculous amount of influence.

In some of these sessions Kepha would stand up to speak to the youths, and in his deep voice, with a big smile on his face, he would ask them what they could each personally do to make peace. The number one answer each time: Pray. As powerful an answer as this usually was, we of course wanted some more practical plans to be laid out, and so the students said they would make peace by: respecting each other; reconciling with other communities; actually going to other communities to show that they are friendly neighbours; encouraging intermarriage (and not fighting in-laws who are from other communities); participating in civic education; and understanding that our differences are unique and beautiful. One of the older students with whom we were speaking stood up and said, "We have to love each other because, from the beginning of the world, there were two people: Adam and Eve. Were they tribal? No, and so these tribes should not divide us either."

Kepha would then continue with his questions and ask, "What would happen to our beautiful Kenya if there was peace?" The students responded that there would be development; there would be more freedom of movement; people would be more willing to share ideas with each other; they would be happy; there would be no war, no violence, and no discrimination; incitement would end. It dawned on me that their words, their ideas, were universal and spoke to the desires that anyone, anywhere in the world, would want. They are also ideas that were echoed in the peace treaty we drafted just days earlier as a group that encouraged Kenyans to live together peacefully as one. The fact that those who had drafted the treaty were now teaching a crowd of students with the exact same dreams and desires spoke tremendously to the capability of all those who came together for change.

The answers and comments we received from the student participants were remarkable. The students at these schools realized that they made up the largest demographic grouping in Kenya, and they understood that they had a role to play in the future of their country. They vowed that the mission of these peace clubs was to get Kenyans to love each other, and one student even said, "We are each passing by in this world, so we have to leave it a better place than how we found it." The students talked about tribalism and how there are stereotypes, but instead of focusing on the negative aspects of these differences they said that differences should unite the country. Another student said, "We must think about the strengths of each community: the Kalenjin can bring milk; the Kisii can bring bananas; and the Luo can bring chicken and fish," to which Kepha declared, "and then we can all have a delicious supper together!" This comment was met with a roar of laughter throughout the group, and exemplified the unity that is most often found in these school settings.

At the close of each session, two of the youth leaders would then announce that our goal was to create a peace club, and they would outline what the expectation of these clubs would be. They told the students that they were looking for volunteers to help run clubs on their own campuses, and reassured the students that the youths who had spoken to them that day would be coming by frequently to help and give them ideas on how to succeed. We had decided that we were looking for 16 volunteers from each school to form these clubs, and reaching this number was not difficult at all. As we saw the hands go up, we went around collecting the names of the volunteers to use both for their own purposes and also to give to the school administrators, so that these students could be recognized for their participation and desire to get involved in extra-curricular activities. Once each list was collected, we asked the volunteers to come to the side to get their picture taken, and we asked the headmaster to close the session with some words or a brief prayer.

While listening to these sessions and furiously trying to write down whatever I could, I always tried to glance over at the headmaster and at the teachers standing behind their students listening to what was being said. It was a different sort of setting and students are often, in all cultures, more comfortable saying certain things to others that they are uncomfortable saying to their teachers. I wondered what those educators thought about this exercise and what they were feeling as a result. Were they surprised by what their students were saying? Were these ideas ones they had heard before? Were they looking at their students through a tribal prism or were they simply looking at a group of students who were proud of what they were able to produce?

I spoke to some of the teachers as we wrapped up our seminars and many were pleased by the results of our visit. Though the headmasters generally remained aloof and distant, they thanked the participants of the workshop for coming and gave them some words of advice for the future. I watched as the teachers approached the ambassadors with a trace of elation in each of their smiles, and thanked them for conducting this exercise. It seemed that although these teachers, who were meant to be teaching math, science, English, Swahili, or religious studies, tended to remain on topic, seeing their students address issues that were not typically spoken about in a classroom made them proud that those whom they had been educating were taking this education to heart. They told the ambassadors that at various times they had a chance to see their students exemplify different characteristics that they did not always see expressed in the classroom, and that the sessions we had been running gave them the opportunity to see their students as something more than just students. One teacher even told Kepha that he had seen the future of Kenya in our seminar that day, and that it had made him optimistic about what the future holds. "We pray to God to give us *amani* (peace)" that same teacher later told me, and he shared with me the sense of excitement and pride that he felt while watching his students at work. He was thrilled that so many of them had volunteered to help start the peace club at his school, and said that he would do whatever he could to ensure the group's successes.

The Youth Ambassadors for Peace have been keen facilitators of these peace clubs and I often receive photographs taken on their visits to watch these clubs in action. The photos I receive show pictures of Kenyan students sitting diligently at their desks, in their clean white shirts, ties, and grey pants, holding signs they have just made. Some signs ask, "Is there peace in Kenya?", "What will I do to make peace in Kenya?", and some appeal directly to me, asking "Mr. Adam Hummel, why did you want to make a peace project in Kenya?" These signs make me proud of the Youth Ambassadors and make me think, even more than some of the other projects we are involved with, about why this all began.

Despite my time spent in Kenya, I still often feel like I am completely clueless about the situation on the ground there. It is not easy for an outsider from Canada to understand the history, culture, nuances, transportation, traditions and practices from spending just two months there. I know that there is conflict and there is hatred, but I share the belief with others that the most effective way to understand a situation is through the eyes of the younger generation. The answers that we received from the students we met all had one thing in common: honesty. They were not there to impress anyone (as they were not speaking to their teachers), nor did they necessarily stand to gain anything from raising one type of question over another. We stood there and asked these students bluntly what they thought was wrong, and they suggested to us not only what they thought was wrong with Kenya, but what they thought was the best way that they personally could take a role in helping. If I were to answer the question that they posed to me, I would say that this is the reason why I chose to do this: to enable them to enunciate these goals in their own words, and then work towards that goal on their own. These school sessions, like so many other aspects of the project, did not require me to have any guiding role, as once they got started it was abundantly clear that they were able to do this on their own. If it was a boost that I was able to offer, then that is what I was there trying to do, and if it was the money that I was able to raise, then that is what I would commit myself to finding for them. The impetus for this project however, and the idea for it in general, came from the youths themselves who felt that creating these clubs was the best way to instill the values of peace and hope in the younger generation.

On these visits, the Youth Ambassadors for Peace themselves actually became teachers, if only for a short time, and if I may say so, they excelled. They excited the students involved, got them thinking, encouraged them to volunteer, and pushed them to step up for both their own and their country's futures. The renowned historian Jacques Barzun once said, "In teaching you cannot see the fruit of a day's work. It is invisible and remains so, maybe for twenty years." I hope that this 'twenty years' is not quite that long, and that hopefully the Youth Ambassadors will be able to see the fruits of their work by the time the next general election comes around in March 2013. In the meantime however, the continued facilitation of these clubs and the effort that goes into making sure that students turn their attention to both academic and non-academic issues is the process of planting seeds that will one day bear the fruit that will assist Kenya's future. At the time of writing, we have set up clubs in 8 different schools and are looking to expand. Seeing the conflict through the eyes of the students was one of the most insightful and valuable exercises of this entire endeavour, and the work that these clubs continue to do is yet another integral part of a grassroots movement designed to shape and improve the future of Kenya.

LIKE CUTTING DOWN A TREE
WITH A RAZOR BLADE

Being a part of the small Jewish community of the world means that wherever you go it's nice to discover other Jews. Being Jewish guarantees a bond with another Jew, no matter where in the world you are, and this is the result of the Jewish population today numbering only approximately 13 million. Even if you grow up in an extremely Jewish community, like I did in Toronto, when you travel and find another Jew or find a small Jewish community somewhere unexpected, I have always found that your Jewish identity suddenly emerges. You come to appreciate the fact that Judaism is not simply a religion, but that it is what people always say it is: a community, a history, a heritage, a culture, and a link with the past. Even if you do not identify with the Jewish community as much as your mother would like you to, as soon as you see a synagogue in a foreign city, or spot a Hasidic Jew walking around, in a way it may seem to relax you, and that's how I feel. I expected my experience in Kenya to be a number of things, but Jewish was not one of them.

My experience with Judaism in Kenya had two distinct parts. The first is my visit to the synagogue in Nairobi. My second experience was totally different and removed from the typical-visit-a-synagogue-in-a-foreign-city experience. It took place in my small, quiet village of Kiptere, in a school classroom to be exact, on a Saturday morning. This experience involved me being asked the questions, and was indicative to me not only of my knowledge, but also of my faith. This was an entirely unexpected experience of my visit but was however one that I will not soon forget.

On one of my first days in Kenya I was wandering through Nairobi trying to find the supplies I needed for the bulk of the peace project. This shopping spree involved heading mainly to stationary stores, bookstores and even some grocery stores, which took me all over Nairobi. While walking around accompanied by my friend Cecilia, I had suddenly remembered that someone had mentioned something to me about a synagogue in Nairobi. I asked Cecilia (Ces) if she knew where it was, and she told me that it was around the corner from where we were. We then quickly made our way over there, concerned that it had already closed as a result of the late hour. Fortunately, we made it on time. This short trek necessarily involved jumping over some fences, running across streets narrowly avoiding being hit by buses and taxis, all while schlepping my bag full of stationary.

Nairobi is a city that is busy, bustling, dirty, filled with people, and vibrant. There are parts of the city that are not really recommended to visit since Kibera, one of Africa's biggest slums, is a suburb of Nairobi. Some places are affluent and taken care of while others are slums, dirty, and attract people you typically would not want to bump into on your way to synagogue. Like London for example, in Nairobi you tend to walk, get lost, and just follow the roads. This means that you never really know where you will end up, which can be good or bad depending on that ultimate destination. This area I had not yet been to and it was near the University of Nairobi. As we approached the area everything seemed a little quieter, a little calmer, a little safer, a little cleaner, and a little nicer.

What I expected of the synagogue based on the rest of the city and what I imagined the condition of a sub-continental African synagogue to look like was not what I found. What I discovered suddenly was a huge piece of land, surrounded by a ten-foot wall with security, sitting within the lushest looking garden I had seen in the city. As I approached the main gates I spotted a giant sign on the wall that read "THE NAIROBI SYNAGOGUE", not hiding anything, and we made our way to the security gate.

As is the case with most synagogues today, there was a security team tasked with protecting what looked to be a Jewish fortress. As I walked over to the security desk with Ces, three men quickly stood up to greet us. I approached, said hello, and asked if it was possible to go inside and see the grounds of the synagogue. The conversation went something like this:

Adam: *Habari*! I was wondering if it would be possible to see the synagogue.
Guard: (Looks me up and down, stares at me straight in the eyes) Are you Jewish?
Adam: Yes sir I am (smile).
Guard: Can I see your passport?
Adam: It says I'm Canadian, not Jewish, but umm sure! Here you go.

Guard: Ok (flips through pages). No one is here.

Adam: Can't I just take a walk around? I just want to take some pictures and see what the building looks like?

Guard: Let me go find out.

Cecilia (to the other guard): Why so much security for a synagogue? We don't have this sort of security at churches.

Guard: Everyone hates them (pointing at me). Just ask him (pointing at me again).

Adam: (Turning to face Cecilia) Well . . . he's not totally wrong . . .

Guard: We've found someone to show you around. His name is Harrison. Leave your bag here.

The gates opened up, and standing in front of us was Harrison. He was Kenyan, probably around 5-feet tall, and has worked at the synagogue for 30 years. A local from Nairobi, he has initially sought employment at the synagogue primarily because he needed a job, but soon his love began to grow, as he said, for the Jews of Nairobi. Twenty years is a long time to work anywhere let alone a synagogue and in that time he had picked up lots about the religion, customs and institution which he increasingly found himself to be a part of.

As we walked into the grounds of the property, we were greeted with a garden. The first fun fact I learned from Harrison is that the gardens of the Nairobi Synagogue were once voted the most beautiful synagogue gardens in the world, and it's instantly clear why (plus I never realized that there was a group who voted on the world's top synagogue gardens). Inside the garden are palm trees creating an almost ceiling over the entire property with acacias and other trees stretching their limbs out over you like outstretched hands. On the ground there are shrubs, rose bushes, thick green African grass and a stone path laid into the ground that leads from building to building.

You can immediately see four buildings, a parking lot, a basketball court, a playground, and an open grassy area. Aside from what I saw, I was also struck suddenly by what I heard: nothing. In the middle of noisy Nairobi there was suddenly less noise and less chaos, and it seemed like I had just stepped into another part of the country.

The first building that I was taken to was a banquet hall called the Vermont Memorial Hall. A typical white little building with a hall inside, it had some chairs still set up with balloons and posters about Israel on the walls. I was told that there had been a party in the banquet hall a few days prior to my visit for *Yom Haatzmaut*, Israel's Independence Day, and that the Jewish community had been celebrating all night. Though information about this synagogue is difficult to find, there is a website for it (http://www.nhc.co.ke) which explains a number of interesting facts about the various buildings. The Vermont Memorial Hall, which I was currently standing in, was built in 1938 and to the best of anyone's knowledge Simon Vermont was a member of the Nairobi Jewish community in the 1930s who sat on the building committee of this soon to be built banquet hall. When he passed away he gave his downtown Nairobi property to the building fund of the synagogue, which essentially financed the building of the new hall. It was Simon's brother Isaac who suggested that the hall be named after him.

The information about this hall and the party for Israel's independence led me to my first questions for Harrison: how many Jews are there in Nairobi? And where did they come from?

Harrison told me that the Jewish community in Nairobi is made up of approximately 300 to 400 people. This number, primarily made up Canadians, Americans, Israelis, and Britons, fluctuates significantly, but the approximate number stays the same. They all come from a variety of backgrounds and though many are in Nairobi on business, the Jewish community in Nairobi is already over 100 years old.

Actually, maybe at this point I can provide a quick overview of the history Nairobi's Jews.

Political Zionism was born in the late 1890s by a man named Theodore Herzl. In 1895 the Dreyfus affair was unfolding in France whereby Alfred Dreyfus, a Jewish member of the French military had been accused of spying for Germany. Overwhelming numbers of the French population let loose some outrageous anti-Semitism as a result, and many of France's Jews were harassed and assaulted, being made to feel entirely uncomfortable in the country where they had, for the most part, assimilated into the general population. In the courtyard of the École Militaire in Paris on January 5, 1895 in front of hundreds of onlookers, Alfred Dreyfus had been found guilty of espionage against the Government of France, was stripped of his military credentials, and sent to prison. Among the onlookers in the crowd on the Champ de Mars was Theodore Herzl, a young Jewish Viennese newspaper reporter who made the stark realization that

Jews were not safe in Western Europe and therefore needed a homeland of their own. In 1896 Herzl published a book entitled *Der Judenstaat*, which called for the creation of a Jewish homeland in Palestine, the historic homeland of the Jewish people. In 1897 the First Zionist Congress was convened in Basle, Switzerland and political Zionism was born.

The Third Zionist Congress in 1900 proposed the plan that the Jewish state perhaps not be established in what was then Palestine. As a result of pressure from the Ottoman Turks who at the time ruled the entire Levant, a potential alternative location was proposed: Uganda (and part of what is now Kenya). In response to this potential arrangement, at the Sixth Zionist Congress in 1903, the British colonial secretary Joseph Chamberlain actually offered the necessary land in Uganda and Kenya to the nascent Zionists. At almost the instant of this suggestion, a number of eager European Jews picked up their scant belongings and traveled all the way to Eastern Africa to help establish what they hoped would soon become a Jewish state (perhaps they wanted to make sure they at least had some streets named after them too).

History telling us the rest, the "Uganda Plan" of course was quickly dropped and the land of Palestine was ultimately chosen to be the home of the Jewish State. Probably feeling pretty abandoned these early Jewish settlers remained in Kenya however and carved out a small home for themselves in the midst of Nairobi, a city that was at the time a large British trading centre in East Africa. By 1913 there were only approximately 20 Jewish families living in Kenya, but as World War Two approached a larger number of Jews escaped Europe to East Africa. The population grew further following the Holocaust at a time when Jews did not feel welcome back in their original European cities, and so the Jewish community in Kenya started therefore to expand.

It was the original eager families who headed down to what would later become Kenya who built the synagogue I was now standing in. Two founding stones lay near the entrance of the actual synagogue building. The first reads "Nairobi Hebrew Congregation Founded 1904". The second is inscribed with, "This foundation stone was laid by his Excellency the Acting Governor of the East African Protectorate Charles Calvert Bowring C.M.C. on Thursday June 20th, 1912." Here was the literal writing-on-the-wall about the foundations of this community and synagogue, and as a history student it truly moved me. My knowledge of Zionism has always been the culmination in the State of Israel, and the Uganda Plan is always regarded as a sort of Plan B that was quickly discarded. I did not realize however how quickly people had acted on the option and that it had even been a legitimate offer from the colonial powers in East Africa at the time. In a sense it proved to me the desperation that some of the Jews were obviously feeling as early as the beginning of the 20th century to find a place to belong, coming at a time well before atrocities like the Holocaust could even have been contemplated. Seeing the foundation stones and what would follow truly left an impression on me of how Judaism is a religion that can grow and flourish almost anywhere in the world.

As we entered into the main sanctuary of the synagogue complex I was impressed by how modern it was, having just read that it was founded in 1912. I found out though that in the 1950s there had been some renovations done to the building and that there was now constant upkeep of the building.

I was intrigued when entering by how much it looked like any other synagogue sanctuary that I am used to seeing in Toronto. It is laid out approximately 20 rows of seats facing the front with an aisle down the centre. On both side of these rows is a short wall, and behind that wall there are three rows on either side facing the centre. This mirrored most Orthodox synagogues where men and women sit separately, and here in the middle of Nairobi it was no different.

At the front of the sanctuary there was the main stage, or *bima*, and at the wall was the ark in which the Torah scrolls are housed. As it is the tradition of facing Jerusalem to pray, this ark was facing north, as opposed to east, which is what I am used to from North America. The windows of the synagogue were stain glass, and the larger windows depicted traditional visions from the Bible such as the burning bush that Moses found or the rainbow that God showed Noah when the flooding of the world has subsided. Around the rim of the ceiling there were 12 smaller windows, each with the name of one of the 12 tribes of Israel written on it in Hebrew with a picture logo of each tribe.

The building was spacious, and I could almost feel what it would be like to join a service in this sanctuary on one of the holidays. Harrison gave me the chance to look around and explore, and I took some time to explain some of the customs and traditions, as well as parts of the religion to Cecilia. Harrison stood on and watched, nodding his head every time I said something that he either agreed with or already knew. I also found out from Harrison that there is no permanent Rabbi in Nairobi, but a visiting Rabbi from America conducts High Holiday services for the Jewish New Year and Yom Kippur.

The synagogue's website contains some interesting information about the history and the roots of the synagogue. Though the website is not frequently updated, the information it does contain speaks to what sort of a community there is in Nairobi.

In the section titled "News and Events" (updated 2005) there are details about births, celebrations and deaths. A look at the surnames of those mentioned shows that there are Jews involved in the synagogue from all different parts of the world. There are many Israeli surnames but there are also a wide variety of more North American Jewish surnames. The births section says who was born and where they were born, and these locations include Nairobi, Israel, Canada and America. These same locations, including the United Kingdom, are mentioned in the weddings and deaths section.

There is a section that welcomes six new couples to the congregation, and says good-bye to seven couples who have recently left. In the section for family events there are seven bar or bat mitzvahs (for boys and girls) and even one first haircut (in Judaism one's first haircut is a big deal—we'll take any opportunity to make a huge meal). The section writes that at that moment of update in 2005, membership included 51 couples, 29 singles, and 62 children.

Most notably, to give some idea of the sorts of events that are held in the synagogue aside from the usual religious services, in 2005-2006 the synagogue held: a lecture on Yemen and Jewelry, an event held for the Israeli Rescue Unit that traveled to Nairobi to assist with the recent collapse of a building, an event to note the UN Commemoration of the Holocaust, a party to celebrate the holiday of Purim including a reading of the Book of Esther, and a Sabbath dinner at the Vermont Hall at which 90 guests were in attendance.

After the sanctuary, Harrison pointed out a building that was once used as a school for some younger kids, and then took me to see the *mikveh*, the ritual bath, which was found behind the sanctuary. The *mikveh* is used on all sorts of occasions in Judaism, such as before the holiest of holidays like the Day of Atonement (*Yom Kippur*); women use it before they get married and after they finish their menstrual cycle, and a variety of other purposes. I was extremely impressed that there was actually a *mikveh* built in this synagogue and when Harrison opened the door I was surprised to find it filled with water and ready to be used.

We left the *mikveh*, walked past a playground area that contained a *menorah*, traditional Jewish candelabra, made out of tree branches, and near the entrance a beautiful 4-foot tall Star of David made of glass and mosaic stood hanging within a metal frame.

As we wrapped up our tour and I was able to get in a few last questions about the synagogue, Ces suddenly turned to Harrison and said, "You seem to know so much about Judaism and the synagogue. Have you ever thought about converting to become Jewish?"

At this point, Harrison turned to her and pointed to a palm tree that we were now standing next to. Without stopping to think about an answer, he said, "you know, Judaism is a beautiful religion, but it is a hard religion. It requires much perseverance, dedication, and knowledge. I have thought about converting but it's very hard to be Jewish, right Adam? It's like trying to cut down this tree with a razor blade."

It was so interesting hearing Judaism described from this perspective, especially coming from someone helping a Jewish community in a seemingly far off land without too many Jews present. He just spent the last hour talking to me about the ins and outs of the religion, about the *mikveh,* about why there must be 10 adult males, a *minyan,* in order to make a proper Jewish prayer service, who the 12 tribes of Israel were, and the history of this synagogue. He appreciated the religion and understood many of its intricacies but also appreciated that Judaism, like every religion, required dedication, commitment, an understanding of the history, the faith, and an understanding of the consequences of becoming Jewish (aside from the, well, you know . . . snip snip).

As we left the grounds of the synagogue, I was invited to come to services on the coming Saturday morning. Though I was unable to attend that exact Saturday, I decided that when I was next in Nairobi in about four weeks' time, that I would try to make it for the service, which is what I did.

On that Saturday morning a few weeks later when I woke up to go to synagogue, two things were troubling me. The first was that I was going to try get downtown on my own, and I was worried about how long it would take and whether or not I would get lost in one of Africa's largest metropolitan cities. The second troubling thing was that after spending a month in a little rural village with no running water or electricity, I was a bit stumped as to what I could possibly wear to services. Hoping that the congregants would overlook my attire and rather appreciate the gesture of me trying to get to the service in any case, I put on the cleanest t-shirt I could find, a pair of cargo pants and running shoes, and went to find a *matatu* to take me to the synagogue.

I was told that the services started at 9:30 on a Saturday morning but when I approached the same security gate at 9:15, I was told that I was already an hour late for services and there was no point in me going in because they were wrapping up. After persisting to a number of people to be allowed in, them checking my religion in my passport again (which, again, was absent from the document) the security guards held onto my backpack again and I walked into the sanctuary and sat down at the back as quietly as possible.

I had not realized that the day I was there was actually a holiday called *Shavuot*. This holiday is the culmination of seven weeks of counting from the start of Passover to celebrate the day that the Jews who had just escaped from Egypt were given the Ten Commandments from God at Mount Sinai. This meant that there were more congregants than usual that morning, and my curiosity to see what kind of people attended this synagogue's services was finally satisfied.

As I sat down at the back corner of the last row I was thankful to realize that the service was only about half way through and that there was still plenty of time left. At the front leading the services were a group of men and by their accents it sounded like they were both American and British. There were a few Israelis (thankfully dressed similarly to the way I was), two girls who looked to be around the same age as me from North America, and to my surprise and delight, a local Kenyan family.

Sitting to my left were the elderly father and son, and the rest of the family was sitting in the women's section: the mother, her daughters, and their daughters. There is a popular story told about the fact that Jews are so different everywhere in the world. The story basically goes that there are a group of American businessmen on a trip to China and they decide to go to services on a Saturday morning at a synagogue in Beijing. As they are walking in, the visibly

Chinese rabbi is standing greeting people at the door. They approach him and he says "are you Jewish?" and they look at each other and say "Yes, of course we are," to which he looks at them with a puzzled look and says "funny, you don't look Jewish."

This was what suddenly struck me sitting next to this Kenyan family. To my delight, since I had neglected to grab a prayer book on my way into the sanctuary, the father noticed that I was lacking reading material. He handed me his book and pointed to the spot in the services where we were, in Hebrew.

I sat through the service and even though I maybe should have focused my attention on the prayers themselves, I seemed to be more interested in observing my present company. As I mentioned before, this was an Orthodox synagogue, yet it took no time at all to realize that those in attendance did not necessarily practice an Orthodox lifestyle. This quickly became apparent when every few minutes a cell phone rang, and one of the men leading the services would step out and speak on his phone. According to the Orthodox observances, no use of electricity or technology is permitted on the Sabbath, so the jig was up. Nevertheless, and not being able to be too judgy since I had broken plenty of the rules on my way there that morning, I sat in the service for just over an hour and was then invited to join the congregation for a quick bite to eat outside in the garden before everyone left.

Outside I took the opportunity to meet some of the people in attendance. I met an American businessman who does work in Kigali, Rwanda, but comes to Nairobi every Friday and Saturday for the Sabbath. I met the two younger observant girls who were doing some volunteer work in Nairobi, and also met a Canadian with whom I tried to play a short but unsuccessful round of Jewish geography (Oh you're from Canada? Do you know the Goldbergs? What about the Steins? No? Not even the Grossmans?!?). Apparently we didn't mix in the same circles. Finally, I built up some courage to go and speak to the Kenyan family, and approached the father and son who had been sitting next to me in the service.

I introduced myself, told them a little bit about what I had been doing in Kenya, and then asked them: "I don't mean to be rude, but are you Jewish?"

Both of them looked at each other, smiled, and looked back at me and said, "No. We are unable to properly convert to Judaism because there is no permanent Rabbi in Nairobi, but *Baruch Hashem* (a VERY Jewish way of saying 'Thank God') we have found our way."

I found out from speaking to them that though the family started out as Christian as most Kenyans do, they had gradually learned more about the Jewish faith through research and talking to the rabbi who comes to Nairobi for the holidays, and decided that this would be the family's religion moving forward. This idea was extremely intriguing to me, and though I was impressed by their determination to break away from the mainstream faith in Kenya I was by no means surprised as a result of an experience I had had in Kiptere only a few days prior to this encounter in Nairobi. This encounter takes me to my second Jewish experience in Kenya.

When I first traveled to Kiptere on my first visit to Kenya, I was pretty ambivalent about telling the people there what religion I was. Being Jewish always requires a modicum of hesitation when it comes to saying outright what faith you belong to. This comes from the obvious history of global anti-Semitism as well as the uncertainty of how people in different parts of the world perceive Jews, especially those who have likely never met a Jew before. After speaking to one of the organizers from Nairobi and gently dropping the issue of religion into a conversation with him, he told me that the youths in the village would be thrilled to know that I was Jewish. He told me that they were a religious group of Christians who saw Judaism as the "older brother" of the Christian faith, and would likely just want to learn as much as they could about it.

When one of the elders in the village heard about the Jew in their midst, he asked his daughter Marion to talk to me about it. When she first came to speak to me about it, she broached the subject by asking me if I knew what the *parsha* of the week was. In Judaism there is a tradition of reading from the Torah every week, and each week you read a new *parsha* or chapter, which tells a new story contained in the Bible. Her use of this word was obviously meant to demonstrate to me that she knew something about Judaism, and it actually stunned me speechless for just a moment while I came to consider how on earth this girl from the middle of rural Africa would know about a concept like that.

After speaking to her for a while, I found out that her family was essentially Messianic Jews, in the sense that they believe in many of the older traditions of Judaism, but that when it comes to our belief in the coming of the Messiah, they believe that Jesus was the Messiah and that he will be coming again sometime soon. Given my understanding of history and her explanation of how they practice their Judaism, I would place their historical practices in around the 1st and 2nd centuries CE, between the time that Jesus was killed—let's say 30-40 CE—and the Council of Nicaea in 325 CE when modern Christianity was codified and given many of its modern symbols and practices.

This was by no means a common practice by other members of the village, but her family, under the guidance of her father, was apparently in touch via email with a rabbi in Miami, and he seemed to be nudging them in this direction. Her father asked if I could come and speak to him because he had never met a Jew in person before, and he had some questions that he wanted answered.

One Saturday morning near the end of my stay in Kiptere I agreed to go and visit Marion's father. I was told that we were just going to be traveling to their home and that I would sit with him and try to answer some of the questions he had. In this way I could just have a quiet conversation and see if I could put some of my religious knowledge to use. To get to our destination required a half-hour walk, hitching a ride on a motorcycle, hitching a ride in a taxi, and walking for probably around 20 minutes until we reached a school. Apparently I had misunderstood the point about going to visit their home, and we were going to speak to her father in the classroom of an empty school. It was, after all, Saturday.

As we walked into the classroom I found it filled with members of the family who were singing a Swahili song. I smiled politely, walked in and sat down at the back of the room to just observe what was going on. I didn't realize that there would be 20 other people in attendance and suddenly had zero idea what to expect from this visit. As the singing ended, Marion's uncle stood up in front of everyone, wearing a tweed jacket, button down shirt, green cardigan and dress pants, and got everyone's attention. "Shabbat Shalom everyone!" he said, using the traditional Hebrew Sabbath greeting, catching me TOTALLY off guard. He then announced that, "Brother Adam is here today to answer our questions about Judaism! Please, Brother Adam, come and stand up at the front of the room, we have prepared many questions for you." In my head I've just finished adding up the thousands of dollars my parents have paid for my Jewish education. I'm hoping all those years of Hebrew school paid off, giving me the ability to answer the questions of some wannabe-Jews spouting off Jewish phrases in an abandoned schoolhouse on the outskirts of Kiptere. It turned out that my reluctance to stand up there was unnecessary as I was more equipped than I had thought.

Not to toot my own horn, but given the circumstances and the nature of the questions asked I think I did a pretty good job answering what they were able to throw at me. When I first got up there I was a bit nervous, not in terms of the setting that I now found myself in, but more in terms of the context, and the content of what I thought they thought I was going to talk about. In order to clear both my own conscience and make sure that things were good between the man upstairs and myself, I spent the first good chunk of my presentation sharing with the family both why I could not help them (for religious reasons) establish any kind of a church, and delicately explaining to them why I and the rest of the Jewish community did not believe in the divinity of Jesus Christ. I had totally underestimated their knowledge about the subject, and amidst them bursting into laughter at my tip-toeing around the issue of our non-belief in Jesus, they assured me that they completely understood what I was saying. "Still," I said, "I prefer to be safe than sorry so that I don't get into any trouble with . . . you know", pointing my finger up to the sky, "and so let me just finish this awkward introduction by saying that I am here only to teach you about Judaism, and what you do with that information is entirely outside of my control. Ok there, I said it. Let's begin." They laughed again, teased me about my fear of divine retribution, and the Kenyan version of *Who Wants to be a Jewish Millionaire* proceeded.

The next three hours (yes, three hours) can easily be counted as some of the most fulfilling hours of my life. Not only was I able to teach, which as I'm sure is abundantly clear by now, I love to do, but I was able to genuinely reflect on my religion in a thoughtful and comfortable way. Here I was teaching a family about my religion, but despite the fact that they did not belong to this religion in the traditional sense, or in any sense at all, they sort of really wanted to. They had done their homework, they had written down questions, and they were not interested in simple answers. They wanted me to think, and I in turn got them to think, and this entire exercise enabled both this family and me to walk away from the schoolhouse with a new found appreciation for the Jewish faith.

The first thing I did when I walked out of there was write down all the questions that I had just been asked. I looked over the list and marveled at the complexity of some of these questions and noticed again how in depth their inquiries had been. These were not basic questions that people often hear about Judaism, such as: Why do you not believe in Jesus? Why do you have your Sabbath on a Saturday and not Sunday? Why do so many people hate you? And what is the recipe for your bubbie's matzo ball soup? (Ok, I may have made up that last one). They were asking me questions designed to better understand the Jewish faith from a religious, spiritual and practical point of view, and I was thoroughly stunned by how much they had already internalized about my faith. These are some of the inquiries they made:

Why are Jews so opposed to intermarriage? Why is Judaism divided into so many streams like Orthodox, Conservative, Reform, and Humanistic? Are there Black Jews? Where do they come from? Why are the Ten Commandments arranged in that order? What is the difference between being Israeli and being Jewish? Do you have to be both? What are Jewish women supposed to wear to remain modest? Why are there 613 *mitzvot* (commandments) in Judaism? What happened to the Jewish Temple in Jerusalem? How old do Jews believe the world is? Who will be the Messiah from the Jewish perspective? Why do Jews not practice proselytization? Are there churches and mosques in Israel? Why do Jews place so much value on the role of the woman in Jewish life? Why is it so important to slaughter animals in a way that they feel no harm? Why is the Torah read aloud every Saturday, Monday and Thursday morning? Why do Jews bow back and forth when they pray? Where did the three Jewish tribes come from (Israel, Levi and Cohen)? Are these tribal differences the same as the differences we find here in Kenya? What is the importance of Zion in

Judaism? Does the Jewish community have the equivalent of a pope?

While I was trying to come up with thoughtful and true answers for all of these questions, I was really taken by what they knew and how intense their questions were. One of the most memorable experiences from this session was when Marion's uncle (the same one who stood up to greet everyone with "Shabbat Shalom!") stood up and said "Adam, in my research I have come across a poem that I find repeated many times. If I tell you this poem, do you think you would be able to tell me what it means and why it is significant?" As my high school English teachers can probably confirm, poetry is not my strong suit, but I was on a roll at this point so it was worth a shot. He started to recite the poem, verse by verse, without breaking eye contact, having totally memorized it, and speaking in perfect clarity. After the first verse, it hit me what he was saying:

> As long as deep in the heart,
> The soul of a Jew yearns,
> And forward to the East
> To Zion, an eye looks.
> Our hope will not be lost,
> The hope of two thousand years,
> To be a free nation in our land,
> The land of Zion and Jerusalem.

He was reciting *Hatikva* (The Hope), the national anthem of Israel. The way that he had memorized it, the setting of where I was hearing it, and the fact that though I know it in Hebrew I would NOT know how to say it in English myself, all went straight to my head. I suddenly felt elated and unbelievably privileged to be living in that exact moment. I told him that it was the anthem, and told him the only thing that I knew about the poem itself, which was that it was written by Naftali Imber in the Ukraine in the 1870s, and that it epitomized the desire of the Jewish people to return to the land of Israel. My Judaism, and even my Zionism, comes from many different places, but to be able to experience it in this setting with outsiders, who are both sincerely interested and unflinchingly supportive of my beliefs and motives, made me feel both proud and lucky to be Jewish at the same time.

Having lived through a number of anti-Semitic experiences and being aware of what happens on a daily basis in the world to some members of the Jewish community, it is experiences like these that genuinely warm my heart. I think however when you look at it from a purely religious level, in today's world many of us are actually able to get along. At York University I always remember that despite the fact that there were so many fights in the hallways between different political supporters and those who were for or against Israel and its policies, the one group that I always felt the most comfortable in was York's Interfaith Council. In this setting we were able to have real discussions with each other, respect each others' beliefs and faiths, and talk about our views from the more respectful, spiritual and mature level. Many things have changed throughout history, and we could argue that we are at the point now where politics divides, but for some people, religion is actually a factor that unites (I realize that this is an overstatement and acknowledge as well the hugely divisive role that religion is playing in the world at the moment as well). This was the experience that I had in Kenya with locals who embraced my religion and

337

its history, and they were so excited to meet someone from a faith that they had not yet personally encountered. They genuinely believed that my faith was the older brother of theirs, and I was just relieved that I was actually able to provide them with some of the answers and insight that they were looking for.

One of my favourite people in Kenya is named Geoffrey. He is a retired school principal with cerebral-palsy, so today he spends most of his time at home as his mobility is severely limited. He comes from one of the wealthier families in the village, owns a huge piece of farmland, and actually lives in a two-storey brick house. On my first visit to Kenya I had the privilege to meet him and while speaking to him I sat marveling at the way he spoke and the extent of his knowledge. Here was someone who had never really left his immediate surroundings and had certainly never been out of Kenya, but he was talking to me about European politics, American sports teams, and even asked me "What is this thing called a 'sasquatch' that you have in North America?" He does not own a computer or Blackberry, and gets his information and news from reading books and listening to the BBC World Report.

At the end of our first visit together I got up to go and shake his hand as I was leaving and he inquired as to whether I would be attending church the next day. I told him that I was actually Jewish so I wouldn't be, and then waited to see what his reaction would be. He looked up at me, looked to his wife, a wide grin formed on his face, and he said "Ah, one of God's chosen people. Then excused from church you shall be." I laughed, and we stood speaking some more. He told me that he had heard on the BBC an interview with some Holocaust survivors and told me that he knew that Jewish people were special, because people were always trying to get rid of us. "In every generation," he said, "the Jews face a new enemy. But you are God's chosen ones, so you arise from the ashes and are able to put everyone else to shame! Good for you Adam!" Laughing, and not wanting to take all the credit for the hard work of my co-religionists, we spoke some more and I was soon on my way.

On my next visit to Kenya, I made sure to go and visit Geoffrey, who had heard that I was in town again. As I approached his house, I saw him standing at the window on the second floor of his house, just over his front door. As I arrived at the door, the words I heard from just above me were, "Adam . . . Shalom!" An immediate smile came to my face, and the warmth and joy that emanates from Geoffrey instantly took over. We sat on his couch catching up, and at one point I said to him, "Geoffrey, I just cannot believe how much information you know! You sit and talk and you just seem to be so well informed about everything! I'm honestly truly impressed." He told me that ever since he was diagnosed with cerebral palsy he has tried to make sure that he reads everything and learns as much as possible, so that life did not change much from the days when he was immersed in a school environment. He quoted Gandhi who once said, "Live as if you will die tomorrow, and learn as if you will live forever," and this is exactly what he has done. He said to me, "I must always maintain a positive attitude otherwise you should just bring a pastor here next time you visit and recite hymn #100 to me!" In reference to a verse that a priest recites to someone just before they die, Geoffrey laughed in his deep throaty laugh, and then quickly reminded his wife that I had been sitting too long waiting for my tea.

He told me that he remembered that I was Jewish at which point I gave him a copy of the Leon Uris novel *Exodus*, which I had brought to add to his collection of books. He thanked me and when I finished telling him what the book was about (essentially the founding of the State of Israel) he told me that he had actually read a book about the Entebbe Raid, which had occurred in 1976. Very briefly, in 1976 an Air France plane was hijacked by a Palestinian terror cell that rerouted the plane to the Entebbe Airport in Uganda. The terrorists kept hostage all the Jews who had been on board, but after one week the Israeli government sent an undercover army team to raid the airport and rescue the hostages. He recounted to me all the details that he remembered, including the name of Doris Bloch, one of the passengers on the plane who had also been a Holocaust survivor, and he expressed his deepest regret that something so awful could happen to someone twice. I asked him when he had read the book and he responded that he read it in 1980! Almost 30 years and he had remembered almost every detail of what he had read.

Feeling a little inferior at this point and wanting to impress him myself, I tried to tell him that the current Prime Minister of Israel, Benyamin "Bibi" Netanyahu's brother, Yoni, was the only Israeli commando killed in the raid. I started to say, "Well, do you know that the current Prime Minister of Is . . ." I was quickly interrupted by, "Yes! Well the Prime Minister, Bibi, as the people in Israel call him, his brother Yoni was the only one killed. This is very very sad, but very good that he has now become the leader of the

Jewish country." Left almost speechless, it was experiences like this that left me wanting more. I spent many hours talking with Geoffrey after that and learned much from his wisdom, guidance and genuinely positive outlook on life.

As a mobile religion Judaism can now be found in all parts of the world. Thanks to movements like Chabad who have set up houses in the smallest cities, towns and even the remotest of villages in places like South America and Southeast Asia, there are places for Jews to go and find other Jews wherever they are traveling and attend a Friday night dinner or synagogue service. For those who may travel to places where there are no Chabad houses however, or where there are not too many other Jews at all, it is these experiences that I have noted above that are truly able to leave an impression and make us remember, maybe for just a second, where we come from. As I have said, I am always impressed by the way some others view the Jewish people, in a sort of archaic, traditional sense, as if we have just stepped off the pages of the Old Testament, and this old-school perspective of who we are is always a good source of understanding, as well as laughter.

One night I was sitting with one of the youths in Kiptere having something to eat, and I asked him if he could teach me some swear words in Swahili. Though childish of course, you can't tell me that you haven't once asked someone to learn a swear word in a new language that you've learned—everyone does it. He sat with a piece of paper and wrote down some (I must say pretty vulgar) words, and had me repeat after him as he said them, and then told me the definition. As we were working on this language exercise, Jessica walks in, heard one of these words come out of my mouth, and instantly put her hands to her ears. "Adam!" she shouted, "You are an Israelite! These words are not to be used by your people!" We laughed and laughed at her reaction, she gave me 'the look' and stormed off, and I went to find her later to apologize for disobeying her direct request to cease and desist the Swahili swear word lesson. I was, as she said, "one of God's chosen people, and chosen people DO NOT speak like that."

Nevertheless, this was her first reaction, and many feel the same way—especially devout Christians in the most rural parts of Africa. Though this is perhaps more of a message to my Jewish audience, I think it may be useful to everyone as well: not everyone hates Jews. People hide behind politics and religion and yes, there are of course some hardcore anti-Semites who subscribe to that exact sort of hatred that we have known for too long. This is not however something that we need always fear as there are plenty of people around the world who understand as we do the beauty of our Judaism and the ins-and-outs of our religion, and it is not simply because our religion is different and therefore fascinating. It is because our heritage is innately tied to the history of Western civilization and our development is tied to many developments that have been witnessed by the whole world. As other religions have developed as off-shoots of Judaism, those people who value faith and a global tapestry of belief systems are willing to put aside political differences and historical rumours to embrace others who may not only be different, but also those who come from the same history. I have always considered myself extremely fortunate to be a member of the Jewish faith and community, and my experiences in Kenya have strengthened my resolve to not only learn as much as I can about the religion, but to always ensure that I am capable of acting as a reliable makeshift Jewish ambassador.

Many people do not know that *Hatikva,* Israel's national anthem, is only the first part of a much longer poem written by Naftali Imber in 1878. In the last verse of this nine-stanza poem, he writes,

> Brother listen far away
> The single voice, our vision
> Because only with the last Jew
> Lies also our last hope.

These few lines, appealing to those who live far away and in places that perhaps do not have any Jewish presence, impart the idea, as I read it, that a desire to return to Israel and continue the lineage of the Jewish people will last even until the moment when there is only one Jewish person remaining. This desire does not only manifest itself in the existence of a community, but can and should be found within the soul of every single Jewish person. Out in the middle of nowhere I found myself sharing the lessons of my faith with those who were most interested and I felt that there should never be talk of a 'last hope'. As long as there are those who are willing to love their neighbours as they love themselves, then hope will never be lost, and a young Jewish volunteer will always have the opportunity to stand in the middle of a deserted school building, in front of a family of quasi-Jewish-Christians, and discuss the meaning of a 140-year old poem about hope.

Conclusion:
Love, Hope and Optimism

On a sunny Friday morning, Kepha, Courtney, Joe (another volunteer), a friend named Milicent, and I decided to hire a private *matatu* since we would be taking a three-hour drive through the countryside and, well, we just didn't feel like sharing. Our destination was a small village called Kipkelion, and we had received an invitation to visit a local elementary school called Victory Primary School from the principal, Elikana. We were going to visit the school, see how they were working with the students, and the only information I had been given was that there were some orphans at the school too. I realize that this was a pretty vague description to encourage me to spend three hours on the bumpy Kenyan roads, but in hindsight it was one of the best decisions of my life.

The drive was squished and though I usually do ok on long drives where the scenery is nice and distracting, I got really antsy in the car. Courtney was sitting up front with the driver, while Joe, Kepha, Milicent and I were crammed into the back. The second half of the journey was bumpy, and I made the mistake of leaning forward at one point, meaning that when I tried to lean back again there was no more room because three other people were also squished into one little space and there was no room for all our shoulders. With my back hurting and my endless nagging questions of, "When will we get there?" being answered every time by, "We're almost there", I decided to wiggle my way over the seat behind me and into the trunk of the car, where I sat cross-legged for another half hour even-more-bumpy ride.

When we arrived in Kipkelion we noticed that it was a tiny village and many of the buildings were recently constructed. Our driver actually commented that this was so because the village had been affected heavily by the post-election violence, but to what extent we were not entirely sure. As we slowly approached the front of the school, we all took a double take at what stood waiting for us at the front of the driveway. Getting out of the car (I crawled out of the trunk) we were greeted with approximately 30 students singing and dancing, welcoming us singing an upbeat African song. A number of them held flowers in their hands that they rushed over to hand to us as we emerged from the car, while we simultaneously shook hands with Elikana, the principal, who proudly stood next to his students.

He asked us to please follow him to the school, said something to the students, and they began to dance in three rows down the road towards the main gate, singing and shouting. Walking behind them we all quickly pulled out our cameras to take videos and pictures of what we were seeing, and as we continued our walk down the dirt path we were greeted with every other student at the school, standing, lining the road, clapping, singing, and grinning in anticipation of our arrival.

This incredible display of excitement was not the welcome that we had expected, and we were told that we were the first visitors at the school, which also implied that we were definitely the first white people to come by too. As we continued down the path, we were blown away by how many students there were, and near the gate stood parents and the village elders, who greeted us with more flowers and put a sort of plastic Hawaiian lei around each of our necks. While shaking hands, greeting people, and trying to take in what we were actually experiencing, Elikana said something to all the students who then suddenly stopped singing and all ran to sit at each of their desks in their classrooms.

The scenery surrounding the school was magnificent, and in keeping with the expectations in the Rift Valley, everything was either green or brown, with the sun shining through the clouds and overhanging trees. There was a large field just outside the main gate of the school with cows freely wandering through it, and as we walked through the school gate, there was a nice big courtyard, surrounding an L-shaped school building. The school was built out of planks of wood and tin sheets. It was a building of bare essentials, and a simple dirt path surrounded the building leading from class to class. Despite the otherwise lacklustre nature of the building, in anticipation of our visit the students had been encouraged to decorate, and they did so with purple flowers picked from a nearby field. Some flower petals had been stuffed through the cracks in the wood, while others had been strewn around the school grounds to add some purple to the usual green and brown. The flowers inside the cracks of the walls had a really beautiful effect and the added colour made you forget that this school was literally just wood and tin, coming together to form seven classrooms. There were also flowerbeds and hedges surrounding the building, and to the right of the main building there was another structure that served as the kitchen, and another to the right, which was the pit latrine.

After first visiting the office of the school, where we were asked to sign what I can only imagine was the ninetieth guest book of my visit, Elikana wanted to take us to meet the students.

We started with the six year old students in the grade one class. We stepped over the little wooden threshold into the room, and as we walked in, every student dressed in their white and blue uniforms stood to greet us. In front of them I said with a big smile on my face, "Good morning everyone!" to which they replied in perfect unison, "Good morning sah!" We laughed and the students remained standing. I asked them to please sit down, and as they did Elikana asked if they were excited by our visit, to which they all responded (again in unison), "Yes sah!" We met their teacher, one of ten at the school, and we spoke to the students and asked them some questions. This was what we did in each class from grade one to eight, and the reactions of the students in each class were very similar. Every time we walked into a class they each stood up, at which point we told them to please sit down, and then when we asked them questions, whoever answered stood up to speak, and finished with "thank you."

In the third grade class we asked what they were studying and they responded English and math, and I told them that they were probably better at math than I was. The teacher then joked and said that I was welcome to stay and join the lesson, at which time I stepped into the class and sat down at a bench next to three of the students. This got a big laugh, and an even bigger laugh when the teacher asked me an easy math question and I had to think for a second about the answer, while six hands shot up around me.

Each class had around nine benches attached to tables, and there were three or four students per bench. The classes were decorated with crudely made posters of the multiplication tables, how to count in English, information about the eco-system, the ecology and topography of Africa and Kenya, and other information that you'd expect to find on the walls of a school. If you actually looked beyond the posters however you could literally see the other classes on either side, as the walls were just planks of wood crudely nailed together in a row, so you could hear what was happening in each adjacent class.

A popular question that Joe began to ask in the classes we spoke to was, "What do you want to be when you grow up?" In the fourth grade class a young boy stood up and told us he wanted to be a pilot, while a girl in the back of the class stood up and said she wanted to be an engineer. In the seventh grade class the girl who had earlier been leading all the students in song told us that she wanted to be a magistrate, while another one of her classmates told us that he wanted to be a teacher and if not a teacher then a lawyer. These answers and the hope that laced each one was really quite moving, and it made each of us optimistic that although these kids were learning in literally the poorest of circumstances, they remained positive and believed, truly, in the power of education.

After we visited each class, I asked Elikana to explain the circumstances of these students to us. He told me that there were 190 students at this school, and that almost half of them were orphans who had lost both their parents either because of the post-election violence and sporadic fighting between 1992 and 2008, or because of HIV/AIDS. He told us that Kipkelion had indeed been ravaged during the post-election violence, and that despite the secluded nature of this small village, it had been one of the first places in the country to be completely torched. Many were killed and as a result, the number of orphans in and around Kipkelion was high. Many who were not orphans had lost one parent or were living with relatives or friends. He said that some of the students do not receive any meals at home, and though they try to raise money for proper lunches for the kids during the day, much of the food they receive for lunch, usually corn and beans, is donated by local farmers. I was told that to feed all 190 students a proper lunch would cost the equivalent of $100, a day.

Elikana told me that he had been trained as a teacher and that he saw an opportunity to assist the kids of the community, and so set his sights to building this school.

They were recently accredited by the Ministry of Education in Kenya as a legitimate elementary school and the teachers who work there do so for a very minimal salary that is paid by the guardians of a number of the students. Otherwise much of the work at the school is done on a purely voluntary basis, and it is always an uphill battle to find resources and funds. When I asked him what he needed more than anything, without even blinking he said "textbooks." He said that right now they have very few books, and though ideally they would even be happy having a few books so that groups of students could share, the cost of purchasing approximately six books per student for them to study from would be around $6000 total. This is of course a large amount of money, but considering that its around 1140 books, it works out to around $5 a book. He also told me that the majority of the students walked approximately 4-5 kilometres every morning to get to school, and pointed out two brothers who run 12 kilometres to school each day (walking would just take too much time).

As he continued to give details, we left the school grounds and walked to the field just next to the main building, where every student, and many adults, had begun to gather. In preparation for our visit the students had expressed their desire to perform for us, and so each class had prepared either the recitation of a poem or performance of a song or skit. As we got to the field we found a table with a nicely knitted tablecloth on it, as well as three chairs set up for us, with a similar cloth over each. There were some other chairs set up for the elders, principal, and some other notable community members. As we took our seats at the front feeling a lot like judges from *American Idol* I told the others firstly that I wanted to be Randy, dawg, and secondly that we had to find a way to help this school. In front of us the kids were gathered sitting so that there was a space in the middle of the grass to perform, and to our left and right sides were adults from the community.

When they called me up to speak after each grade performed the first thing I said was that I wished we had learned to do something like this in our schools at home. I said that if we had learned to perform and act like this from such a young age, then many of us would be more outgoing, more confident, and understand that excelling at school should not only be evaluated by your performance in English or science, but also by your performance in the arts. I was reminded of a TED talk I once watched, during which the lecturer spoke about how priority in education is always given to the sciences and traditionally academic courses, whereas liberal arts like drama and art are always considered tier two forms of education. This experience on a field in Kenya helped me realize the importance of a properly rounded education. I told them that their performances had left an indelible impression on me and that when I get back to Canada I would tell as many people as I could about this school.

Their drama and poetry performances were wonderful. The first grade class stood up together and recited a short poem in perfect unison about the importance of family. The third grade class sang a song about how HIV and AIDS affects their country and loved ones, and warned about the dangers of unsafe sex . . . in grade three. The fourth grade class recited a poem about how they had lost loved ones during the post-election violence, and described the acts of barbarity that Kenya witnessed at the time. They concluded that they hoped they had seen the end of violence in Kenya. The grade eight class performed a song about the importance of school and how nothing else matters except for receiving a good education at the hands of effective teachers. A boy from the grade six class dressed up with a scarf, sunglasses and baseball cap and sang a song about Jesus while he was afterwards joined by the grade eight class to sing another popular gospel song. Class after class we were blown away by the passion and thoughtfulness of each performance, and could not believe either their level of English (which we were told was taught from a very young age) or their ability to simply perform so effectively and emotively.

Despite the sadness of what they were singing about, these kids were upbeat. They were enthusiastic, excited to meet us, and happy. After the performances we got a chance to just walk around and speak to them one on one, and though they were being given lunch, they each wanted to take their turn to shake our hands (and of course touch and pull out my leg hair). When asking them to pose for pictures they all put their arms around each other, smiled nice and wide, some of them making funny faces, and asked us to stay and visit their classes again. We were in a rush to get back to town for a few other things we had planned, and so when we announced that we were leaving, the song-leaders from the grade eight class quickly gathered everyone together in the middle of the courtyard to start singing another song. The principal laughed and quickly told them that they did not have to keep singing, but despite this they persisted and sang a beautiful African song asking us to come and visit again.

As we walked back to our car, we were all pretty quiet. Elikana thanked us for visiting to which we all instantly responded, "No no no, we should be thanking you for this experience," and the first thing I did when I got into the car was pull out my Blackberry and start emailing people to see if it was possible to organize a fundraiser.

I wanted to finish my book on this story because I believe that the Victory Primary School represents a hope and potential for change. Despite what these students have endured, and despite their current circumstances of eating a small lunch that is donated and walking five kilometres to school every day, they smile, they laugh, they're happy, and they have dreams. Hearing what they want to do with their lives warmed each of our hearts, and although this school had little to do with our actual peace project, it was another phenomenal example of how people live in Kenya.

The purpose of this book has been to demonstrate the enthusiasm and ability of youths to take their future in to their own hands and to ensure that those in positions of power do not dictate their lives. The peace project that we have been fortunate to initiate in the small village of Kiptere has started to spread to other communities, and the progress that has been made to date has been astonishing. One of my biggest fears in beginning this endeavour was that it would be difficult for the youths with whom we were working to separate Adam from their projects. This was a fear I initially had when they started naming projects after me and I thought that although they had the determination, they would simply be relying on me and the money I raised to move things forward. In the last three years since starting this project, I have been pleasantly surprised however, and know now that if I said to them today that I wanted nothing to do with this project anymore, then they would have few problems continuing on their own.

The Youth Ambassadors for Peace have created an office in the Kisii village of Matongo that serves as a youth centre and community gathering point. With some of the money we have raised there are now three computers and a small printer and photocopy machine that is offered to community members for a small usage fee. The money charged for using these computer services goes to pay the rent for the office that is minimal, and the leftover money is reinvested into projects and used to buy supplies for our other activities. Some old donated digital cameras are used for the purpose of documenting our activities but they are also now used for other services, like taking passport photos for those who need them (and of course helping people update their Facebook profile pictures). The local Ministry of Health even comes around and gives the office boxes of condoms to distribute in the community in their attempts to be proactive about the HIV/AIDS crisis and they rely on us to help the wider community as well. The office is brightly painted with the name of the group and is situated in the middle of the village so that many people and cars pass by it every day, and they have come to use it as a community centre of sorts. The plan is to develop this office into a proper youth centre, and we will be holding events like lunch-and-learns and perhaps even movie nights if we are able to find the requisite supplies now that there is electricity freely flowing to the village. A new group has donated two new computers with the understanding that we will hold computer lessons for a number of local orphans, and a bee keeping project for honey and candle-making is now also in the works.

The chicken farm is clucking amazing and at the time of writing there are approximately 130 chickens that lay almost 50 eggs daily. Half the eggs we sell to raise money for the chicken feed and other materials for the farm, whereas the other half we donate to members of the communities in which we work who have been diagnosed with HIV/AIDS. I am constantly updated about the visits that are made to the communities to distribute eggs, and each visit is met with a group of mainly elderly women who have difficulty fitting into a community that is still largely ignorant about the true nature of HIV. Whereas many of their co-community members refuse to shake their hands or even speak to them because of their medical circumstances, they get excited when youths from our group come to visit and distribute the eggs. I even saw them singing and dancing after our visit one day, when they received only six eggs each.

We continue to expand the network of high school peace clubs, and at the time of writing we now have eight clubs set up in high schools around the Rift Valley and Nyanza Provinces. The groups of students are visited frequently by Kepha and other members of the Youth Ambassadors, and aside from just working with high schools, Kepha and others who have taken the lead on the project are also trying to reach out to other youth groups to spread a common message and find groups with missions similar to ours because in Kenya, there are plenty.

As we continue to brainstorm more ideas, the project is becoming more than just a peace project. Those who have felt the momentum of the projects and have had an active role in helping us move forward have now started looking beyond the March 2013 elections, and want this organization to become a youth group with a common voice and common message dictated by the youths of Kenya. Though our primary goal remains a peaceful March 2013 general elections, the planning, brainstorming, and rhetoric that I hear coming from the mouths of those who just three years ago were quiet and passive, sitting on the side of the road in their respective villages, is, as I continue to say, inspiring. These youths do not want to resort to violence and they thankfully do not have to. They live in a democratic country and know that if they can propose decent programs, engage others, and get the attention of the world, that they can affect change through peaceful means. This is not to say that there is not still widespread pessimism throughout the country when it comes to politics. Kenyan politicians are to their people the personification of corruption, and a peaceful election campaign will not necessarily change that, and for that reason perhaps it is good that the members of the group are now looking beyond the elections. However, we must be cautious in not biting off more than we can chew, and we look to specific landmarks to make sure that we are hitting our goals.

Throughout this book I discussed what life is like for the majority of Kenya's population, and have discussed the political situation. I have detailed how disenfranchised youths can become engaged and active in small social movements, and have hopefully demonstrated that they are not apathetic, but rather tired of Africa as usual. Poverty is rife, HIV/AIDS is present, corruption is mainstream, and the people are anxious. Kenyans want something more and want to re-establish their country as the powerhouse of East Africa, and believe that this is possible if politicians could only check their own greedy impulses. But as we all know, it takes much more than that. It takes movement, from the ground up. This starts with the masses of those shepherds and fishermen on the coast of Lake Victoria, spreading through to the tea farmers and taxi drivers in the Rift Valley Province, to the businessmen and politicians in Nairobi to the Maasai warriors in the South and those dying of poverty and starvation in the Northeast.

What we have started in Kenya is just that, a start, but achieving peace in Kenya is something that will require the involvement of the entire country. What we are trying to prove is that the youths know what they want, and they are willing to take a leading role to make Kenya great again. To reiterate a point I made earlier, when people realize that they have the ability to take action, they then hopefully realize that they have the responsibility to take action, and this is the idea that we are trying to instill in this generation of Kenyan youths.

The late Jack Layton, head of the National Democratic Party of Canada and briefly the leader of the Official Opposition, wrote in an open letter to Canadians just weeks before he passed away, "My friends, love is better than anger. Hope is better than fear. Optimism is better than despair. So let us be loving, hopeful and optimistic. And we'll change the world." On the day he passed away these words were written on streets in Toronto, all over the social media world in Canada, and will no doubt be remembered as his last great words to the population of his country. And they should be. They are powerful and they speak to a desire that many have at a time when we see the world crumbling around us.

It is 2012 and aside from the onslaught of natural disasters that we have experienced over the past year from tornadoes in the South of the United States, to the Japanese earthquake and tsunami, to the drought and famine in the Horn of Africa and China, we have seen our share of human evil as well. Massacres and human rights violations in Syria and Libya, militias withholding food from starving Somali women and children, arguable and continuous genocides in the Congo and Darfur, and numerous other human rights issues that plague the world leave us feeling like the world has turned upside down. It is for this reason that words like 'loving', 'hopeful' and 'optimistic' are so catchy, because we want the world that they envision, but we all hope that someone else will bring it to us.

Near the end of one of our workshop discussions, one of the youths put up his hand and said, "May I please add some salt to the soup?" which made me laugh, but I was told it meant that he wanted to contribute to the conversation. The idea that I had when first starting out to write this book was just that: adding some salt to the soup and contributing to the discussion about efforts to change the world, how to make a lasting impact, and attempts at resolving critical issues that we can no longer ignore. There are plenty of ideas out there and the greatest minds in the world have dedicated their wealth of knowledge to peace movements. The ideas that I have mentioned are neither necessarily unique in their inception nor brilliant in their execution. They have however made a difference, and that is all that world peace needs: an effort, a chance, an attempt, a dream, a goal, a desire, a wish, a push, a boost, and a start. We found our start in a muddy village called Kiptere, where the food was plain, the ground was wet, and the night was quiet, but the motivation was there. We gave it a shot, we found the right people, and we have started something that we hope will continue. All that is required is for others to do the same and then it becomes clear that peace is both possible and contagious.

Popular Israeli singer Idan Reichel said,

> Our ability to live in peace with each other depends first and foremost on our ability to accept all that is different between us. I want to get closer to you, but let me be who I am. I welcome you coming closer to me, while respecting who you are. On our own individual paths we are all looking for the bread, the water, the wind and a dignified life. And yes, we all cling to love.

There is much more to do, and there is no one way to do it right. It is not what we do however but how we do it that will determine our successes, and we hope that with further achievements we find more people to help, more voices to speak out for peace, and we crave a peaceful Kenyan general election in March 2013. In the meantime we try our best, we share our ideas, and we go about our lives but we do it with the message of hope in our eyes and the spirit of peace in our hearts.

APPENDIX – PEACE TREATY

<u>Youth Treaty of Hope, Reconciliation and Peace</u>

Drafted by: The Youth Ambassadors for Peace
Kiptere, Belgut, Sigowet Division, Kenya

Preamble:

The Youth Ambassadors of Peace assembled in order to state that they are dissatisfied with the current situation in Kenya.

We believe that there is an opportunity for change in our country, and that only by coming together is this change possible.

We believe that identification on tribal grounds is a relic of the past that only breeds division. To overcome such division, we seek a bright future that unites, rather than divides. Elections are a natural political process that must not tear this country apart when they occur, and it is the role of the youth to ensure that conflict does not strike this country again.

We believe that peace must first be found internally before it can be spread externally. Once peace is found inside the heart of every Kenyan, then conflict will become a distant memory.

We believe that peace is possible, and we believe that united as Kenyans in harmony, we will serve as a model for the African continent.

Part I: Goals and Visions

To unite Kenya, clear goals for the future must be established. There are a variety of visions for what the future holds, and the unifying factor in all these visions is the dream of a Kenya free from conflict.

We therefore declare:

1. That communities in Kenya live in a peaceful and friendly manner by ensuring that,
   - Each community will respect one another,
   - Every person in a community has free movement within the community, surrounding communities, and the country,
   - Any Kenyan can live and work anywhere they desire,
   - Communities can choose a particular political party to support free from pressure, persuasion and manipulation,
   - Communities have freedom of speech, and the ability to share their views, within the concept of freedom of expression, free from manipulation or pressure,

- We ignore issues like ethnicity and tribalism, and foster an atmosphere of coexistence and equality,

2. That youths play a vital role in the peaceful future of this country, and we must ensure that,
   - Youths are empowered and able to take on leadership roles in future elections to ensure that their voices are heard and accounted for,
   - Youths make efforts to create work for themselves and others, to avoid the detrimental effects of idleness,
   - Youths are elected to public office so that they can bring the voice of this majority to the official level,
   - Youths are empowered to lead seminars, workshops, conferences, and activities to spread the messages of peace, reconciliation and harmony,
   - Youths are also empowered to speak about the elements that harm society, such as manipulation, corruption and poverty, and take steps to ensure that there are mechanisms in place to protect against these elements,

3. That diversity is a blessing that must be used to unite, rather than divide. What is important is that we recognize our shared values, and this is what makes us unique,

4. That when any problems arise, they are confronted in a reasonable, civilized manner. People must

come together at times of conflict, and solve issues amicably. Violence is never an option,

5. Those who strive to bring peace to Kenya—peacemakers—must be role models in their day-to-day lives, and must embody the ideals of peace.

Part II: Definition of Peaceful Relations

To foster an atmosphere of peace, there must be a clear understanding of what peaceful relations are in Kenya. Clear definitions can foster clear roles and clear goals.

We therefore declare:

1. That peaceful relations mean that people can travel and work freely throughout Kenya, by ensuring that,
   - Exchanges of goods and ideas can occur without the need to consider a person's particular tribe,
   - There is no favouritism between tribes,
   - Natural resources are equally shared,
   - There is an effort to minimize the gap between rich and poor,
   - There is full equality with regard to gender, tribe, age, and profession,
   - Intermarriage is encouraged between tribes,
   - People can express their legal rights in a safe atmosphere,
   - Defensive attitudes are no longer employed by tribes, and that attitudes become inclusive,

assuming only the best in others, not the worst,

2. That elections must occur free from political patronage, bribery or manipulation, by ensuring that,
   - Civic education occurs regularly, especially before a national election, and that this education teaches positive forms of expression and freedom,

3. That we have a moral imperative to find compromise in situations that may otherwise end in violence, such as,
   - Business transactions,
   - Land disputes,
   - Electoral results,

4. That people must strive to find the value of the individual in the process of living together as Kenyans.

Part III: Regional Framework

An atmosphere of reconciliation must occur within a general framework, understanding that even though only some communities may be affected at a certain time, we are always connected to the rest of the country through a variety of elements. Understanding our role in this regional framework is essential.

We therefore declare:

1. That education is of utmost importance, and
    that there is a reform to the education system, by
    ensuring that,
    -   There are national education units that
        address relevant issues for peace,
    -   There are all inclusive civic education projects
        that are funded by Non-Governmental
        Organizations,
    -   People have the ability to influence the way
        laws are created, and that these laws are geared
        towards national cohesion and peacebuilding
        through affirmative action,

2. That issues that affect one part of the country easily
    affect other parts of the country, such as,
    -   Health,
    -   Security,
    -   Economy,
    -   Transportation,

3. That each part of the country has a chance to assess
    their goals and visions to create a united goal of
    peace,

4. That the media is utilized responsibly to ensure
    accountability and enlightenment free from bias,
    and to ensure that local governments are truly
    working for the people,

5. That religious mechanisms are utilized to spread
    ideas of unity and togetherness, and that ideally,

religious leaders will be politically neutral in their message.

Part IV: Rehabilitation

Previous conflicts have left many affected by the results of war. It is up to us, as peacemakers and visionaries of the future, to ensure that those who require assistance, are cared for, and those who can help, do help.

We therefore declare:

1. That rehabilitation efforts are made to better the situation of Internally Displaced Persons ("IDPs"), fighting communities, women who lost husbands or children in the conflict, and children who lost parents or guardians in the conflict, by ensuring that,
    - Trauma counseling is available for everyone who feels they require it, to discuss what they experienced, what they saw, and what they did during the conflict,
    - IDPs are welcomed back into their various communities, that we seek their forgiveness, that we help rebuild what was taken from them, and that we demand that the government helps reimburse these costs,
    - There are sports events and national prayers for reconciliation throughout the country,
    - There is a national holiday established for IDPs so that we will forever remember what happened and work towards a brighter future,

- We establish a National Reconciliation Movement, as well as a National Forgive and Forget Movement,
- There is a Mercy Train effort, that collects donations for the poor, such as food and supplies, and delivers these goods to those who need it most,
- There are fundraising efforts throughout the country to help ensure that people who feel the effects of war feel that they still belong to the community, and that these efforts are done by Non-Governmental Organizations, not the government,
- There is always a form of human contact for those affected by war, either by utilizing the Church mechanism or other social mechanisms as human contact is a supremely valuable commodity that cannot be lost as a result of war,

2. That government sponsorship is available to help rebuild communities, but that this sponsorship comes with full representation of all aspects of society, and aids people from all tribes and both genders,

3. That sports and entertainment programs are regularly held to unite communities,

4. That intermarriage is encouraged,

5. That former enemies will endeavour to work together through joint ventures, whether they are social, economic or religious.

Part V: Peacebuilding

Peacebuilding is a critical element of moving forward and creating peace. We affirm that peacebuilding is the effort to build bridges and links between communities that require these links to thrive, and we endeavour to create these links in the most productive manner possible. These efforts should harmonize youths nationally, and should spread the word that there is a "Youth Ethnicity" which is an extremely valuable commodity for moving forward.

We therefore declare:

1. That workshops are held throughout the country to bring tribes together in order to help understand the similarities and differences of all Kenyans, and that our collective experience is used to guide the future,

2. That mobile clinics are created to share the achievements of communities with successful efforts to build peaceful connections, and that these clinics help facilitate,
    - Cultural events for people to highlight the traditions of their own communities, and cultural centers to hold these events,
    - Forums for peace dialogue,
    - Intermarriage,

- The creation of youth centers in each community,
- Educational programs that stress the importance of individuals, communities, and civic education,
- Remembrance programs, so that we never forget what happened so that it does not happen again,
- Events that stress the ideas of shared values,
- Movies, music events, festivals, and methods of artistic expression to demonstrate how peace can be achieved,

3. That efforts must be made to utilize the United Nations International Day of Peace, September 21, to spread the message of peace throughout the country,

4. That creativity and innovation should always be encouraged since any minor idea can become an idea that may set us on a successful path to peace.

Part VI: Creating a Culture of Peace

We believe that in order for a long lasting peace to thrive in our country, efforts must be taken to ensure that a culture of peace is created. There are a variety of aspects to this culture of peace, and we believe that they stem from a number of factors. We believe that it is important to smile and greet other members of society, regardless of their background. We believe that we must respect every community's culture, and accept, appreciate and admire that culture. We must act as role models who embody the ideals of peace, and we must believe in peace with all our hearts, and this belief should be embraced and implemented through positive programs. We must also embrace the idea that for the country to survive, we must believe that we can all live together in peace, solve problems together, believe in our commonality, and express daily our national identity. Coexistence is an important value that must never be lost sight of, and we must always believe, as a country, that we are all Kenyans.

Part VII: Security and Implementation

To ensure that this treaty is adhered to and implemented, we must create awareness through civic education efforts that eradicate stereotypes, prejudice, and negative presumptions. We believe that there must also be education efforts about how artistic expression can lead to peaceful expression, and that this expression is always valued over violence. There should be efforts to educate about weapons safety, and we believe that citizens should be able to turn over weapons to the proper authorities free from risk of detention or fines. We wish to create positive relationships with politicians, so that our dreams can be expressed in ways that can perhaps turn into official policy, and hope that politicians reciprocate this goodwill. Finally, we will endeavour to create a mentorship program, so that those who lack guidance can find that guidance through community leaders. We also believe in a culture of "Just Say No to War." We believe that these efforts will lead to the full implementation of this agreement, and we believe that as a result, peace is on the horizon.

Signed, this day, the 17th of May, 2009
Sondu, Kenya

ACKNOWLEDGEMENTS

As with all projects, I have so many people to thank for their assistance. Their help has come not only in the production of this book, but throughout the time that it has taken to get the Youth Ambassadors for Peace set up and going.

Firstly, I must thank the people in Kenya who have been so incredible to work with, and from whom I have learned so much. Kepha Nyambegera in particular, for making this entire project come to life, I cannot thank enough. I must also thank all the members of the Youth Ambassadors for Peace, who by now are too many to list, as well as the members of Adam's Youth Group, who have put so many projects into place. They are: Albert Masisa, Ledmark Okari, Sheillah Moraa, Winny Kerubo, Inkled Moraa, Wycliffe Monigi, Joachim Onkware, Duke Mweresa, Handson Monari, and Millicent Magoma. Others whose help has been immensely appreciated are Weldon Kiplangat, Jescah Chelangat, Robins Ochieng, and Geverson Kipkemoi. I must also thank those individuals in Nairobi who made me feel comfortable in every *matatu* ride that I took, and in making me feel so at home in Nairobi: Ronnie Mdawida, Serah Mucha, Cecilia Mueni and Leonard Gacheru.

My appreciation also goes out to all those individuals in Kenya who have opened up their homes to me to sleep in, who have fed me, looked out for me, taken me in, shown me around, and have provided me with the materials required to put this book together. You have shown me a special form of African hospitability that I believe is truly unique in Kenya, and have illustrated that true happiness comes not from the amount of goods one possesses, but from one's state of mind, and state of heart. The laughter and smiles that we have shared together while I have tried new things with you and tested my limits with respect to what food and drinks I am willing to try, will not soon be forgotten.

Courtney Toretto, who I have mentioned throughout this book, has been the one person to join me in Kenya and help move this project forward by engaging directly with those on the ground. All of us who are involved with this project owe her immensely for bringing her enthusiasm, patience and creativity to the table and pushing us forward.

At home in Toronto, so many people have helped make this project the success it is. Primarily, my parents, David and Denise, my brothers, Mikey and Justin, my two grandmothers for being exceptional proofreaders, and all my aunts, uncles and cousins have been so constantly supportive throughout this entire endeavour and I must thank them for their generosity and their ability to challenge me and help me make this project what it has become.

I must also thank those who have assisted with fundraising and logistics on this side of the Atlantic: Hillel of Greater Toronto and in particular Zac Kaye, Harvey Erlich, Steve Muzzo, and countless others like (but not limited to) Jenn Green, Marc Grosman, Jon Champagne, Matt Reingold, Amy Schreiber, Carrie Nadler, and Jess Spring, who have contributed and provided additional support to ensure the success of this project.

For their help in producing and editing the content of this book, thanks to Jeanette Jacobs (for her constant and unrelenting support in everything I do), Nikki Greenspan (also for her support with the chicken project), Esther Hummel, Laura Griffin, Leah Walters, Esther Marcus, Anna Grosman, Ashley Zaretsky, Erin Caplan, Meghan Servais, Bianca Canave, David Weisz, Noah Kochman, and Naomi Max.

My inexperience with marketing and branding was saved by Elliot Cowan who deserves huge thanks for his constant support from the start of this project, and for designing all form of materials, from business cards, to the Youth Ambassadors for Peace logo, to the phenomenal cover of this book. I must also thank Hilary Sher for her tireless work in keeping our website (www.kenyapeaceproject.com) looking amazing. Also thanks to Jason Rose for graphic design assistance.

Thank you also to those who continue to write to me with messages of support for this project, and for those reaching out to help create a network of peace groups throughout Kenya. Those who have offered to assist me in helping move this project forward, you have given me added motivation, which is always required. I hope that we will continue working together and that others will also be able to assist in our endeavour at helping affect a functional and lasting peace in Kenya. Thank you to all.

CPSIA information can be obtained at www.ICGtesting.com
Printed in the USA
LVOW060413190512

282367LV00002B/2/P